STILL BARKING

Friendship, Brotherhood,
and 25 years of The Sports Junkies

John-Paul Flaim

5editorial

Silver Spring, Maryland U.S.A

MORE PRAISE OF "THE SPORTS JUNKIES"

"The Junks are everything you were told in broadcasting not to be. They work because they're unique, and their originality defines them. I knew they had something when they created their own language. Their story is bazilly."

— **Mike O'Meara,** *"The Mike O'Meara Show" podcast*

"I still listen to The Junkies every day. I sit in my car and interact with them like I'm in the studio with them. I still fantasize about being the Fifth Junkie! Theirs is a great story. They're awfully lucky, and so are we, the listeners."

— **Tony Perkins,** *News Anchor, WUSA-TV*

"I thought I understood fandom due to my time as a player in the league. I quickly found out I was wrong. The Junkies' ability to give voice to the opinions of the 'every person'—right, wrong, heartfelt, completely absurd—is unmatched."

— **Jason Wright,** *President, Washington Football team*

"The Junkies set the standard in camaraderie and fun. This book perfectly depicts everything good in sports, friendship, and what it means to truly live the dream."

— **Mike Rizzo,** *General Manager, Washington Nationals*

"To say 'The Sports Junkies' are an institution is an understatement. You haven't made it in the D.C. sports scene unless you have spent time with these guys. The first time I joined them in the studio, I had an 'I Love The Junkies' shirt made because getting ribbed and having fun with them was a milestone for me."

— **Lindsay Czarniak,** *Sports Anchor, Reporter*

"They are part of the reason I got into blogging. I saw guys making jokes and talking about sports for a living and decided that's what I wanted to do. Twenty-five years later, they are still the best in the biz."

— **Eric "Barstool Nate" Nathan,** *Podcaster, Blogger, Poker Player*

"I've appeared on 'The Sports Junkies' show more than 200 times, and I'm just happy to survive four voices coming at me. I still can't tell them apart, but J.P. sounds the smartest, at least."

— **Rick Snider,** *Columnist, 106.7 The Fan*

"I do not have any apologies for the home team, and my home team has been The Junkies for years. They were the first show to cover us when we were in the midst of a nasty fight with the NFL, and having them in our office on the day we were locked out set the tone for our friendship ever since."

— **DeMaurice Smith,** *Director, NFLPA*

"I've appreciated and admired the way The Junks cover sports. They have a unique ability to give their audience a different angle on athletes and our lives on and off the field."

— **Ryan Zimmerman,** *Washington Nationals*

"Nothing makes me feel more connected to the D.C. sports scene than The Junks. I started listening in the summer of '96, when I was home from college, and I immediately thought, 'This is us!' This is my buddies and me chopping it up about D.C. sports, pop culture, and nonsense. And, that's what makes 'The Sports Junkies' work. Whether I was living in Bethesda or California, these dudes have been a part of my morning routine for 25 years."

— **Dan Hellie,** *Sports TV Host and Play-by-Play*

"To have three friends since your 20s is amazing, but to work with them four hours a day, five days a week is incredible. The chemistry these guys share is unthinkable. My wife and I have separate bedrooms, and we're soul mates."

— **Rich Vos,** *Comedian*

"They're my guys, I love them dearly, and they reflect the influence of their moms, who were always free with our opinions. But they did not get their filthy potty mouths from us."

— **Paulette Auville Murray,** *Cakes's mom*

Still Barking
Friendship, Brotherhood, and 25 years of The Sports Junkies
Copyright ©2021 John-Paul Flaim

ISBN -13: Softcover 13 978-0-9982771-2-7

Cover artwork copyright ©2021 Doug Stevens, Flyboy Graphics, Ellicott City, Maryland

Composition by Jenine Zimmers, San Diego, California

Back cover and promotional photos courtesy Aaron Schwartz, Schwartzy LLC

Editing and publishing by Dennis Tuttle, 5editorial, Silver Spring, Maryland

All rights reserved. No part of this book may be reproduced or transmitted in any form or by any means, electronic or mechanical, including photocopying, recording, or by any information storage and retrieval system, without permission in writing from the copyright owner.

This book was printed in the United States of America

10 9 8 7 6 5 4 3 2 1

For bulk or promotional copies of this book, visit:
www.stillbarking.com

For my wife Jessica, and my children Kelsie, Dylan, and Isabella.

CONTENTS

Foreword by Marc Roberge 11
Prologue 13
1. The Brotherhood 17
2. Wayne's World 26
3. Working For the Weekend 32
4. Not For Everyone 43
5. Failure Is Not an Option 51
6. Can't Contain Genius 62
7. Road Trip 68
8. The Future of Radio 71
9. Frat Party 83
10. The Homies 91
11. Mo' Money, Mo' Problems 97
12. The Untouchables 103
13. Steppin' to the A.M 120
14. Heartbreak 135
15. Never Ask For Double 140
16. Adios Means Welcome Back 147
17. Monsters of the Midday 156
18. Gibbs 2.0 164
19. Accidental Shock Jocks 171
20. Chasing Rocky 179
21. Attention Dollars 190
22. Haircuts Suck 196
23. Brothers Fight 205

CONTENTS

24. Change Is Inevitable...........................210
25. Drab Is the New Black......................226
26. RJesus 235
27. Skits and Bits 240
28. Everybody Loves a Parade 248
29. No Sports, No Problem? 257
30. Social Distance..................................262
31. "I Love You, Ita"................................270
Junkies Greatest Moments........................277
Junkies Chronology...................................302
Where Are They Now? 305
Junkies Glossary..307
Acknowledgments 309

FOREWORD

By Marc Roberge, Lead Singer, O.A.R.

Being from the area, we already knew who they were.

They were the guys from the neighborhood who started a cable access TV show in the basement and proceeded to weave their way deep into the fabric of our world that was Rockville, Maryland. They had made it happen.

We were five guys from the neighborhood who made songs in the basement about our friends after school. We ran around the country playing shows anywhere we could find a gig, now standing on the edge of our journey into the zeitgeist of early 21st century Washington, D.C.

We were about to make it happen.

And as we hurriedly pushed our way down a half-lit hallway to our first interview at the legendary WHFS, I remember scanning my brain nervously for any relevant local sports knowledge that may have survived my four years away at Ohio State. I knew every one of our friends and family would be listening, and we had to hold our own.

This was the dream. We were about to go on-air with "The Sports Junkies" and talk about playing at the 2004 HFStival. Unreal.

Guess what? I don't think we talked about sports at all. I remember laughing—a lot. We had much in common. And we walked out of that interview with a full pass stamped by the gatekeepers themselves.

The guys we had cheered for every time they made a move in radio were now cheering for us. We were becoming part of the fabric.

All we ever wanted. We'd found our champions.

We can trace back to a handful of moments in our career that accelerated our climb into the music business. Our performance of U2's "Sunday Bloody Sunday" at the HFStival became one of the station's most-played songs the following year. Our fanbase grew, and so did The Junks. Their inclusion of O.A.R. into their story and that radio station gave us a home for our music, a springboard to fly out into the rest of the country, and the confidence to be a couple of guys from the neighborhood making it happen.

We've sweat it out together on rooftops singing songs to the world, celebrated our parallel milestones with sold-out shows at the 9:30 Club, and chopped it up on Table Manners while always cheering each other on, always proud to represent the area that's given us all so much.

So congratulations on 25 years of laughs, craziness, and convictions of the heart. We call you legends already because you have earned it, not because there isn't so much more to come.

PROLOGUE

"Look at where we are. Did you ever think we'd have this?"
— Vincent Chase, "Entourage"

Twenty-five years. It's truly incredible. And nobody could have predicted it would happen. What started on a whim became our passion and, ultimately, our profession. From the moment we began yapping into a microphone, we knew sports talk was our calling.

People ask what's our secret. I don't have all the answers, but the way I see it, this one is pretty simple: We are four life-long friends—brothers, really—who have had a ton of fun being ourselves. We've been honest and authentic, regardless of how it made us look, and we've never hidden that from our audience.

After all this time, our listeners know us as well as we know each other. We never bothered to create fake radio names, and we never staged arguments. Instead, we fought each other, made fun of each other, and laughed at each other in plain sight through the highs and lows of our lives.

The beauty is our secret sauce has always been we each bring something different to the table. Individually, who knows if we could carry a show? We're not stand-up comedians. We're not professionally trained broadcasters. "The Sports Junkies," however, have always been more significant than the sum of our parts.

Would *Entourage* have been an HBO smash hit if the show was only about the handsome lead character Vincent Chase? Highly doubtful, but we have a Vincent. Jason "Lurch" Bishop looks and sounds like a professional sports anchor picked straight out of central casting. And much like with Vincent, life always seems to have a way of working out for him. Sure, he's suffered countless bad gambling beats and the tragic loss of his mother, but in the end, the sun always seems to shine on Lurch. Who else would be invited by a stranger to fly on a private jet for a boys' weekend of drinking and golf in Pebble Beach—for free?

We have our Johnny Drama, too. Eric "E.B." Bickel has always let it all hang out, unfiltered and raw. Maybe because he's been a radio enthusiast since he first discovered Howard Stern long before we'd hit the airwaves, but E.B.'s unvarnished on-air personality and charisma has provided vital flavor to the show. His passionate opinions can sometimes infuriate and seem baseless and ridiculous. He might even forget his original stance during the process. But much like Johnny Drama, E.B. makes things interesting.

Cakes is our Turtle. He's lovable, funny, and brings balance to a show full of alpha dogs. He's comfortable blending in and not creating a ruckus. But without Cakes's charm, his zings, and light-hearted attitude, "The Sports Junkies" aren't the same. Who else walks down 29 flights of stairs wearing only their boxer briefs to a casino hotel lobby so they can retrieve a key to their locked room?

That leaves me. I'm boring Eric "E" Murphy, Vincent Chase's best friend and manager. And I'm okay with that. Without E pushing his childhood friend, Vincent might never have become a worldwide Hollywood star. Everybody plays a role on a winning baseball team. Not everybody can hit the home run or close out the game with the save, but you can't win the World Series without a composed, competent, and consistent set-up man in your bullpen.

In the end, just like on "Entourage," our show is about brotherhood and friendship. And that friendship existed long before "The Sports Junkies." That's what makes our story unique. We grew up attending the same birthday parties, had the same teachers, and knew each other's families.

We were there when Jason missed a big free throw in DeMatha High School's upset basketball victory against the No. 1 team in the country. We were together for beach week in Ocean City after graduating from high school, and partied together in college. We've spoken the same lingo most of our lives.

We're still just four friends from Prince George's County, Maryland, who love to hang out and talk sports while listening to rock and hip hop music. Our kindred bond can't be duplicated. It's storybook. That friendship bonds us and drives the show, and that friendship reaches out and grabs the audience.

In December 2019, sports talk legend Mike Francesa, who dominated the New York airwaves on WFAN for decades with Chris "Mad Dog" Russo before they split, joined us to promote the Adam Sandler movie "Uncut Gems." After talking about his role in the film, Francesa began interviewing us. He asked how we decided who was going to speak and whether we ever fought. He also wondered if we had ever broken up.

Nope. We're still barking.

1

THE BROTHERHOOD

"You don't have to have anything in common with the people you've known since you were five. With old friends, you've got your whole life in common." — Lyle Lovett

It all started in October 1973. My mom, Lourdes Nieves Flaim, had been invited to the new neighbor's house. The Rev. Carl O. Bickel, his wife Shirley, and their 3-year-old son had just relocated from Champaign, Illinois, to their new two-story colonial in Bowie, Maryland, a middle-class suburb about 20 miles outside Washington, D.C.

There was no way to predict how intertwined our families would become for nearly 50 years. My mom, who had just given birth to my younger brother that May, prepared brownies for a welcome-to-the-neighborhood visit. Meanwhile, Mrs. Bickel made chocolate fudge cookies that she had pulled from the oven, ready for our arrival. The waft of the freshly baked goods greeted us at the door.

Once inside, I met a skinny, blond-haired boy named Eric, the same as my new brother, for the first time. But, as our moms seated us next to each other for snack time, we didn't say much. Ironic.

Shortly after, we were running around the yard like hellions, probably on a sugar high. And just like that, we became best friends.

★ ★ ★ ★

More than 20 years later, on April 29, 1995, our friend John Auville, who grew up just down the street, was about to get married. Like Eric and me, John was born in 1970, attended "Play Day" preschool and then Pointer Ridge Elementary.

As kids, we played sports together and attended each other's birthday parties. Each of us had younger brothers. Our crew of eight boys included me and my brother Eric; John and his brothers, Marc and Ross; and Eric and his brothers, Chad and Matt. When it snowed, the eight of us would build igloos and sled for hours. Other times we would play epic games of hide-and-seek or tackle football in the front yard. It was the best of times.

But now we were all together, witnessing the first of our tight-knit childhood gang to get married. Though I was a groomsman, I felt so different than my pal John. While he was about to embark on a huge new chapter in his young life, I was finishing my first year of law school at Temple University in Philadelphia. Getting married was the last thing on my mind. I still had finals coming up in the next few weeks.

After my exams, I came home for the summer and interned with the Honorable Glenn T. Harrell Jr. on the Maryland Court of Special Appeals. The internship made sense for me. It's what you do after the first year of studying for your Juris Doctor. Law school made sense for me. I was a type A personality with an interest in politics who never shied from a good debate.

Still, I had no real idea what I wanted to do with the rest of my life. I just knew I had to do something different than my first job out of college. I had graduated from the University of Maryland in 1992 with a degree in international business. It wasn't that I loved business. I didn't. But I figured being bilingual—my mom is Puerto Rican, and my Italian father spoke six languages—would give me an advantage when I entered the real world. *Wrong.* On my first day as a document control coordinator for B.F. Saul Mortgage company, my boss chewed me out for making copies too slowly. I couldn't believe four years of college had led to this nonsense.

Even as I was promoted and started making more money, all I could think about was where to go for lunch and how there had to be something better. Law school was my ticket.

Unlike the mind-numbing days working inside a cubicle, law school was interesting and challenging. Beyond the classes, I was having a ton of fun living with one of my best friends, Mike Fraser, yet another childhood friend from the neighborhood. In our free time, we played tennis, basketball, and Wiffle ball. Most nights, I would stay up to watch ESPN and study just enough not to embarrass myself if the professor called on me in class. Best of all, I loved that there was just one final exam that counted for 100 percent of my grade. I could coast most of the year and cram at the end.

★ ★ ★ ★

"The Sports Junkies" were born out of friendship. Of course, that's not entirely unique. Many successful businesses have been the product of friends and family. But did Ben and Jerry grow up across the street from each other and attend the same preschool? No, but that's beside the point. "The Sports Junkies" started on a whim, and our show wasn't a plan we hatched as kids. I didn't study broadcasting or journalism. That is what's crazy about our story. We just wanted to have fun together. We weren't thinking about our futures. We simply shared a common bond. Sports.

As kids, we watched games together, and traded baseball cards. Our closeness continued through high school, college and into young adulthood. We played co-ed soccer on a team full of weekend warriors. We attended games as a group, and Eric and I shared season tickets to the Baltimore Orioles.

In the summer of 1995, I was learning about the "but-for" test, John was married and working as a manager at Toys R Us, and Eric was in graduate school. We were in our mid-20s and a moonshot from jobs in sports journalism. We had no idea radio was our destiny. But when I reflect on our highly unusual beginning, "The Sports Junkies" would not have happened without...

1.) Rev. Bickel moving his family halfway across the country to become pastor of the United Parish of Bowie;

2.) Eric's future mother-in-law planting the seed for a talk show;

3.) "The Sports Junkies" show defying some pretty significant odds.

That's why I decided to write this book. Those odds? One in a million. The story of "The Sports Junkies" is about as likely as being struck by lightning.

Twenty-five years later, we're still going strong. Sure, there have been ups and downs, but our friendship has persevered. More than anything else, brotherhood has propelled us to where we now sit, the preeminent sports talk radio show in the nation's capital. But nothing is ever guaranteed.

Over the years, "The Sports Junkies" has switched from weekends to nights to mornings, from cable access TV to two different radio stations, and dodged being fired during format changes and the financial fall-out of the coronavirus pandemic. And through it all, we have adhered to the same basic principle since the very first show, taped in my old bedroom at my parents' house in Bowie. Have fun together.

By the time I returned to Bowie in the summer of 1995, my best friend Eric "Bic" Bickel had just finished his first year of graduate school at the University of Maryland, where he was pursuing a master's in school counseling. Like me, Bic didn't fall in love with his first "real" job. How could he? His job duties included counting the steps of the elderly in an assisted living complex. Wanting to escape, he would take the newspaper sports pages into the bathroom during work hours and emerge 30 minutes later. We often met for epically long lunches to bemoan the drudgery of our terrible jobs.

College had been so much more fun. Bic was my roommate our junior and senior years. Though he graduated with a psychology degree, it wasn't because parsing mental processes were his dream. His major required the least number of credits, so he took electives such as bowling and theory of coaching basketball.

Bic was a basketball junkie. As juniors, we shared a shabby apartment and played pickup hoops constantly. While some of us went drinking on weekends, Bic often stayed back to watch his beloved Washington Bullets. Maybe he thought John "Hot Plate" Williams and Tom Hammonds would help make them a championship contender, or perhaps he realized the rest of us were foolishly in an endless cycle of getting wasted, but he chose the game over partying.

As seniors, Bic joined the gang more often for late-night shenanigans. Sometimes drinking would lead to pickup games. Still, Bic was an even bigger Maryland Terrapins basketball fan. Walt "The Wizard" Williams dazzled on the court, and Hall of Fame coach Gary Williams was intense, demanding, and mesmerizing on the bench. He was a god in Bic's eyes. A Maryland alum, Williams had returned to his alma mater in 1989 to rebuild a program ravaged by NCAA probation. Under his leadership, the Terps held open practices that Bic regularly attended.

But what Bic recognized was Williams's meticulous game preparation and razor-sharp ability to counter his opponent's strategy. Gary was a brilliant Xs and Os tactician whose lesser talent routinely beat the other Atlantic Coast Conference blue bloods. Bic tried to implement some of those philosophies to coach his younger brother Matt's travel team in Bowie. I served as his assistant. Though we didn't win many games—talent usually trumps coaching—Bic got the most out of our guys. He was a prepared, caring, and fiery leader who seemed destined to coach in high school.

Coaching would have suited Bic well. He was passionate about sports. As kids, we were energetic and a handful to our parents, so when we were old enough to play for the South Bowie Boys' and Girls' Club, they registered us for soccer, basketball, and baseball, ensuring we were on the same teams.

In baseball, I aspired to be like my favorite pitcher, Jim Palmer. I would start most games on the mound with Bic behind the plate doing his best Johnny Bench impersonation. We were quite the battery. Youth baseball rules only allowed the starting pitcher to throw three of the six innings, so Bic would close out the games after I was done. Neither of us perfected throwing a curveball, but we still won a bunch.

Baseball was our early obsession, including writing articles for our little magazine previewing the 1982 Orioles season. Since Bic was born outside Chicago, he was raised a Cubs fan. Me, I loved the Orioles. So, each summer, our dads would pack all of the boys (there were five of us) into Mr. Bickel's behemoth of a Chevy Impala, affectionately known as the Clunker, and head to Memorial Stadium and watch the Orioles live. Those games were the highlights of our summers.

As kids, we were inseparable. We had the same teachers and played on the same sports teams until travel teams started recruiting us. When I tried out for the South Bowie Bears select soccer team, Bic wasn't allowed to play. Games were on Sundays, and he had church.

Eventually, his parents relented, and he started playing travel baseball and basketball. He also became an avid tennis player. This was the era of John McEnroe, Jimmy Connors, Martina Navratilova, and Chris Evert Lloyd. Tennis was huge back then. Young superstars like Boris Becker and Andre Agassi were bursting on the scene. Bic remained a McEnroe disciple with a mean serve and volley game at DeMatha Catholic High School in Hyattsville, Maryland.

DeMatha was a smaller all-boys private school, a sports powerhouse best known for its nationally ranked basketball team coached by Hall of Famer Morgan Wootten. There, Bic relished the family atmosphere where everybody "joaned" on each other. Barbs and insults were hurled constantly, but all in the spirit of fun.

Bic loved the verbal jousting, especially when it was about his favorite football team, the Washington Redskins, perennial Super Bowl contenders during the Joe Gibbs era. Even though he played saxophone in the band, Bic hung out with the jocks, including Jason "Bish" Bishop, a 6-foot 6 sharpshooter. Bish had chosen DeMatha to pursue his hoop dreams.

★ ★ ★ ★

Growing up in nearby Lanham, Bish lived alone with his mom Peggy, who worked in the White House as a stenographer. As a kid, he thrived in baseball before focusing on basketball as he kept growing taller.

Off the court, Bish was a rabid Washington Capitals hockey fan—Dennis Maruk and Rod Langway were his favorites—but his true love was the University of Maryland teams. His mother's boyfriend Ernie would take him to basketball games at Cole Field House and football and lacrosse games at Byrd Stadium. Bish knew all the players and revered basketballers such as Adrian Branch and Len Bias.

Far from a homer, Bish became an obsessive Boston Red Sox fan as he visited Fenway Park with Ernie. He also loved the San Francisco 49ers. With Joe Montana at quarterback and Jerry Rice at receiver, that wasn't a hard choice. The Niners won 104 games, most of any NFL team in the 1980s, plus three Super Bowls, and Bish loved winners.

Picking winners soon grew into his biggest addiction. His best friend Scott had parents who loved to gamble. So when Bish visited, he would watch Scott's mom pick games on a betting sheet as she shouted lines to her husband and son. That whet Bish's appetite for betting. It would never leave.

On the court, Bish became a starting forward on a stacked DeMatha team that included Jerrod Mustaf, later drafted by the New York Knicks. On Dec.

12, 1987, in arguably the biggest game of his senior season, DeMatha faced the nation's top-ranked team, Archbishop Molloy from Queens, New York. Every basketball fan in the area wanted to be there, so I joined Bic and his DeMatha pals for the mega matchup.

Junior Molloy point guard Kenny Anderson, a future NBA All-Star, sped up and down the court that night, scoring a game-high 26 points. Still, DeMatha led 68-66 when Bish was fouled with three seconds to play. Though he missed the front end of a one-and-one free throw opportunity, DeMatha held on for the upset. Afterward, we celebrated at a nearby McDonald's, reveling in the colossal win.

As a senior, Bish's DeMatha Stags squad claimed another D.C. championship, helping him earn a scholarship from the University of Richmond, which had gone on a Sweet Sixteen run the year before. Unfortunately, the lanky freshman's first year in college didn't go as planned. Bish struggled in the classroom, that is, when he went to class. On the court, things didn't go much better. Bish dealt with a back injury that led to surgery and a lack of playing time.

After his freshman year, he transferred to Grossmont Junior College on the outskirts of San Diego. Bish's basketball swagger returned as he averaged nearly 15 points a game. Though he loved San Diego (with occasional trips to Tijuana), the west coast wasn't home. Bish longed for a return.

For years he had dreamed of playing for the Terps. Now it seemed like his dream might come true. Bish was set to be a preferred walk-on. Unfortunately, the university's academic requirements had tightened after the Terps went on NCAA probation in 1990. Bish was denied admission to the school.

So, he headed to the eastern shore of Maryland to Salisbury State University. With basketball practices kicking off at 5:30 a.m., Bish decided to hang up his high tops and dabble in broadcasting.

At first, he worked as a deejay, spinning tunes on the "S.S.U. Café," where he would play bands like New Order and The Cure. Later, Bish would host a sports talk radio show called "Sports Wrap," which was only heard on the college's cable access television station, WSUR. There weren't many listeners, but Bish, also known to the audience by his gambling handle "Mr. Seven," was honing his broadcasting skills. The show managed to land some heavy hitters as guests, including point guard Bobby Hurley from Duke's back-to-back national champions.

In addition, Bish served as the sports director and dipped into play-by-play, where he called Seagulls basketball and football games with his partner, Greg Jewell, offering "color commentation," as Bish described. He wasn't exactly the next Jim Nantz, but he was on his way to a career in sports.

After graduating from Salisbury State in 1994, Bish moved in with a friend in Bowie and started working as a courier. At the same time, he began editing sports highlight packages for Reuters news service and serving as an unpaid intern at WTEM, Washington's only sports talk radio station. Though Bish had no idea where he was headed next, at least he had his big foot in the door.

When I finally tried out for the South Bowie Bears travel soccer team when I was 9 years old, it was because my friend John Auville was already on the team. On Sundays, we often traveled over an hour for regional games and visited places like Greensboro, North Carolina, where John and I would room together as the home team would host us for tournaments. I'll never forget when John had to warn one of the moms that he still wet the bed on occasion. He's never heard the end of that confessional.

While Bic joined Bish at DeMatha, John and I passed the admission test to Eleanor Roosevelt High School in Greenbelt, Maryland, a science and technology magnet school. For both of us, Roosevelt wasn't about education. It was about attending a free public school versus our parents paying for private—and a school that started at 9:30 in the morning instead of 7:30. And, it was also about a school with girls, not that either of us had much success with them.

Our time at Roosevelt was a blast. While I played soccer in the fall and baseball in the spring, John played for the Raiders' tennis team. Dina Chin was John's mixed doubles partner. One year John asked her to homecoming because he didn't have a date. They went purely as friends. A few years later, our friend Bic started dating Dina. He never dated anyone else.

Meanwhile, the magnet program at Roosevelt pushed us academically, and we struggled. Geometry was John's biggest foe. His dad Gene, who served in the U.S. Navy before working at the U.S. Patent Office, was a no-nonsense man who wouldn't accept failure, so he hired a tutor to help his son. It didn't matter. Geometry was a nemesis John couldn't defeat.

It's entirely possible, and probably likely that John and I didn't study enough. Instead of hitting the books far too often, Bic and I walked down the street to John's house and played video games. Occasionally, his dad would answer the door wearing nothing but his tighty whities, embarrassing John.

His dad was a proud, headstrong, opinionated man who didn't mind butting heads with his son's best friends. Bic and I affectionately called him "Mean Gene" for his aggressive delivery, but we loved bickering with him. He pulled no punches, and we'd laugh as he passionately argued Larry Bird of the Boston Celtics was overrated or Notre Dame got all the calls. Though

John cringed, it was cool his dad engaged us in sports debates.

When I wasn't at John's place, he walked over to play ping pong at my house. Usually, he would have to wait. The Flaim family dinner was later than most. My mom didn't get home from work until 6:30, and often I would arrive later from soccer and baseball practice. That meant we weren't eating until 7:30ish, and so was John. My parents wouldn't take no for an answer, so John would have to sit down with us and stuff his face with arroz con pollo or spaghetti.

After dinner, the two of us often retreated to the garage for those ping pong battles. Sometimes Bic and my brother Eric, a fellow DeMatha Stag, would join the matches, but they couldn't play late like John and I. DeMatha started two hours before Roosevelt. So we'd play until 10 or 11 at night. It was during these epic battles that I dubbed him Johnny "Cakes" for no other reason than it flowed.

Though Cakes wasn't a math wizard, we were impressed by his ingenuity. As a senior, he served as a teacher's assistant, giving him access to permission slips. To get out of running during physical education, Cakes would grab a permission slip, hand it to the gym teacher, and head to the cafeteria for a second lunch. Genius.

For college, Cakes landed at Towson State in Baltimore County. Two of his suitemates were stud basketball players on the Tigers team that reached the NCAA Tournament. They were also big partiers. Cakes got caught up in the lifestyle and had what you would call a "lost semester."

When Mean Gene learned his son didn't even have a 1.0 grade-point average, he threatened to enlist him in the Army. *This was during the Gulf War!* Luckily, John's mom Paulette wouldn't allow that to happen. Instead, he switched majors from accounting to mass communications, and his grades improved.

Before graduating, Cakes met Amy Wertheimer. Amy was on her way to becoming a teacher, and he quickly became her man in shining armor. They fell in love, and now, just a few years later, they were about to get married.

★ ★ ★ ★

As Cakes stood before his friends and family about to wed the beautiful Amy, he never looked happier. Sporting a full head of hair and a broad smile, he proudly said, "I do." Those two simple words put him on an entirely different stratosphere than the rest of his friends. We were in awe.

Moving to the reception at the nearby Crofton Country Club, a group of us marveled that we now had a friend who was married. It blew our minds. Cakes had a wife. Cakes had a real job with health insurance and a retirement plan. Cakes was making and saving money. And, he was just 24 years old. The rest of us were still in school, trying to figure out where our lives were headed.

Sure, Cakes was officially a grown-up with adult responsibilities, but we also knew that he took just three job interviews when he graduated from Towson: Taco Bell, Foot Locker, and Toys R Us. We weren't in awe anymore.

2

WAYNE'S WORLD

"I always liked those moments of epiphany, when you have the next destination." — *Brad Pitt*

Several weeks after the wedding, while I was staying with my parents during the summer, Bic popped over one night after leaving his girlfriend Dina's house. His future mother-in-law had planted an idea that was rattling around his brain.

"Do you want to start a TV show?"

Bic and Mrs. Chin had seen some kids we knew doing a political talk show on Bowie Community Television, or BCTV, and their chatter reminded her of our circle of friends. "This is a joke—you guys can do better," Mrs. Chin declared. Our parents had long witnessed our endless verbal exchanges. None perceived loud-mouthing as a viable occupation. So, I was Bic's first pitch for a TV show, and I was all-in right away. Sports were our passion, so we wouldn't be talking politics.

Excited by the prospects, we weren't sure if we could make this idea work. We were fans of opinion shows like "The Sports Reporters" on ESPN that featured some of the best columnists in the country, including a few of our favorites—Tony Kornheiser, Michael Wilbon, and John Feinstein of the *Washington Post*. But we had never tried our raucous, spontaneous sports takes on camera. Neither of us studied journalism or took mass communications in college, but we knew somebody who did.

Cakes joined Bic and me in the more private orange bedroom at my parents' house within an hour. With Bic's oversized video camera in tow, the three of us started jabbering away for a rough screen test. The content didn't matter. We were on fire with the presentation. We couldn't stop laughing, we had a ton of fun, and we quickly believed in our potential.

Still, we needed a name for the show. During the brainstorming session, Bic suggested "Sports-A-Rama." Cakes and I joaned. Then I proposed "The Sports Junkies."

Boom!

The next day, I called Bowie City Hall for information and requirements. What would it take to get on BCTV? Not much. All we had to do was take one class. And this wasn't a class that would require weeks. It was an hourlong instruction on how to operate their equipment. Then we would choose a time slot and producers to help us on the technical side.

On Thursday, August 17, 1995, we taped our first real show. "The Sports Junkies" would air on Friday nights at 9 p.m. on Channel 15B and rerun on Tuesday and Wednesday afternoons. The show lasted 30 minutes. We were nervous, we were excited, but we were ready. Producers Sean Benedict and Scot Randol would help on the technical side from the control room. Mr. Chin, Dina's Dad, would run one of the cameras. And Dina designed a poster board sign displaying the show's name: "The Sports Junkies."

With the help of the producers, Bic and I created a short intro with graphics. Gary Glitter's "Rock'n Roll Part 2" boomed during the opening credits. Since we were huge Spike Lee fans—Bic had filmed some goofy shorts on his camera a la Spike's character Mars Blackmon in the Michael Jordan Nike commercials—we called the show a J.P./Bic Joint. Maybe that was foreshadowing? Cakes called us a few hours before our first taping and said he had to work a double shift at Toy R Us.

Pondering a two-man show, Bic had an idea. Bish was living just a few miles away and knew sports better than anybody we knew. Plus, he had broadcasting experience. Best of all, he was available. So, we told Bish to grab a dress shirt and tie and join us at the studios housed inside a former elementary school converted into Bowie City Hall.

Armed with a clipboard and a list of topics, I got behind the blue desk that we dressed up with my white Phoenix Suns Charles Barkley jersey, Bic's burgundy Heath Shuler Redskins jersey, and a couple of Bic's hats. "The Sports Junkies" sign was behind us on an easel popping between me, Bish, and the blue screen backdrop. An observant viewer might have caught a glimpse of Bish's shorts as we crammed in behind the desk, but we positioned ourselves best as possible to look professional.

The overhead lights were hot and intense. As we waited for the producers in the control room to count us down, we were predictably anxious. Luckily, Bish was ready. He snuck vodka into the studio, so we took a shot. Then it was lights, camera, action! "The Sports Junkies" wasn't a concept anymore. We were an actual show.

Prepared with a cheesy rhyme, I opened the show: "Hi. Don't turn that dial. Stay tuned for a while 'cause we're about to get funky. We are 'The Sports Junkies.'"

Then I looked down at my clipboard with the list of topics I had meticulously prepared. I teed up my partners on everything from the upcoming college football season to Cal Ripken Jr., who was just two weeks from breaking

Lou Gehrig's streak of 2,130 consecutive games played.

I asked Bish about Phil Regan, manager of the floundering Orioles. With deadpan delivery, Bish responded: "A stiff as a manager and would probably be working the streets in another two months." We all laughed. While Bish brought wit, Bic brought passion and energy. He screamed with blind optimism about his Terps, anticipating a Mark Duffner turnaround entering his fourth season as their football coach.

Incredibly, during our segment called "Word Association," Bish flippantly predicted the No. 1 overall pick in the NFL Draft would get hurt. That was Ki-Jana Carter, Heisman Trophy runner-up from undefeated Penn State, which won the Rose Bowl. Carter had been selected by the Cincinnati Bengals and given a $19.2 million contract. Less than an hour after Bish's prediction, Carter blew out his left ACL on the third carry of his first preseason game. He was never the same and managed just 1,144 career rushing yards.

After the show, it was evident Bish was the most comfortable on camera. He had a commanding presence and knew what he was doing, but we weren't going to Wally Pipp our lifelong friend Cakes, and replace him. Instead, we asked Bish to become a permanent member of "The Sports Junkies."

★ ★ ★ ★

During the fall of 1995, we began to tape a few episodes of "The Sports Junkies" each month. With Cakes joining us, our group dynamic was complete. We knew how to push each other's buttons, and we became looser.

After the Maryland Terrapins football team opened their season with wins against Tulane and North Carolina, Bic erupted like a lunatic. "Look at the Terps! They'll probably be 3-0 by the time this show airs. But I'm looking at their schedule. I know I had them going 6-5 this season, but I'm revising my pick!" With the three of us snickering, Bic grew louder, and his tirade continued.

"West Virginia at home. *No problem.* Duke at home. *Winner.* At Georgia Tech and Wake. *Winner. Winner.* I'm looking at the Terps going 10-1 this season. At worst, 8-3."

We couldn't stop laughing. The Terps had won just four games the year before. Still, Bic's energy was infectious. Nevertheless, Cakes couldn't let this slide though. "West Virginia will definitely beat Maryland," he declared. A few days later, the Terps improved to 3-0 with a 31-17 victory against WVU at Byrd Stadium. Always bet against Cakes. (FYI: The Terps finished 6-5.)

Soon we began to refurbish our set, making the show look as professional as possible. Cakes' eclectic mix of sports jerseys, including basketball and football, plus hockey sweaters, hung from our new graffiti-lined backdrop.

We also tweaked elements within the show. Bish stole highlights from Reuters that we used for the closing credits with Ice Cube's "Check Yo Self." We added features like Bish on the BoSox—I love alliteration—where he fawned over pitcher Tim Wakefield's knuckleball and slugger Mo Vaughn's MVP run.

Each show closed with our Under My Skin segment where Bic might rip into major-leaguers who couldn't bunt, or I poked fun at O.J. Simpson's ridiculous murder defense while trying on gloves that didn't fit. We were improving, enjoying ourselves, and our personalities were beginning to shine on the screen.

In December, we filmed a holiday special where we donned Santa hats and drank egg nog. I hummed sports Christmas carols for the occasion as I drove from Philadelphia before the taping. Then, to the melody of "Rudolph the Red-Nosed Reindeer," I mocked beleaguered Redskins starting quarterback Heath Shuler and shamelessly crooned:

Shuler, the bonus baby
Had a very large contract
And if you ever saw him
You would see the skill he lacked.

Eventually, we scrapped the cumbersome desk for a more open look and started tossing a football to each other for our closing segment, a verbal passing of the microphone. We taped a new intro during a Washington Bullets practice featuring center Jim McIlvaine and former Michigan "Fab Five" star forward Juwan Howard, who freestyled, *"Yo, Yo, Yo, Yo, Yo. I'm about to get funky on the 'Sports Junkies,' don't turn that dial."*

We loved it.

Though we had no idea if anybody was watching besides our family and friends, we gained confidence by the week. In January, we had a rare meeting to figure out how to take the show to the next level. We divvied responsibilities. Bish and Bic would try to land guests. Cakes would send letters to colleges and pro teams begging for swag to dress up our set, and I would reach out to local media for feedback and see if we might garner some attention.

My task was simple. I could make publicity calls from Philadelphia during the week. First, I connected with Warner Wolf, the legendary New York sportscaster working at WUSA-Channel 9 in Washington. Warner was a pleasant fellow, and he invited me to send him a tape from one of our episodes. After watching it, he sent me a three-sentence note complimenting our chemistry. Nice, but that wasn't moving the ball.

Next, I tried reaching Len Shapiro, the sports media writer for the *Washington Post*. When he didn't answer, I called Dick Heller at the *Washington*

Times. Heller, a D.C. native, had covered local sports since the 1950s, when he worked for the old *Washington Star*. When he answered, I introduced myself and began pitching the story. Stopping me, Heller said, "I've seen cable access before. It's terrible. But I like your story. Send me a tape."

Heller called back a few weeks later. He was surprised by how much he liked the show. Beyond that, Heller loved that we were four friends chasing a dream. "Would you mind if I watched you tape an episode and brought a photographer with me?" he asked. As soon as we hung up, I called my boys with the bombshell news.

By the time Heller joined us at the BCTV studios in late March, Bish and Bic had managed to land a few guests including Bob Ferry, the former Bullets general manager. Cakes had snagged a bunch of gear, too, ranging from a Los Angeles Lakers warm-up suit to Portland Trailblazer ties. The set looked professional. We looked professional. We were prepared and on our game.

Peppered by questions throughout the evening as we taped our 20th show in seven months, we may not have grasped the gravity of the moment. But after a brief photoshoot, we were full of anticipation. When was Heller's article going to be published, and what was he going to say about us?

★ ★ ★ ★

Sometimes your life changes, and you don't see it coming. Other times you have an idea. For me, March 25, 1996, was one of those days.

Despite final exams nearing for my second year of law school, I decided to visit my parents for the weekend in Bowie even though we weren't taping a show. Most of my friends were back home, and it was only a 2 1/2-hour drive from my tiny rowhouse in the quaint Chestnut Hill neighborhood. Besides, mom was still doing my laundry.

This weekend was different, though. I had decided to stay through Monday morning for a copy of Dick Heller's story before I sped back to Philly. "The Sports Junkies" were about to be discovered.

Minutes after waking up, I jumped in my rundown Plymouth Laser and sped to CVS just a few blocks from my parent's house. My heart was pounding with excitement as I asked the lady behind the counter for a copy of the *Washington Times*. As she handed me the paper, my palms were sweaty, so I walked back to my car before searching for the article.

We may not have been on the front page, but on page B12 of the sports section, the three-column spread was anchored by a headline that read in big, bold print: "Sports Junkies" with the sub-headline: "Four longtime buddies talking up a storm on uninhibited cable-access show in Bowie."

Above the headline was a prominent picture of us laughing on our BCTV set with the caption: "Eric Bickel, Jason Bishop, John-Paul Flaim, and John Auville take a loose and looser look at sports." We couldn't complain about that. Our names were spelled correctly, and the caption grasped the essence of the show. But that still left the article. This could get worse.

But Heller didn't let us down. He called our show "very good" and added:

"Their discussions are intelligent, lively, and sometimes argumentative. Most important, they're fun." I re-read sections of the article over and over before I raced onto Route 301 for my trek back to Philadelphia.

The opening passage had truly captured our story: "These four guys had been talking sports since they were kids, see, and they thought it would be cool to do it on TV. So they got this show on a cable-access station—sort of like Wayne and Garth—and now they're knocking 'em dead all across Bowie."

Now we wanted more.

3

WORKING FOR THE WEEKEND

"If you had one shot. Or one opportunity. To seize everything you ever wanted. In one moment. Would you capture it? Or just let it slip?"— Eminem

In the 1990s, radio in Washington, D.C., was diverse and had something for everybody. Nationally known deejay and BET television star Donnie Simpson's silky smooth voice could be heard in the mornings on 95.5 WPGC, a phenomenally successful and hip R&B station. Conservative talk radio featuring icons Rush Limbaugh and Sean Hannity crushed in the ratings on 630 WMAL. There were top 40 music stations, news stations, and country stations as well. After all, this is the nation's capital and a top 10 market. But there was nothing quite like 106.7 WJFK.

Washington's hot talk superstation featured Howard Stern, the most successful morning show in radio history. The polarizing G. Gordon Liddy, a central figure in the infamous Watergate scandal, talked politics in the midday slot. Then from 3-7 p.m., shock jocks Don Geronimo and Mike O'Meara dominated the airwaves. Since high school, we had listened to them when they were "The Morning Zoo" on 105.1 WAVA. Now the show included strip trivia, riveting tales of Don's daily life, and Mike's flawless impersonations during their low-budget "Jeopardy" games.

The controversial Greaseman's show took over at 7 p.m., blending his unique personality and legendary screwball skits. Years earlier, he had been fired for his incendiary comments about the Martin Luther King holiday, but by 1994 his nationally syndicated show based in Los Angeles reached an estimated 2.5 million listeners across the country.

But weekends were a vast wasteland for WJFK, filled with smooth jazz. Ratings didn't matter. WJFK brought in so much money in weekday advertising revenue that weekend content was essentially ignored. That was changing, though. In March 1995, the station became the official radio home of the Washington Redskins after three seasons with the weaker 570 WTEM, the only sports talk station in town.

To complement carrying Redskins football in the fall, WJFK program director Jeremy Coleman created a new weekend lineup. First, he hired former

Redskins defensive end Charles Mann and paired him with Larry Michael, a versatile sportscaster whose range included calling boxing matches on HBO and Notre Dame football. Dan Daly, a *Washington Times* sports columnist, would partner with Earl Forcey for "The Sports Jam." Earl had worked at WTEM. His colleague Rich "The Coach" Gilgallon, who had hosted the popular "Kiley and the Coach" show, would also join his "Soapbox" show set to air on Sunday mornings.

Still, Coleman and assistant program director Jim McClure was searching for talent to finalize the lineup. Fortunately for us, McClure read the *Washington Times*.

After seeing Dick Heller's column, McClure approached his boss and kicked around the idea of adding us to their new sports weekend. Coleman wasn't a sports fan, but he was open-minded, so he gave McClure the green light. We connected very soon after the article. McClure wanted a radio demo so they could determine whether we had potential. Though Bish had tapes from his days at Salisbury, we didn't have a radio demo. Instead, we would have to send VHS copies of our TV show. That weekend, I returned to Bowie and dubbed a few of our best shows together at the BCTV studios. Since I had to return to Philadelphia on Sunday, I passed the VHS tape to the only courier I knew, Jason Bishop.

On Monday morning, Bish headed to the WJFK studios in Fairfax, Virginia, and briefly met with McClure. When he returned home, Bish called each of us with an update. He also mocked McClure. Jim was friendly and surprisingly young—a few years younger than us—but the everlasting first impression he made on Bish was he didn't have a chin.

Pouring through episodes of "The Sports Junkies," McClure was immediately struck by our chemistry. One segment stood out in particular. During our "Give It Up" feature, where we highlighted the positive stories in sports, Bish congratulated PGA golfer Tim "Lumpy" Herron for his first career win in the 1996 Honda Classic. What caught McClure's ear was the way Bish hilariously pronounced "Luuuumpee" with the rest of us joining the antics. Sophomoric for sure, but McClure couldn't stop laughing.

Later, McClure would approach Coleman and lobby on our behalf. After listening to a few segments, Jeremy agreed with his right-hand man. We were relatable, fun, and worthy of a meeting. He tasked McClure with setting things up, and once we got to know each other, we might move forward.

So, on an unusually hot April day, the four of us dressed in our Sunday best in button-down shirts and ties. Piling into my mom's maroon 1990

Buick Century, we drove to Fairfax together. Anxious as we trekked on the Beltway, calamity struck. The car overheated and we had to pull over. There were no cell phones. We were screwed. Luckily, a tow truck arrived within 15 minutes, and eventually we reached the meeting, albeit a little late.

While we were still sweating, McClure greeted us wearing jeans and a t-shirt. The man with no chin—Bish had nailed this description—jabbed, "Why are you guys wearing ties? *This* is radio."

Soon we met Coleman, a slight gentleman who spoke with a calm and measured tone. After talking about the station's powerhouse lineup and what he was trying to accomplish on the weekends, he explained that he needed to hear an actual radio demo before committing to giving us a time slot. Admitting that he was a sports neophyte, Coleman added, "I had no idea what you guys were talking about, but I liked it."

The following Saturday, we returned to cut our demo in WJFK's secondary studio. McClure worked the control board while we crammed around the console. Soon we began to rant and rave with reckless abandon. Much like our cable access TV show, I served as the unofficial moderator and kicked topics to the boys, not that I could harness much control.

As expected, Bish dropped deep sports knowledge on the major league baseball season, which was just underway. Bic brought unbridled energy and enthusiasm as we reflected on The Masters golf tournament, where his favorite golfer, Greg "The Shark" Norman, had choked away a six-stroke lead the week before. And Cakes played to his strength. He blended in, provided balance, and brought well-timed zingers.

When we finished, McClure likened our demo to a train wreck, but he saw the potential for success if we had more direction. Next, he recommended that Jeremy give us a chance. We left feeling upbeat. We had done the best we could. Now it was out of our hands.

Luckily, Coleman respected McClure's opinion and had put him in charge of the weekend sports programming. Had he not, we may have never been given a chance to work on live radio. Jeremy called that Tuesday to offer us the Saturday 5-8 p.m. timeslot following "The Sports Jam." Nothing was guaranteed, but at least we didn't have to move across the country to some podunk town to work in radio. Instead, we would ply our brand of sports talk in our backyard on a radio station we revered.

Knowing that we were the lowest of the low on the radio station's totem pole, there was no room to negotiate pay. When Jeremy offered each of us $75 per show, we thanked him and asked when we would start.

★ ★ ★ ★

Just as my second year of law school ended, "The Sports Junkies" were set to embark on a new journey. We would hit the Washington radio airwaves for the first time as part of WJFK's "new sports weekend" on Saturday, May 4, 1996. In the days leading up to our debut, McClure called with feedback and suggestions. Along with Coleman, McClure thought Bish should be the lead. They pointed to his distinctly deeper voice and suggested he take us in and out of commercial breaks and steer the show. Though Bish preferred to react to topics versus lead the discussion, we didn't have a choice.

My feelings were bruised, but I was a pragmatist, too. Bish's broadcasting experience at Salisbury had given him an advantage, and his voice sounded better. So that week, while balancing law school with prep for the show, I created an outline of topics and segments that I would hand to Bish, our new bus driver.

The main studio at WJFK wasn't big enough for the four of us, so McClure suggested Bish sit in the tiny adjacent studio that housed Don and Mike's newsman, Buzz Burbank. Fortunately, there was a small glass partition on the wall separating the rooms to see each other.

The changeover between "The Sports Jam" and the start of our show was frenetic. There was no time to calm our nerves. As we entered, Dan Daly and Earl Forcey looked at us baffled and bewildered. They had no idea who we were. We had no bona fide credentials or media chops. But there wasn't time to chat. After exchanging pleasantries, they wished us luck and exited the studio.

With McClure springing behind the console while commercials played in the background, the four of us anxiously sat down, grabbed our papers, and peered at each other as we were only minutes from launch. We had chosen Redman's "Time 4 Sum Aksion" as our opening salvo. Mike Tyson had used the same rap classic before his menacing ring entrance during his return to boxing after being released from prison.

When McClure pointed at Bish, the microphones were hot, and it was go-time. After a fleeting introduction, Bish surprised us by skipping the first planned topic on the outline and launching into the Kentucky Derby.

Maybe we shouldn't have been shocked. Bish lived and breathed sports gambling. And though none of us read the *Daily Racing Form* or knew much about the horses, we prattled on about well-known trainers Bob Baffert and D. Wayne Lukas as though we were experts. As we settled in, our sophomoric humor began to flow, especially when Cakes pointed out the horse on post 14, "Built for Pleasure." Then Bic began to puff his chest as if he were an authority on horse racing since he'd bet exacta boxes on harness racing at nearby Rosecroft Raceway. We knew he didn't know jack, so we called him out and ribbed him.

Later, Redskins center Cory Raymer became our first guest. McClure had booked the interview to promote WJFK's status as the team's official new radio home. Bish, always fascinated by where people were from, started the conversation: "So Cory, tell me about Fond du Lac, Wisconsin." The burly offensive lineman chuckled and began to bare his soul about his hometown and fishing on Lake Winnebago.

Then Bic asked what would become a staple of our future interviews: "So did you buy anything cool with your bonus after you were drafted?" Raymer had just finished his rookie season and wasn't the reckless spending type, but we made him comfortable enough to laugh and joke about the oversized TV he purchased.

Three hours flew by quickly. Beforehand, we didn't know if we could fill the time. All we had done were half-hour episodes on BCTV and a train wreck of a demo. Now we had just finished our first radio show and felt good about the performance. We had no idea if anybody was listening, but it felt like we had been prepping our whole lives for this moment.

★ ★ ★ ★

Before Facebook, before Google, before everybody used their cell phones to gather information, newspapers were a big deal. The newspaper was where we got our stories. The newspaper is where we got our stats. The newspaper and the sports pages were the lifeblood of our show. And the newspaper is what changed the trajectory of our lives.

So, during the summer of 1996, as we embarked on our radio careers, I continued to hustle for more press. Though the *Prince George's Journal* wasn't the *Washington Post* or *Washington Times*, why wouldn't they want to cover four friends from P.G. County now heard throughout the District, Maryland, and Virginia?

Sure enough, reporter John Harris III and a photographer joined us at the WJFK studios for a show, watching us spew non-stop irreverent opinions while laughing at each other's infantile jokes. By then, our radio mentors Jeremy Coleman and Jim McClure had branded us as "just four regular guys talking sports," which Bish repeatedly bellowed throughout our shows. So, it wasn't surprising that the opening line in Harris's 26-paragraph feature in the July 3 edition echoed, "They're just four guys talking sports, offering not a lot of knowledge, but tons of opinions."

"Not a lot of knowledge!" Bish was offended. But besides the slight, the article captured our spirit. Over two months on the air, we had improved a reasonable amount. After realizing we were more relaxed while music played beneath us, McClure approved a constant backdrop of rock and hip hop music that added a unique, garage-band feel to the show. We created new features like the "Bad Boys Honor Roll," where we mocked the "cornucopia of criminals" in sports. And we balanced our verbal jousting with interviews of guests we booked ourselves, such as ESPN's Linda Cohn and two-time NBA champion Kenny Smith of the Houston Rockets.

We also started venturing away from sports and into our personal lives, whether it was Bic's upcoming nuptials or our television viewing habits. "Yeah, I watched the National Spelling Bee," Bish scoffed, "That's how dull my life is!"

And though the last line of the *P.G. Journal* article didn't highlight our humility, we couldn't complain. Bish boasted, "I'm not bragging or anything, but I think we have a very good show." He wasn't lying. Momentum was building.

After working Saturday nights for a few months and breaking us into the radio business, Jim McClure returned to his full-time duties running the board for the Howard Stern show while serving as the station's assistant program director. In the early weeks of the "new sports weekend," McClure had hired Brian Cosgrove and Jason Veazey to produce our show on Saturday nights. Amy Szutowicz would answer phones.

When Veazey interviewed for his job, he recalls McClure describing us as "four guys who talk about goofy things who might hear a Bob Marley song playing in the background and then start to sing it." The description didn't inspire confidence. McClure labeling us as irreverent and off-the-cuff gave Veazey the impression we didn't know what we were doing and his run as our producer might not last. To Veazey, we sounded like an experiment that was destined to fail.

His perception changed after working with us the first time. An avid WJFK listener, Veazey found us utterly different than anything he had heard before. Since he was green like us, he was ready to focus on running the board, but we quickly became intrigued by the 6-foot-4, 280-pound Army veteran and began to ask him questions. We busted his balls about flying a helicopter while serving our country. How did he fit in the chopper? Luckily for us, Veazey handled the ribbing perfectly. Instead of becoming defensive, his infectious laugh blended in perfectly with the "goofy guys."

Though we were crass and juvenile on the air, we turned it off around our phone screener Amy, who was gracious and demure. For three hours, Amy mostly sat in a separate room down the hallway answering calls to the show, but she joined us in the studio when we wanted a female opinion. Amy, who aspired to break into the broadcasting business, was happy to oblige, and hearing her voice served as a stark contrast to the on-air boys club. Surprisingly, she seemed to like us.

Building a great team behind us inspired confidence. We were all young and inexperienced but having so much fun. That rubbed off on the listeners. We were amassing a cadre of crazy callers. We didn't have the resumes of the station's other programs, but we led the league in pizza delivery drivers like Ryan from Odenton, who would crack us up every Saturday as he joined our shenanigans. Each week, I compiled a list of show guests and callers for Jeremy Coleman to see if he was paying attention.

We felt more confident after taping over 30 episodes with guests like Redskins quarterback Gus Frerotte and the legendary Maryland basketball coach Lefty Driesell. And it seemed as if we were being accepted, too. We were invited to the company's Christmas party, where we would finally meet the station's weekday superstars.

Dressed in suits and ties, the four of us headed to a posh hotel in downtown Washington. Besides our bosses, a few weekend board operators, and Dan Daly and Earl Forcey from "The Sports Jam," we didn't know anybody at WJFK. Somewhat uneasy, we were looking forward to letting loose.

Curious to meet Don Geronimo and Mike O'Meara, in particular, Bic, who had religiously listened to the duo during his morning commutes to DeMatha High, brought his wife Dina. Cakes was accompanied by his wife Amy, while Bish and I brought our girlfriends. There was no minimizing this night. We were nattily attired and there were free food and drinks. It was going to be a night to remember.

Soft Christmas music played in the background as we walked into the ballroom adorned with holiday décor and majestic chandeliers. Station employees buzzed around the swanky tables and dance floor as waiters greeted them with trays of hors d'oeuvres. Before joining, we were steered to a table by the ballroom entrance to check into the party. Promotions director Tammy Sacks, armed with a list, looked at us and asked us who we were.

"We're the Sports Junkies," we responded smugly.

"Who?" Tammy had never heard of us. We weren't on the guest list and couldn't enter our station's party. Humble pie.

Eventually, McClure spotted us and formally introduced us to Tammy and countless employees, from accountants to sales staff to the station's general manager, Ken Stevens. Everybody was friendly, although it seemed like we were a curiosity to most.

Armed with liquid courage, we decided to make our move after dinner. Bic led us toward Don and Mike, who had been holding court most of the evening. They were the money-makers at WJFK, generating millions of dollars in advertising and lining the pockets of every sales associate. They were the undisputed kings of the ring—and millionaires. We were still making $75 a weekend.

★ ★ ★ ★

Steve Jobs, co-founder of Apple, once said, "My favorite things in life don't cost any money. It's really clear that the most precious resource we all have is time." In the radio business, everybody fights for airtime. There's nothing more valuable.

So, after the Washington Redskins notched a meaningless win over the playoff-bound Dallas Cowboys on December 22 to close their 1996 season, we knew we had an opportunity to expand. Without game coverage, WJFK had a hole in their Sunday lineup. We wanted more airtime and Jeremy gave it to us. The following weekend we cranked out shows on Saturday and Sunday. If anybody wondered whether we could handle six hours of radio, they got their answer. We were building our resume.

Continuing to send letters in a persistent search for more press, the *Washington Post* and their sports media columnist Len Shapiro repeatedly ignored my pursuits. But Kitson Flynn from the *Washington Times* was receptive and wrote about WJFK "beefing up its weekend sports programming since the Redskins' season choked to a close." She explained that the "four raging sports fans bantering about whatever happens to be on their minds" were being upped to two nights a week and quoted me saying, "We got this chance and we want to make the most of it." Now we had to deliver.

It was full steam ahead the next several months. WJFK's sister station in Baltimore, 1300 AM, began to run "The Sports Junkies," and we added a fourth hour to the show. With each of us now making $200 a weekend, our collective haul of $800 was about the cost of a single one-minute commercial on "The Don and Mike Show."

The Redskins' season behind us, the show shifted from doses of heavy football talk to more personality-driven radio. As the weeks rolled on, we became bolder and bolder. For example, when World Championship Wrestling star Diamond Dallas Page joined us on the phone, Cakes asked about his signature move. Sounding deadly serious about how he used his diamond cutter to beat Randy "Macho Man" Savage, I interrupted him. "But wrestling is fake."

My cohorts couldn't believe I had gone there, but we had developed a no-holds-barred attitude during the show. Why would we change during interviews? Cringe radio was riveting radio.

Not all of our interviews were controversial. Former Washington Capitals winger Craig Laughlin became a regular talking about his former team and the NHL. We also built a Rolodex of college basketball coaches who joined us leading up to March Madness. Hearing from Jim Calhoun at Connecticut or Rick Majerus at Utah gave us credibility. And even though people wondered why we would have Delaware coach Mike Brey on the show regularly, he was a Bethesda, Maryland, native, former DeMatha High player and assistant coach, and we knew he was headed to bigger things (i.e., Notre Dame).

Eventually, we held our first remote broadcast in front of fans at former Redskins coach Richie Petitbon's restaurant in Oakton, Virginia. There weren't hundreds in the crowd, more like 20, and that included friends and family. But having attended many "Don and Mike Show" events in the past, Veazey noticed something different about our crowd. There were more Blacks. Maybe it was the music we played or our P.G. County roots and lingo, or our sports content, but WJFK's audience had been primarily white. Adding a new demographic could only help.

While being more inclusive was great, we were relieved that anybody came to see us in person. This experience was new to us, and we were able to put faces to the names of some listeners. Derrick from Logan Circle was a burly African-American man with dreadlocks and an effervescent smile. Anthony from Oxon Hill looked nothing like we expected. He was a baby-faced kid still in high school. Months later, Bic and I were invited to Derrick's house for crabs, and we obliged. Then I attended Anthony's football game as he returned kicks for Friendly High School. The connections were genuine.

We were so appreciative that we even let 7th-grader William Choi interview us for his creative writing project. With his mother listening on the line, he bribed us with beer so we couldn't say no.

As insignificant as those engagements seemed, they struck a nerve with Jim McClure. Even though we ridiculed him constantly by calling him Chinstrap and Jimmy Dum-Dum on the show, we actually respected him. McClure had discovered us, but Jeremy Coleman was a question mark. We didn't know if he listened to the show.

After updating Coleman on our recent exploits, McClure prepared an office memo for the sales staff—the same people who had no idea who we were at the Christmas party—to update them on our weekend endeavors. The memo highlighted our dedication, pointing out we not only booked our own guests but had the "best guests by far of any of the sports shows." In addition, McClure explained that our interviews were fun, pointing to our

April 5 conversation with PGA Tour golfer Billy Andrade, who mocked us for using cheap golf clubs while agreeing to meet for beers.

Most of all, McClure called "The Sports Junkies" cutting-edge personality radio. We weren't just "four regular guys talking sports" anymore. And unlike the other weekend sports shows, McClure wrote in that office memo, "When people talk about listening to The Junkies, listeners were mentioning us in the same breath as the other weekday shows, not the other sports shows," including Howard Stern, Don and Mike, and the Greaseman. We had created a distinct identity, and our bosses were noticing.

★ ★ ★ ★

At the same time, the Greaseman's nationally syndicated show was beginning to flatline. In 1993, he had reportedly turned down a $6.5 million renewal offer from DC 101. Instead, the Greaseman moved to Los Angeles with Infinity Broadcasting carrying his show nationwide. Three years later, affiliates were dropping like flies, including New York and L.A. His syndication deal was in jeopardy. Though the Greaseman was controversial, he wasn't dumb. He could see the writing on the wall, so when 94.7 WARW offered him $1 million a year to host a morning show in Washington that May, he jumped at the chance.

Now WJFK had a decision. Who would replace the Greaseman in the night slot after "The Don and Mike Show?" Everybody from the station's sports weekend wanted the opportunity, but Jeremy Coleman and Jim McClure had their answer. "The Sports Junkies" had separated from the pack. We were generating press, unlike the rest of the weekend shows. Plus, we were making a dent in the ratings, and there wasn't a show that sounded remotely like us. Our bosses felt the buzz.

Soon we were having another meeting in Coleman's office. McClure had told us what to expect, but hearing Coleman officially offer us the night slot felt like a dream. Just a year before, nobody knew who we were. Now we were being offered a daily spot on D.C.'s superstation. How could we say no?

Still, getting the job wasn't automatic. Coleman explained that general manager Ken Stevens wasn't ready to commit fully. Instead, we would be given an eight-week tryout. Then, should things go well, we would revisit and talk about a longer deal.

After our meeting, we headed to Bish's mom's house to ponder our future. Sitting on the back deck, we recognized the opportunity. Bish and I were on board without hesitation. Though I was set to graduate from Temple Law School, I had decided not to pursue a legal job for a year. I wanted to see if radio might indeed be my future. WJFK's offer couldn't have come at a better time. For Bish, a career in sports was always his dream. There was no internal struggle or debate.

On the other hand, Bic and Cakes were in entirely different life circumstances. They were married. Bic's passion for radio was indisputable. He wanted the daily show as much as anybody—so that left Cakes.

For him, there was uncertainty. He had a wife with a baby on the way, and a non-guaranteed offer wasn't a no-brainer. Cakes had security at Toys R Us. If he stayed with the company another year, they would triple match his investments.

As we drank beers on the deck, Cakes, bowing to the pressure from his boys, finally decided, "*Fuck it. I can always go back to selling toys.*" We knew this was our shot. We knew this was our opportunity. We couldn't let it slip. We had to capture it.

4

NOT FOR EVERYONE

"The Four Levels of Comedy: Make your friends laugh, make strangers laugh, get paid to make strangers laugh, and make people talk like you because it's so much fun." — *Jerry Seinfeld*

The next few weeks were a blur. While I still had finals and graduation in Philadelphia, Cakes had to give two weeks' notice to Toys R Us. The last thing he wanted to do was burn bridges. What would happen if WJFK decided we weren't worthy after our eight-week tryout?

Meanwhile, we still had to accept WJFK's offer. We wanted to negotiate for a raise. Though we had no idea how much we should be making, we knew it was more than on the weekends. Unfortunately, I was nominated by my pals to ask Jeremy Coleman for the bump.

Knowing WJFK was charging up to $1,000 per minute for "The Don and Mike Show," I crunched the numbers by estimating our spots might go for $100. If we ran 16 minutes of commercials each hour—a lowball estimate—"The Sports Junkies" would generate $24,000 per week, minimum. So asking for $150 per show seemed reasonable. Each of us would make $750 a week and account for just 12.5 percent of the estimated revenue. And that was a conservative estimate.

Armed with my numbers and notes, I nervously called Coleman. Before talking money, I tried to butter him up. "We just wanted to say how thrilled we are that you've offered us this opportunity," I started. "We couldn't be more excited." As Jeremy listened and waited patiently for an official yes, my angst grew.

"Here's the thing, Jeremy," I continued, "you're asking John to give up his career where he's been making pretty good money, and I'm going to have to put working as a lawyer on hold." I may have been stretching the truth.

"So, we do want to give this thing a shot." Before I could launch my closing salvo, Jeremy cheerfully interjected, "that's great." He didn't fathom that we'd have the audacity to negotiate.

Picking up where I left off, I sheepishly said, "We do want to do this, Jeremy, we really do, but we're giving up a lot for just a tryout. And $100 per show is nothing. For a nighttime show, that's a joke." The silence on the other end was deafening. Tentatively, I pressed forward.

"We know there's a much bigger audience during the week and that you guys will be charging more for commercials, so we think $150 per show would be fair."

The next seconds felt eternal. My stomach was in knots. Clearly, Coleman wasn't moved. Finally, the usually composed programmer countered, "Are you fucking kidding me? This is the opportunity of a lifetime. You guys haven't done shit. And now you want more money. Who do you think you are?"

Gulp! This negotiation wasn't going the way I envisioned. I had never heard Jeremy raise his voice, and now he was cussing at me on the phone. Should I cave and accept the $100 per show? What would my boys think?

Fortunately, cooler heads prevailed. Coleman was playing his role. His boss, general manager Ken Stevens, was notoriously cheap. So, Jeremy didn't want to give four unproven guys a 50 percent increase. Instead, we settled on $110 per show. I took that as a victory.

★ ★ ★ ★

My radio partners did not jump for joy when I told them about our paltry raise, but we couldn't afford to bellyache about it, either. We had to focus. Instead of conducting a remote show before a smattering of fans on Saturday nights, we'd sign on immediately after "The Don and Mike Show," the market's top-rated afternoon drive program. Thousands of listeners would be in their cars tuned to WJFK. "The Sports Junkies" needed to figure out how to convert them into fans.

Our biggest challenge was filling the time. How were we going to do three hours of radio Monday through Friday? It seemed daunting. So we met at Cakes's townhouse to brainstorm ideas.

Luckily, the weekend shows had been a testing ground. Though Jim McClure offered advice, we were allowed to experiment and figure out what worked. By the time our weekend run was over, we had done 77 shows and tried innumerable segments. Some were holdovers from our TV show while others like "Doo Doo Browns" were new. We'd play the song by 2 Hype Brothers and a Dog and rip into the pathetic performances in sports. Callers would suggest their poopy performances, too. "Doo Doo Browns" was stupid but fun.

There were about three weeks before the new show started, but we drafted the format quickly. Bish would lead a daily "Sports Page" and we added an "Entertainment Page," directed by Bic, our pop culture guru who was all over the latest celebrity gossip. We had tried the segment a few times on the weekend, often leading to some of the funniest parts of the show.

The "E.P." was also a way for us to break the monotony of sports talk. We could discuss music, our favorite TV shows, and the latest movies. Tangents always sprang from the E.P. You never knew where we would end up once we heard the theme song from "Entertainment Tonight." Bic might discuss the latest theories about Tupac's murder, or we would debate who was hotter, Jennifer Aniston or Sandra Bullock.

Beyond the daily features, we'd try "Game Show Wednesday." Listeners love prizes. Whether we offered concert tickets or gift cards, the phone lines lit up. We gave away Junkies hats that Cakes's wife Amy designed at the mall. With more station support, we would offer better swag. So we hoped.

Taking a bite from Rush Limbaugh and his "Open Line Friday," we'd accept more calls on "Open Line Thursday." Up to that point, most of our calls sprouted from our dedicated segments. Other times, we dove into a heated sports debate, and listeners would respond. But to date, we had never opened the phone lines blindly to see what might follow.

We had to keep hustling through fresh segment ideas with the dedicated days and daily features as our baseline. We also aggressively sought the best guests possible. With only eight weeks to impress our bosses and win over an audience, we couldn't afford to have listeners change the station.

On May 26, 1997, a Monday, and just a little over a year after our weekend debut, "The Sports Junkies" hit the radio airwaves on a weeknight for the first time. We were nervous but ready. Using his connections, Bish asked his old radio partner Greg Jewell, now a producer at ESPN, for help booking long-time "SportsCenter" anchor Linda Cohn as our first guest. We would also talk with NFL insider John Clayton and reconnect with Bob Ferry, the former Washington Bullets general manager who kept us laughing during an appearance on our BCTV show months earlier.

We were feeling good about our guest lineup, but a minor controversy marred our debut. Dan Daly, *Washington Times* columnist and co-host of "The Sports Jam," quit when he learned we were chosen to replace "The Greaseman." The prickly newspaper columnist had never taken us seriously and figured he deserved the opportunity. Instead of choosing one of the best NFL historians in the country, Coleman and McClure selected four guys who sounded like a bunch of frat boys at the neighborhood bar. Daly was indignant. Instead of forging ahead, he chose to walk away from radio entirely.

Regardless, the pressure was on *us* to deliver. Before our first show, McClure wanted to have a quick meeting. Driving in that afternoon, I popped on WJFK and tuned into "The Don and Mike Show." They had been together for 12 years and were a machine. Don Geronimo led most discussions while his partner Mike O'Meara chimed in with hysterical impressions and anecdotes. Producer Robb Spewak and newsman Buzz Burbank popped in on the conversations occasionally, too. Don and Mike's show was polished, gripping, fun, and sounded so much smoother than ours.

As I plodded through Beltway traffic, I hoped The Junkies' long friendship and natural camaraderie would translate to a much bigger audience. While I was confident in our show, I worried that we might be rejected. My partners felt the same way. But that wasn't going to stop us from giving it our best shot.

Gathered in McClure's office on the second floor, I distributed a detailed outline of our segments and guests, and we went over the rundown together. But that wasn't as important to McClure. We were jittery and he wanted to calm us down.

Though Brian Cosgrove and Jason Veazey had joined our group to run the board on weekends, McClure would work directly with us during our first few weeks. That made us feel comfortable. McClure emphasized that we keep doing what we had been doing for the last year and just have fun.

After the meeting, we moved to the first floor, which housed the studios, offices, and a mass of cubicles filled by sales executives. Overhead speakers played the station's broadcasting feed, so we could hear Buzz Burbank deliver the news. We wondered what Don and Mike might say about us in the transition between our shows.

Since their program was a ratings juggernaut, they were afforded the luxury of doing commercial-free radio for long blocks during their peak hour at 5 p.m. That meant there was still a heavy dose of commercials left to play during the tail end of their show. As a result, Buzz's newscast often ran well past 7 p.m. so they could cram in their commercial breaks. As the clock ticked, we waited anxiously.

During their last break, Mike emerged from the studio to greet us and wish us luck. We had met just once, but his good humor and heartfelt welcome left us feeling more relaxed. Then, as he returned to the studio, Don launched into an unexpected introduction.

We had no idea if they had ever listened to our show. Signing off to his audience after 7:15 p.m., Don closed, "So 'The Sports Junkies' are next," and Mike added, "It'll be money." They knew us, and that had to be a good thing.

★ ★ ★ ★

Pouring into the main studio as Don packed his papers into a brown attaché case, it didn't matter that we had been doing weekend radio for over a year. This moment felt like our first show all over again.

After Don wished us luck, Cakes grabbed a seat next to the wall. I squeezed in next to him with Bic on my right and McClure across from us standing behind the radio board. While the three of us were packed in like sardines, Bish sat alone in Buzz's studio. Nervous energy filled both rooms as the final commercial fired in the cart machine. Finally, when Redman's "Tim 4 Sum Aksion" kicked in, we were ready. We knew this was our once-in-a-lifetime moment. As the beat kicked in, I made the sign of the cross quickly and prayed that we had made the right decision. Who couldn't use some divine intervention?

Though the WJFK audience wasn't accustomed to hearing hip hop music, it was part of who we were. We knew our show was different and didn't sound professional, and our music might not appeal to everybody. But we also knew the constant backdrop of music raised our energy and added flavor to the show.

As McClure potted down the music, Bish opened the show, and we quickly found our groove using the same P.G. County slang we had been using all our lives. A huge Michael Jordan fan, Bish was "cised" that he had poured in 34 points against the Miami Heat in the Eastern Conference Finals two days earlier.

Later, we laughed with Linda Cohn about living in Bristol, Connecticut, a sprawling ESPN complex and not much else. We bounced around topics, ranging from the NBA Finals to her disappointing New York Yankees. Having ESPN's most prominent female anchor on-air with us added legitimacy to our first new show. Similarly, having NFL insider John Clayton as a guest lent more credibility.

Three hours flew by and, in a strange way, the time felt like a celebration. Many of our devoted weekend callers checked in to raise our comfort level during the "Big Hurtings" segment, a "Doo Doo Brown" disciple. Others called to say how "silly" it was to hear us during the week. We felt the weekend love. Cakes responded to one caller with our signature, "it's a show," describing the absurdity of it all. A few weeks earlier, he was close to becoming a vested employee at Toys R Us and destined for a life in retail. Now his job consisted of delivering well-timed zingers.

Perhaps our interview with Bob Ferry captured the moment best. The gregarious guest reflected on sitting down with us the previous March. He couldn't believe we had flipped our little TV show into a paid gig. "Anything is possible," he quipped.

He was right. We finished our first weeknight show on Washington's superstation before passing the baton to the nationally syndicated Scott Ferrall. But instead of waiting an entire week for our next show, we'd be back the next night, and the night after that, for at least two months.

★ ★ ★ ★

We continued to book a wide range of guests during our first week, including PGA golfer Fred Funk, who served as the golf coach at the University of Maryland before hitting the pro tour. Bish and Bic were huge golf fans, and though most sports radio shows didn't dedicate much time to the sport, we didn't care. Our philosophy was to talk about what interests us, and we hoped the audience would follow.

Bic had been following Tiger Woods since his amateur days, so he wanted Funk's impressions of the 21-year-old prodigy winning his first major tournament at The Masters two month's earlier. Tiger had crushed the field by 12 strokes with an estimated 44 million people watching. Funk's perspective on Tiger's future, and impact on the sport, was riveting radio.

Later in the week, we reconnected with an old golfing pal Rick Schuller, who had joined us during our weekend run. A year earlier, Bic persuaded Schuller on the air to be his caddy during the PGA Tour's Kemper Open in Bethesda. This time, Schuller ridiculed Bic's caddying skills because he complained about the golf bag's weight.

Because Bish was obsessed with the weather, we booked Sue Palka from WTTG-Channel 5 to talk about El Niño, the weather pattern wreaking havoc on the mid-Atlantic. The tall, cheerful weather lady had been on TV since 1985, winning local Emmy awards. We enjoyed her stories of chasing tornadoes in Oklahoma.

WJLA-Channel 7 sportscaster Rene Knott surprised us the following week. We hadn't booked him. Instead, the hulking former college football player and all-around nice guy called in while driving home to let us know he was enjoying the show. He had heard our interviews with Pat Gillick, the Baltimore Orioles' general manager, and our conversation with Washington Redskins Hall of Famer Ken Houston. Maybe it shouldn't have mattered that he was listening, but we felt accepted when local media came on the show.

Of course, an article in the *Washington Post* would be different.

Getting into the paper, which each of us delivered as kids, had been our goal since we hit the radio airwaves. Unfortunately, my letters with guest lists and show highlights that I had been sending religiously to sports media columnist Len Shapiro had borne no fruit. Shapiro was either ignoring my pleas for coverage or unimpressed. Perhaps both?

Surprisingly, it wasn't a sportswriter from *The Post* who reached out first. Marc Fisher, a future two-time Pulitzer Prize winner who served as a local columnist when our show was moved to weekdays, was tasked with writing about the four radio upstarts chasing their dream. Fisher's column on June 3, 1997, wasn't a ringing endorsement, but it wasn't half bad either. We were on the front page of the Style section. A picture of us was directly above the column titled, "Four Men and a Mike: On WJFK, Twenty-Something Sports Junkies Talk Trash." Unfortunately for Bic, his name was misspelled in the photo caption. He was Eric *Brickel*.

Nonetheless, the article described what made our show different. "Roll over, Ken Beatrice," Fisher wrote, referring to the long-time Washington sports talk icon. "The Sports Junkies" are fixing to change the way Washington talks sports." That seemed like a lofty goal. We just wanted to pass our eight-week tryout and get an actual contract.

Continuing, Fisher wrote, "This is not the stuff of ESPN. This is not chatter about the Skins' offensive line. This is not even speculation about Marv Albert's nocturnal activities. Instead try tips on cheating in golf, tales of childhood pranks and 'Junkardy,' a 'Jeopardy!'-style game show in which the categories are 'Drunks,' 'Batterers,' 'Babes in Sports,' 'Mets Who Blow' [about former New York Mets caught using cocaine] and 'Creepers' [about guys who've cheated on their wives]." Clearly, he had listened to "Game Show Wednesday."

Then Fisher fired a few shots. "They talk on top of each other, it's hard to tell them apart, they laugh at their own lines, and they often act half their age." It wasn't flattering, but wasn't inaccurate either. Fisher added, "But if shock is what sells on talk radio, they've got it made. Whether the topic is Frank Gifford or big fat baseball players, The Junkies push the envelope."

There were a few lines that vexed us.

"The Junkies are sometimes funny, sometimes far too impressed with their own creative skills," Fisher wrote. "But in an era when talk radio often means little more than listening to somebody shoot the breeze in front of a microphone, The Junkies at least begin armed with a youthful disdain for the rules. The kids take chances. Even if they die out there, it'll be worth listening to them go down with the ship."

Die out there? Go down with the ship? We hoped that wasn't premonitory. Still, the overall image of the show was fair. We weren't established. We weren't experienced. We weren't radio professionals. In the end, it was free publicity. And as P.T. Barnum preached, any press was good press. Hopefully, the Fisher piece would entice readers to give us a listen.

One week later, it was absolute chaos in the studio. That wasn't necessarily a bad thing. On the same day, WRC-Channel 4 sent a reporter to do a story on "The Sports Junkies," and Rick Reilly from *Sports Illustrated* became our first in-studio guest. Reilly, a five-time national sportswriter of the year, was in town to promote his book "Missing Links." Though none of us were voracious readers, the fictional story happened to be about four buddies who hacked it up on their local golf course. We could definitely relate.

The jokes started flying right away. First, there was the issue of space. We barely had any. While Jason sat comfortably in his own studio, the rest of us packed into the small area behind the console. Adding Reilly into the cramped confines only made things more uncomfortable. Reilly was practically on top of Bic while Cakes and I were almost arm-in-arm.

As if that wasn't enough, the cameraman from Channel 4 was there to capture everything, leaving us with less space. So when Reilly found out we had been on the air for just two weeks, he wondered why his publicist had booked him. We didn't mind the ribbing. Reilly fit perfectly into the show format.

Still, he felt like a spectator at a tennis match as we lobbed verbal volleys back and forth, covering everything from his relationship with Charles Barkley to his thoughts on Tiger Woods. Reilly's stories were hilarious—he had friendships with some of the most prominent athletes in the sports world—but after the interview, he looked like a punch-drunk fighter.

Standing in the hallway after his segment, Reilly said he had never done a show with four hosts. He complimented our energy, the frenetic pace of the interview, and the pinpoint questions. Deep down, he may have thought we wouldn't make it past our trial period, but his kudos seemed genuine.

Reversing roles, Channel 4 reporter Suzanne Malveaux entered the studio to ask us questions. A self-described expert on local newscasters, particularly the attractive female reporters, Bish knew all about Suzanne. Though she was just a few years older than us, she had been in the business five years.

Malveaux, who would later serve as a White House correspondent for CNN, began feeding us familiar questions: How did we get started? How long had we been friends? What were we doing before the radio show?

Our story had always distinguished us, as much as the show itself. Not surprisingly, when Malveaux's package aired at the end of the top-rated Channel 4 newscast just before 11:30 p.m., anchor Doreen Gentzler said, "Four local guys are taking sports radio by storm. They grew up together in Bowie, Maryland, and now have given up everything to try and make it big in talk radio."

Truthfully, we hadn't given up much, but the introduction was great. Next, Malveaux's voice came in as she narrated the two-minute piece, interspersed with clips of that night's show and our playful interactions. We couldn't have asked for more. But the most memorable part was the sarcastic parting shot from Gentzler and her co-anchor, the legendary Jim Vance.

Gentzler closed the broadcast with, "They're not for everyone." Without hesitation, Vance added, "You know who you are."

5

FAILURE IS NOT AN OPTION

"Only those who dare to fail greatly can ever achieve greatly."
— Robert F. Kennedy

Doreen Gentzler was right. We weren't for everyone. But that wasn't our job. At WJFK, the mission was clear. The hot talk station's target demographic was men 25-54. The entire lineup—from Howard Stern to "The Don and Mike Show"—dominated that category, finishing atop the ratings almost every quarter. We needed to be there, too.

After just a few weeks, we felt pretty good about the direction of the show. We were booking great guests and producing fun shows. It seemed like the audience was growing. Still, our challenge was to keep things fresh. With the sports calendar slowing for the summer of 1997, how could we get to the college and pro football and basketball seasons with enough content?

WJFK wouldn't care. If we didn't make a dent in the ratings, we would be looking for new jobs. We couldn't afford to fail. So, less than a month into our new gig, we held our first in-studio contest, a talent show.

Radio contests can be a welcome change of pace from the routine of a three-hour program. It also serves as a way to give prizes from sponsors that welcome the mentions. Not knowing what to expect, we hoped for enough listeners willing to participate. Pleasantly surprised, we had nearly a dozen contestants.

Though many of the acts were weak, two stood out. Ray the Puker could make himself vomit on command. As gross as it was to watch him heave at will, it was still impressive. But not impressive enough.

A contestant claimed he could say any word or name in reverse. This seemed inconceivable. How can your brain process a thing like that? We were intrigued. After he correctly said a few random words in reverse, Bic challenged him with the name of the Redskins' quarterback. "How about Gus Frerotte?" The contestant instantly responded, "Torerf Sug." We giggled like school kids.

Still, we weren't sure if he was correct. So our producer delivered validation by turning the audio around to hear the backwards talker in reverse. Sure enough, we heard clearly, "Gus Frerotte." We were blown away. Winner winner, chicken dinner!

★ ★ ★ ★

By the fall, we had become part of the WJFK fabric. Station promos touted the deep lineup of talk shows, closing with "The Sports Junkies at night."

But weeks after our two-month tryout period had passed, we hadn't signed a binding contract. Fortunately, I was replaced as chief negotiator in favor of Bish's uncle, Joe Suntum, a local attorney at Miller, Miller and Canby.

Having somebody unaffiliated with the show representing us was a good thing. Joe wouldn't be intimidated by Jeremy Coleman and scared into submission. Hiring Uncle Joe paid quick dividends as we received a temporary raise from $110 to $150 per show. Though it wasn't a windfall, the gesture indicated WJFK wanted us to be part of its future.

It hadn't taken us long to establish "The Sports Junkies" as the show to follow when it came to Redskins talk, a good spot to be given the team's popularity. Though Washington had been mired in mediocrity during recent years, the three Super Bowl wins still carried a ton of weight. Redskins games were sold out, and their radio and TV ratings were through the roof with a staggering 53 percent of all TVs in use. So when our bosses asked us to be part of the team's official postgame show, featuring former Redskins center and Super Bowl champion Jeff Bostic, we happily obliged. The postgame audience was huge, The Junkies self-promotional value enormous.

Increasingly, the sales staff was asking us to make appearances. On August 27, 1997, we were set up to broadcast from a Redskins preseason rally and cruise held by six-time Pro Bowler Darrell Green, who invited many of his teammates to be part of the charity event. Situated along the pier on the D.C. waterfront, a large 106.7 FM WJFK Redskins radio banner hung behind us. Fans seeking autographs, plus local TV reporters, buzzed around, anticipating the arrival of the team's stars. Most weren't familiar with "The Sports Junkies" yet, but they couldn't miss our signage. And when Darrell Green joined us, they noticed.

With only four microphones on hand, I jumped behind Cakes, wearing a Gus Frerotte jersey and a Redskins cap backward. Then my boys peppered Green with questions ranging from his days as the NFL's fastest man to the team's expectations for the new season. Green, a 14-year veteran and future Hall of Famer, spoke all the usual football clichés. Still, he wasn't accustomed to the rapid-fire nature of our questions, which hit him from all directions.

Smiling throughout, Green was engaging as he wove the famous tale of chasing down Dallas Cowboys running back Tony Dorsett in 1983. Afterward, he politely wished us luck and went back to glad-handing the fans. We would see him again in two weeks when the new Jack Kent Cooke Stadium opened.

A few years before passing away in spring 1997, the charismatic Cooke set the wheels in motion for a new Redskins home. RFK Stadium, beloved by the fans, was badly outdated and seated just 57,000. Cooke dreamed of a bigger, modern stadium with all the bells and whistles—from video boards with advertising to corporate skyboxes to club seating with upscale food and beverage amenities.

Cooke had long admired Giants Stadium in the New Jersey Meadowlands and hired architects to draft a close replica. But then, Cooke couldn't find a place for their sprawling new home, and the blueprints collected dust. Negotiations with Washington, D.C., broke down amid political infighting, and Cooke failed to build the stadium at Potomac Yards in Crystal City, Virginia, and adjacent to the Laurel Race Track in Maryland. He finally settled on a piece of land in Landover, Maryland, just nine miles from where we grew up in Prince George's County.

The stadium design was already outdated when the Redskins would host their home opener against the Arizona Cardinals. Local media fawned over Jack's place, but if you looked closely and were somewhat objective, you realized the stadium was a hastily built concrete dump on a hill. The upper-level seating was closer to the moon than the playing field.

Nevertheless, we were asked to host the broadcast for the stadium dedication. We couldn't believe we were sitting in the same booth where Frank Herzog and legends Sonny Jurgensen and Sam Huff would call games on the vast Redskins Radio Network.

How many games had we heard them call? How many historic Redskins moments had they witnessed? Herzog had been the Redskins' play-by-play announcer since 1979, and their chemistry and camaraderie were unparalleled. Countless fans who watched Redskins games on TV would turn off the volume so they could listen to the beloved trio on the radio.

Sitting in their chairs was a big thrill, but so was our guest lineup. John Kent Cooke, who had taken over for his father as owner, joined us first, followed by NFL commissioner Paul Tagliabue. Less than two years earlier, we were happy to book Keith Cavanaugh, editor of the *Terrapin Times*, on our TV show.

Later, we reconnected with Darrell Green, but that was just the beginning. The guest lineup was stacked—from Gus Frerotte to "Head Hog" George Starke, who had been part of the team's first Super Bowl win in 1983. Defensive coordinator Mike Nolan joined us to preview their game against the Cardinals.

Then, a lesser-known name called into the show for the first time. Ryan Keuhl, an undrafted defensive tackle from the University of Virginia, had latched on with the Redskins a year earlier. Keuhl had become a fan of "The Sports Junkies" during his commute from American University, where he was taking summer courses toward a master's degree. Just two years younger than us, Keuhl attended Walt Whitman High School in Bethesda, Maryland. Just as we were trying to make it on the radio, Keuhl was trying to make an impression with his hometown team.

There was something meaningful about Keuhl's call. A Redskins player was listening to us and had called unsolicited. This was the first time all four of us got on board for one player. Ryan Keuhl was our new favorite Redskin.

★ ★ ★ ★

Beyond meeting some of our heroes, one of the perks of a radio show is getting things free. Quickly, Bic and Bish built a network of connections, including local golf pros, meaning they would rarely have to pay for a round. Bish was so adept at schmoozing and angling for free stuff that we began to call him "The Angler."

Part of the radio game was making clients and sponsors happy. When Jim McClure and Jeremy Coleman decided to give us a shot, one thing that stood out to them was how appreciative we were of our advertisers. If Subway dropped off a tray of sandwiches, we'd carry on about the great food. When Bic said, "I get cised for pickles," it somehow became a sound drop prominently featured on the show. This made the sponsors even happier.

Working at night lent itself to countless food drops. Restaurants would get their mention and we'd get free food. It was beautiful. But there was nothing like our connection with Britches Great Outdoors. Shelly Lawrence, a marketing rep, saw the four of us as the perfect fit to hawk their Polo rugby shirts and preppy casual clothing. When we were invited to one of their nearby stores, we jumped at the opportunity. While I snagged a free pair of jeans and a new shirt, Cakes walked away with an entire trash bag of new clothes. It wouldn't be the last time.

So, we had to oblige when Britches asked WJFK if we could do a remote broadcast from one of their stores. It was strange to do a show with listeners standing in front of clothing racks, but we made it work. NBA player Dickey Simpkins, who had played high school ball at Friendly High School in nearby Fort Washington, stopped by and talked about winning championships with Michael Jordan and the Chicago Bulls.

While we were broadcasting until 10 p.m., customers and listeners tuned in for the better part of three hours, indicating we were building a weeknight audience. McClure, who had helped set things up, was impressed. But most of all, Shelly was happy. Our pipeline for free clothes kept flowing.

A few weeks after Jack Kent Cooke stadium opened, Bic called me for the silliest of reasons. Having rapped 16 bars in honor of Allen Iverson's arrest for speeding and possession of a firearm in August, Bic wondered if I might be able to pen a new parody.

Marv Albert, legendary sportscaster, had just pled guilty to a misdemeanor count of assault and battery. Though he wouldn't serve jail time, he was fired by NBC, and embarrassed as the whole world now knew the sordid details of his kinky sex life.

It was an easy request for Bic. He wouldn't have to find the right background music or write any lyrics. Still, I was inspired, so I went to work.

Settling on "Mo' Money, Mo' Problems" by the Notorious B.I.G. and Puff Daddy, I worked feverishly to write lyrics that fit the beat. This time, unknown to my cohorts, I would write parts for each of them. If I was going to feel the inevitable wrath of callers mocking my rap performance, why wouldn't I spread the wealth?

Hours later, I arrived in Fairfax with my opus. My new ditty included a chorus down to the exact same number of syllables in the hit rap song. I did need some help though. Who would sing the chorus?

Working my way through the cubicles on the bottom floor, I asked two of the women on the WJFK sales staff to lend a hand. Michelle and Julie were amused, and happily obliged. A few minutes later they were in one of the production studios harmonizing the chorus.

Then, when my boys arrived a half-hour later, I sprung the news. I needed them to rap. They weren't exactly thrilled. Still, one by one, they entered the production studio. We knew it wasn't going to sound like "Self Destruction," the 1989 rap hit featuring the best emcees in the game, but that wasn't the point. Now our producer just had to pull it all together.

After previewing the Redskins' upcoming game against Jacksonville for the better part of an hour, the conversation shifted toward Marv's predilections and the fallout from his conviction. Then we introduced the rap, readying ourselves for ridicule. After the beat kicked in, Michelle and Julie crooned:

Marv copped a plea, say good-bye to NBC
It's like he knew there were more women that might say he was guilty
Marv liked it rough, Marv liked to bite
It's like the more booty he came across, the stranger sex he liked.

Michelle and Julie crushed it. That's when I jumped in trying to sound hard:

Now, who spit, who bit, tell me who quit
Who pays for whores? You tell me who scored.

I may not have hit my marks, but I didn't want to sound soft and corny like I did during the Iverson rap, so I mustered as much attitude as possible. Next up was Bic, who was starting to be known more by his initials E.B. He clumsily started…

E.B.'s on the mic and let me give you the scoop
You won't see Marv calling no hoops
He copped a plea, so now he'll suffer
No cash money, things will get tougher.

The lyrics were choppy, but E.B. made the best of it. Dividing the song into two sections, the chorus followed with Cakes joining next:

I'm the C to the A to the K E S
I'll do my best, to describe the mess
From my eyes, there was a test
Put Marv on the stand, and he would confess.

Listening to the loveable heavy metal fan stumble his way through eight bars was hilarious. Then Bish closed the show…

I'm a little bit shocked, I thought it was a lock
I thought the bitch, was as dumb as a rock.

My mom wasn't going to like the "B" word, but it fit.

Soon all eight phone lines exploded. Surprisingly, some listeners actually lauded our efforts. While some complimented our delivery and told us who they liked best, most mocked. That was okay. We expected that. It didn't matter. Mission accomplished.

★ ★ ★ ★

Though Jeremy Coleman usually allowed us to work unfettered, there were times he sprang into action. When he learned our overeager intern had been harassing some of our sponsors for free food, he summoned Thomas Block to his office.

Block was an 18-year-old freshman majoring in communications at nearby George Mason University. An avid WJFK listener, he had impressed us when we held intern tryouts that summer. Impressing us didn't take much, really.

Block had listened to E.B. weave a classic tale from our college years. E.B. claimed, "I've seen Jason order two footlongs from Subway and pummel them." While Bish declared it was an exaggeration, he didn't deny E.B.'s allegations that he opted to use public restrooms because of his propensity to destroy toilets. True or not, we howled with laughter at the thought.

Armed with the information and knowledge that we used a toilet sound effect to flush away bad callers, Thomas presented Bish with a toilet bowl keychain that made a flushing sound effect. That's all it took to win over Bish, who convinced us Thomas should be named our first intern.

Soon we dubbed him "The Blocker" as he became our on-air whipping boy. Working alongside our phone screener Amy, who was professional, gracious, and stuck to her job duties, The Blocker couldn't be more different. Instead of staying in his lane, The Blocker tried hard to ingratiate himself into our fraternity, like an annoying younger brother.

Still, The Blocker was never in danger of losing his unpaid gig—until we discovered he had been going to various restaurants, including some of our advertisers, posing as a member of the show asking for discounts and free food.

Much to The Blocker's surprise, Coleman was furious. Suggesting the behavior was detrimental to the show and our relationships with sponsors, Coleman promptly fired him. Begging for free chicken wings at Hooters had cost The Blocker his job.

Nevertheless, Jeremy suggested our young intern pay his penance on the air. We exposed the drama and promoted a "Torture the Blocker" Friday night special where our shamed minion would face a firing squad.

Listeners lined up to throw pies at The Blocker's face in our studio, which we had wrapped in plastic to protect the equipment. The stunt became a public flogging when audience members showered him with everything from Hostess apple pies to homemade cream pies. The glee from listeners was palatable as they poured soda, chocolate syrup, and even feathers over his head. By the end, The Blocker was wholly covered in syrup and shame.

Shivering in his shorts and t-shirt, The Blocker had gotten what he had always wanted. He was the star of the show. Unfortunately, it was his last.

During our weekend run, we did 77 shows in a little over a year. While that seemed substantial, it was nothing compared to the weekday grind. Six months into our new gig, we had recorded 120 episodes. Charlie Casserly, the Redskins general manager, joined us every Monday. Our new pal Ryan Keuhl would frequently call, too. Our relationship had blossomed to the point that when Casserly suggested Keuhl might want to start practicing long snapping, he listened. The recommendation ultimately helped Keuhl forge a 12-year NFL career, and hefty pension.

Beyond our Redskins insiders, we had built a connection with Craig Laughlin, who talked Capitals hockey, and Darvin Ham from the Washington Wizards. Still, as great as it was to have them call in regularly, there was nothing like an in-studio visit. And there was nobody like Oksana Baiul.

When the 1994 Olympic gold medalist stopped by for an on-air visit on November 11, 1997, we didn't know what to expect. While we thought we'd talk about her exploits on the ice and get the inside story on the infamous Nancy Kerrigan and Tonya Harding rivalry, the interview quickly devolved into innocent flirtation. Baiul, petite and pretty, swooned us. After saying she loved being in the studio, Bish asked, "Why?" Oksana replied, "Because I'm surrounded by four beautiful men."

Known to drink, Baiul seemed half loopy when she spoke to us with her thick Ukrainian accent. Baiul had been dropped from the Champions on Ice tour months earlier because of her drinking problem. She shrieked and squealed in laughter throughout the interview, delving into such trivial topics as her hairstyle and boyfriends. Though she dodged which one of us she liked best, it was fun to put her on the spot.

Then E.B. surprised us all as he attempted to say "I love you" in Russian. He may have butchered the delivery, but Baiul cried in laughter. Later we sang "Happy Birthday" to Oksana, who had turned 21 that weekend.

Twenty minutes with the Olympian felt like a blink. And though we didn't unearth any great revelations about figure skating, we didn't care. Oksana had charmed us into giddiness.

★ ★ ★ ★

One year earlier, we asked program director Jeremy Coleman for our Saturday night ratings. We had no clue where we stood. Though Jeremy argued they didn't matter, that seemed counterintuitive. Maybe there was a reason he didn't want us to see them. They could be disastrous. Even so, we insisted that we receive a breakdown.

A few days later, Coleman passed along a memo that outlined our numbers. We had taken a 0.3 rating in men 18-44 and raised it to a 1.2. Quadrupling WJFK's numbers on Saturday nights seemed impressive—until Coleman put them in perspective. The top station, WPGC, netted a 10.1. Two rock stations, WHFS and DC101, notched an 8.5 and 8.0, respectively. We weren't close.

Still, Jeremy tried to paint a rosier picture, "I think it's reasonable for your show to grow to at least a 3-share. But I know it will take time, so take pride in the fact that you are on your way. Now please throw this away and stop thinking about ratings."

Now, one year later, we couldn't stop wondering. Our ratings loomed larger than ever as we were starting to feel the pressure of being part of a radio station generating an estimated $50 million a year in revenue, more than any station in the country.

We hoped the 1997 Fall ratings book would be reflective of what we felt on the air. We had met hundreds of listeners during our remote broadcasts. Our phone lines were jammed constantly. We had booked great guests. We had been joined in studio by a local rock band, Jimmy's Chicken Shack, which was blowing up on MTV with their smash hit "High." We had poured our hearts and souls into the show.

That's why our first Fall ratings book felt so significant. Sure enough, we weren't wrong about the buzz. "The Sports Junkies" hit No. 1 in our time slot with men 25-54. We scored a 7.2 rating, more than double what the Greaseman had a year earlier. We had grown the ratings in our period by more than 300 percent and maintained a 26 percent advantage over the second-place station.

We may not have been making the money of other hosts, but we were ecstatic. And so were Jim McClure and Jeremy Coleman, the two guys that had given us a shot. Still, we had to needle Jeremy, "I guess we've grown to a three share." But nothing was going to wipe off his smile. In just our second full ratings book, we had exceeded all expectations and hit No. 1.

Even though we were still working without a contract, but we had proven to be so much more than an experiment as we passed the eight-week tryout period with flying colors. "The Sports Junkies" weren't a novelty any longer.

Maybe we were influenced by Howard Stern, but the longer we were on the air, the more comfortable we felt exposing our private viewing habits. E.B. even bragged about his extensive collection, which he kept in a JanSport backpack. So when local video company MVC started running ads on the show, opportunity struck. The hottest star in the adult film industry, Jenna Jameson, was promoting an appearance in their store and joined us in the studio. Days before we'd meet, E.B. broke down her performance with Randy West, age 50, who wasn't exactly carrying a baseball bat like most men in the industry.

As exciting as it may sound, having porn stars on the show can be incredibly awkward. Sometimes the starlets don't look as good in person as they do in their movies. But that wasn't the case with Jenna. The 23-year-old blonde, bathed in perfume, was wearing tight turquoise spandex pants and a white halter top nearly bursting at the seams. Her outfit left little for the vivid 20-something male imagination. She was gorgeous.

As stunning as Jenna looked, she was equally captivating on the show. An experienced radio guest, she had appeared on Howard Stern's show numerous times and appeared as herself in his movie "Private Parts." She was among the first entertainers of any genre to monetize the internet in the 1990s, and her autobiography spent six weeks on the New York Times bestseller list. While we talked about her mainstream success, we didn't want our interview to sound like others. Many of our listeners had probably heard her story, so we needed a different angle.

After asking some common questions like how she broke into the business, whether she was having fun, and what Randy West was like, we got to our pressing topic: What did she think of the Pam Anderson sex tape?

The "Baywatch" superstar had married Motley Crue drummer Tommy Lee, and it seemed the entire world had seen them in action… that is, except Jenna Jameson. We had to right that wrong. So, after quickly getting a copy of the tape, we popped it on a TV that our producer hooked up in the studio. Then, Jenna offered her expert opinion—from Pam Anderson's technique to Tommy Lee's manhood.

Jenna didn't mail in her appearance with us. She killed it, and we figured our audience loved it, too. At least, that's what we hoped.

A few days later, I received a letter from E.B.'s mom, who is extremely devout. Even though her husband was a pastor, I always felt I could joke around with him. Mrs. Bickel was different. I've never seen her take a drink. I've never heard her curse. She is so much different than "The Sports Junkies."

That's why my stomach became queasy when I started reading her letter. Mrs. Bickel wrote, "My dear Junks. You say you always like to hear from 'the honeys' out there. Well, here's one honey who thinks about you every day. In fact, you guys disturbed my sleep this a.m. so I decided to write you this letter."

Uh-oh! This couldn't be good.

"You fellows have so much going for you. Why? Because you get so ecstatic over these sporting events you watch. You're not unbiased, and you just explode with emotion over what you see happening [or not transpiring] at these various events."

I felt a "but" coming.

"Of course, you're articulate about the contests, but it's the fun you have among yourselves interpreting the different plays, the players and the coaches' actions that makes it interesting. You put one another down and yet come across as real friends. You're creative—inventing games for the listeners, writing and singing your own rap, and you keep adding different segments to the show."

That's when she dropped the hammer.

"I personally don't think your increasing talk about 'getting buns' or watching adult videos is what attracts people to your show."

Boom! There it was. She had gone where none of our moms had gone before. Though we relished being completely open and laughing about visiting adult video stores, having one of our moms confront us about it was unsettling.

Later, Mrs. Bickel referenced G-rated comedians such as Red Skelton and Bob Hope. She felt they were examples of entertainers who never relied on "Howard Stern-type questions and titillations." She feared we might be selling our integrity for ratings. She claimed we were role models and asked us to perceive what our future children might think of our shows.

The letter was heavy, mentioning the apostle Paul having admonished the Corinthians. The passage was over my head, but I was filled with guilt. We had just come off the high of interviewing Jenna Jameson and felt we had knocked that segment out of the park. Meanwhile, Mrs. Bickel was castigating us, asking…

"Is the giving of one's body merely a three-minute conquest, and, therefore, the latest 'sport' to be covered by the Junks?"

This wasn't the first time I had heard such a complaint. My mom was not fond of the language we used. She would tell me not to lower ourselves into the gutter, but we were four 27-year-old guys, and that's how we talked. But what if our moms were right?

6

CAN'T CONTAIN THE GENIUS

"Winning is only half of it. Having fun is the other half." – *Bum Phillips*

Pam Anderson once said, "It's great to be a blonde. With low expectations, it's very easy to surprise people." Finishing No. 1 in our time slot of the fall ratings was gratifying, but it also set an extremely high bar. We had to prove it wasn't a fluke. Expectations were sky-high.

Fortunately, we had a great team supporting us behind the scenes. If we delivered good ratings, our program director Jeremy Coleman would leave us alone.

We didn't even see him most nights. He headed home before we arrived.

Somehow, we saw our general manager even less. But Ken Stevens, who also ran WYSP in Philadelphia, a highly rated rock station featuring Howard Stern, was famously frugal. That didn't bode well for contract negotiations.

Jim McClure, our radio mentor, had moved back into his management role and mostly served as a cheerleader for the show that he had discovered. Though he would pop into the studio occasionally, his primary role was to be the liaison between the sales staff and promotions departments.

Based on our success, the salespeople went into overdrive. Advertising rates shot up, new sponsors were secured, and we made more appearances around D.C., Maryland, and Virginia. Since we weren't making much money and remained radio neophytes, we weren't in a position to say no. We didn't want to, anyway. If we could make $150 promoting the lottery at a gas station for two hours, why wouldn't we? Accept the extra cash and meet some of our listeners.

During one such appearance at The Barbershop & Company in Springfield, Virginia, we met Chris Kinard, a freshman at American University who stood in line for an autographed black and white promo picture. Chris, a WJFK fanatic, listened to us religiously on the weekends and was a huge fan of Howard Stern and "The Don and Mike Show."

The shy 18-year-old had listened to our Torture the Blocker segment and wondered if he might be able to fill our intern void. Impressing me with his radio knowledge and drive—Chris was set to work at WJLA-Channel 7 during his winter break—I jotted down his number. Two months later, he was hired.

We dubbed him C.K. and began to pepper him with questions about college and his dating life. C.K.'s embarrassment and awkwardness made him an easy target, but he handled the razzing well. And why not? C.K. would be able to say he "worked on the radio." Even if his job duties were menial, the job sounded cool. At the very least, it was a conversation starter.

As C.K. screened phone calls, he recognized a familiar voice. Chad From Burke was a regular caller who seemed to know more about "The Sports Junkies" than our families. Chad had been C.K.'s classmate at Lake Braddock High School, where he was part of the theater group. Now C.K. was putting him through so he could make us laugh with obscure references and inside jokes. The depths of Chad's knowledge scared us. When we learned he kept meticulous notes in a blue composition notebook and had a manilla folder full of post-it notes about the show, Chad From Burke became Chad the Stalker.

While we couldn't take our foot off the gas pedal on the air, we needed to solidify our team behind the scenes. A rotation of producers had worked with us. Brian Cosgrove remained a part-timer and Jason Veazey was available less often after taking a deejay job at a nearby country station. McClure had to hire somebody else.

That's when Joe Ardinger, a likeable Rolling Stones fanatic, joined our gang. Joe had filled in running the board for us, but it wasn't smooth sailing. When Joe failed to enter the names of our callers fast enough, E.B. became flustered and began to shout, "What's going on with the phones? How hard can it be to type up names?" Cakes prodded, "He's not doing it right!" Exasperated, E.B. barked, "No. Just go to break. Go to break. He's doing them too slow. He's too slow. Slow Joe."

We all laughed. As we went to commercials, Bish repeated, "Slow Joe, Slow Joe." We now had a new target, a new show character, and Joe had a new nickname that he would never shed.

During the infancy of the show, because we were so unique, the attention from the press kept coming. We figured it could only help, so we were happy when Patrick Butters from the *Washington Times* joined us in the studio to write a feature about "The Sports Junkies." The two-page article appeared in the February 3, 1998, editions and was the most in-depth look at us yet.

"They came, they saw, and now the Sports Junkies are conquering," Butters started. Even if the words were hyperbolic, the rest of the article painted the picture of a show on the rise that covered more than just sports.

Butters continued: "Yet other pressing topics creep in, such as whether President Clinton's accuser, Monica Lewinsky, rates a '10,' the merits of Sony PlayStation or callers' most embarrassing roadside moments. Although they're classic Generation Xers, The Junkies rapid, rabid banter—against a screeching hard-rock soundtrack—is fast pulling in non-sports fans, baby boomers, and beyond."

Though we weren't sure what it meant to be a Gen-Xer, Butters enjoyed his visit so much that he inserted himself into the article. After hearing us mock his hairstyle and wardrobe during his commute home, Butters closed: "Later, when someone mentioned 'failure,' another cracked, 'Yeah, like that guy who interviewed us!' I've got to admit, though, that was the funniest part of the show."

★ ★ ★ ★

Slowly but surely, we built a strong connection with our audience as we exposed more about our personal lives. For example, Bish was a consummate sports fan who loved to gamble. Over time he revealed countless stories about his gambling losses with a photographic-like memory of his bad beats.

One of his best tales harkened to college when he had fallen into such debt that he begged his uncle for money to pay off his bookie. Then there was the time he was able to evade another bookie who thought Bish was African-American. Later, he told us about the time he and his pal Scott shorted yet another bookie by the name of Dickie. Instead of paying off their $600 debt, they threw an envelope with a $100 bill and ones underneath to Dickie before speeding home in their car. When Dickie realized the envelope was light, it was too late.

Bish's voice was distinctly deeper than the rest of us on the air, so it was easier for the audience to recognize him. We also gave him a new nickname. Because he stands 6 feet 6 inches tall, we began to call him Lurch for "The Addams Family" character. Though he wasn't fond of the new moniker, the reality was, he's a big lurch. Cakes and I are just 5 feet 9 inches tall, while E.B. is slightly above 6 feet. So Lurch towers over us like a street light.

Soon listeners followed our lead, leaving Bish no choice but to adopt his new nickname. So he began to refer to himself as "The Lurch Papa."

While we enjoyed sports, Lurch *lovvvved* them. An avid college basketball and football fan, Lurch also closely follows the NFL, NBA, and PGA tour. However, his *lovvvve* of the national pastime truly set him apart from us.

During the 1998 season, Lurch kept a baseball pager attached to his hip that alerted him with the "charge" tune every time someone hit a home run. The pager constantly buzzed with Mark McGwire and Sammy Sosa chasing Roger Maris's single-season home run record. Occasionally we'd hear the chime while on the air. We could only shake our heads. Lurch wasn't willing to silence his baseball pager while at work. The information was too important to him.

Behind the scenes, Lurch lobbied for more interviews with athletes. Occasionally he would voice his frustration. He believed we spent too much time on non-sports topics, ranging from adult movies to our bathroom habits. Lurch argued for more sports content. After all, the name of the show is "The Sports Junkies." He couldn't get enough.

Ironically, Lurch was open about his home life. Unlike his three partners from Bowie, he had grown up without any siblings or a strong father figure. Though we didn't know all the details, his relationship with his dad and stepmom was strained. Still, when he joked the only Christmas present he received one year from his dad was an iron-on Celtics t-shirt, we couldn't help but giggle. But Lurch laughed with us, too, albeit with a hint of pain.

His deep love for his mom was apparent. Having been raised by a single mother, he spoke with pride about her job. Peggy Suntum served as the White House director of stenography for nearly 30 years. During her tenure, she was omnipresent to record every word spoken by presidents since the Reagan administration. She was there with Reagan and Gorbachev, Clinton during the Monica Lewinsky scandal, George W. Bush on 9/11, and Obama at the 50th anniversary of the Selma-to-Montgomery marches. She was widely admired and loved in Washington across both political parties, and Lurch has pictures made with Reagan, Clinton, and Dubya. He also was able to visit the White House regularly.

We couldn't imagine growing up with a mom who dated. Peggy was strikingly tall with thick auburn hair and bright blue eyes. She was also generous with hugs and widely revered among White House staff. Though it was perfectly normal for a single mother to have boyfriends, we always found it amusing when Lurch talked about the men who lived in the basement of his childhood home.

First, there was Ernie, a huge sports fan who would take Lurch to Maryland Terrapins games. Ernie also introduced Lurch to the Boston Red Sox, even taking him to Fenway Park. While his biological dad had given him an iron-on t-shirt, Ernie had taken Lurch to see Fenway Park and its Green Monster left-field wall in person. Then, he watched his favorite baseball player, right fielder Dwight Evans, which ignited Lurch's passion for the Red Sox, which still runs strong.

Ernie would ultimately move out of the basement as things didn't work out with Lurch's mom. Later, Peggy would date Reggie, a member of the Secret Service. On one trip to California, Reggie took Lurch to see one of his close friends, Pro Football Hall of Famer Marcus Allen. Visiting the running back's house, Lurch saw Allen's 1981 Heisman Trophy up close.

Maybe it wasn't intentional—he preferred to talk sports—but whenever Lurch opened up about his personal life, it was interesting radio. Over time, we'd learn, along with our audience, that he had some very compelling stories, too.

★ ★ ★ ★

Even though tangents were often the best part of "The Sports Junkies," our disagreements were never scripted or concocted on our daily show outline. We had different and distinct personalities, and we could fight over anything and everything, but our arguments were organic and real. Sometimes we'd fight over the most ridiculous hypotheticals. No matter how absurd, we have passionate and fiery debates—the instance of the shark versus the crocodile notwithstanding.

By 1997, Steve Irwin's show "The Crocodile Hunter" had become a pop culture phenomenon. The Australian zookeeper appeared on "The Tonight Show with Jay Leno" regularly. Naturally, we were fascinated by the charismatic Irwin, who wore his signature khaki shorts and a utility vest while sticking his hands in the jaws of saltwater crocodiles.

How could Irwin tangle with crocodiles without any protection? But was this behavior as dangerous as the marine biologists who swam with sharks?

Since he was a kid, Cakes has long been fascinated by sharks, authoring book reports about great whites in elementary school. He argued sharks were more dangerous. That's all it took to stoke the fire of a debate that would rage for almost an hour.

So we created a hypothetical match between a fully grown great white shark and a 25-foot crocodile. Cakes spouted with confidence, "The shark would absolutely pummel the croc." Despite his certainty, Lurch disagreed vehemently. "You think a great white shark is going to escape a croc's bite?"

The next thing you know, Lurch was prattling on about the jaw strength of crocodiles and their thick, leathery skin as if he were an expert. Lurch argued, "It'll be over, Johnny, before the shark even gets started."

The beauty of the inane debate is there was no right or wrong answer. While Lurch may have watched "The Crocodile Hunter" on television, E.B. and I weren't buying what he was selling. We were Team Shark. As our producer scrambled to find the theme music from "Jaws," I jumped into the fray.

"The shark could attack from every angle. The croc wouldn't know where he's coming from." Then E.B. piled on, "Don't crocs have those short, stubby legs? Shark meat!"

Soon the phone lines were jammed. Some callers sided with Lurch, while others agreed with me, E.B. and Cakes. We could have done an entire three-hour show about this hypothetical bout. The whole dialogue was so stupid, and yet our audience was enthralled and engaged. Can't contain the genius.

7

ROAD TRIP

"When you go on a road trip, the trip itself becomes part of the story."
— Steve Rushin

After hitting No. 1 in our time slot at WJFK, we were excited to hold some equity with management on our first road trip: broadcasting from the 1998 NFL Draft in New York City. Though the Redskins didn't have a first-round pick—they had traded it to Cincinnati for defensive tackle "Big Daddy" Wilkinson—we couldn't wait to be there.

That didn't stop E.B. from complaining about the prep we needed to do. Since we had to be on the air for four hours, we'd have to study the entire league, individual team needs, and all the potential picks. We were knee-deep in Mel Kiper's famous draft book in the weeks leading up to the big day.

The national debate surrounding the draft was who should be picked No. 1 overall. The Indianapolis Colts would choose between quarterbacks Peyton Manning, who starred at Tennessee, and fellow Heisman Trophy finalist Ryan Leaf from Washington State.

Sure enough, the four of us weren't in agreement and began to argue vociferously. As a Colts fan, I was leery about my favorite team drafting Manning. Though his stats were undeniable and his lineage impressive—father Archie was a legend at Ole Miss and played 13 seasons in the NFL, mainly for the New Orleans Saints— Peyton sported an 0-4 Southeastern Conference record against the Florida Gators. That meant something to me; namely, he couldn't win the big game against an elite team.

Lurch was incensed. A hardcore college sports fan who bet incessantly on football, Lurch had watched Manning play much more than I had. "You're a moron if you think his record matters," he argued. The name-calling wasn't going to change my mind.

Round and round we went, growing louder and louder, yet another classic Junkies verbal free-for-all. And much like the crocs versus sharks segment, there was no correct answer. Even NFL scouts and TV experts were split. This draft also produced Hall of Famers Charles Woodson, Randy Moss, and Alan Faneca, plus 30 future Pro Bowlers.

So when we arrived at the Theater at MSG that Saturday morning, we knew we would have plenty to talk about when the commissioner announced the first pick. We settled in our seats on radio row near several other programs. While Jim McClure, elevated to operations manager at WJFK, helped set up our equipment, we pulled out our cache of notebooks and papers to get ready for the main event.

Sitting there, we marveled at the stage and ESPN's grandiose set. We couldn't believe we were there. But that didn't stop us from joaning. Lurch told us ESPN's Chris Berman was notorious for pummeling Doritos, so we watched to see if the rumors were true. Though we didn't see any chips from where we were perched, that didn't mean the snacks weren't there.

Regardless, once we jumped on the air, we brought our typical fast-paced, high-energy banter. The adjacent radio shows eyeballed us like we were lepers. They weren't accustomed to our volume and frenetic pace. We didn't care. Strange looks weren't going to change how we conducted our shows.

Finally, NFL Commissioner Paul Tagliabue stepped to the podium and announced, "With the first pick in the draft, the Indianapolis Colts select quarterback, University of Tennessee, Peyton Manning." The arena erupted with cheers and a smattering of boos.

We quickly reacted to the team's decision and watched the 6-foot-5 college star walk on stage wearing a new blue No. 18 Colts jersey. Though I wondered if he was the real deal, I was a Colts fan, so I hoped for the best. It was a no-lose situation for me. If Manning became a star, I'd be thrilled. And if he stunk, I could rub it in Lurch's face. I knew he'd do the same to me.

Not long after the selection, we were interviewing the top pick. Dressed in a custom-tailored gray suit, Manning was impressive. He looked us in the eyes when he talked and was highly polished. Though I may have called him a dork before the draft, it's impossible to dislike him. He's genuine, decent, and extremely likable.

Later we interviewed Curtis Enis from Penn State, drafted No. 5 overall by the Chicago Bears. The 6-foot, 240-pound running back was sculpted like a god. We couldn't stop fawning over him and were convinced he'd become a star. Our enthusiasm was infectious, and our talent evaluation skills a bust. Enis lasted only three seasons with the Bears and Browns, plagued by injuries and poor production.

Nevertheless, we had poured our hearts into the draft coverage. I'm not sure we have prepared harder or deeper for a show. Our homework left us sounding like draftniks, but it was our passion that separated us from the pack. Throughout our broadcast, producers from other radio shows across the country approached McClure, asking who we were.

When our show came to a close at 4 p.m., we were exhausted and retreated to our hotel for some rest before dinner. A few hours later, we devoured expensive steaks on the station's dime. Reflecting on the afternoon, we were confident and giddy we had delivered a great show. Not only had we brought energy and fast information, but we had done so in our balls-to-the-wall style. Pretty cool.

Draft talk behind us, we headed to Greenwich Village for a late night of drinking, which we had done together since high school beach week. Instead of slugging terrible Matilda Bay wine coolers, we were now pounding Guinness beers in the middle of an Irish pub. We were 10 years older, but we still loved getting hammered as a group. The difference now was we had a new drinking partner in Jim McClure.

Raising our glasses, we toasted the guy who had helped change our lives. If it weren't for him, we might still be toiling in obscurity on BCTV. Instead, we were partying together in New York City after covering the NFL Draft. This successful road trip would lead to so many more in the coming years.

We attended Super Bowls, baseball spring training, U.S. Open Tennis Championships, and even the Grammys. We also hosted poker tournaments in Atlantic City and Las Vegas, and appeared at Ultimate Fighting Championship and boxing matches across the country. We were truly blessed.

THE FUTURE OF RADIO

"Success is no accident. It is hard work, perseverance, learning, studying, sacrificing, and most of all, love of what you are doing or learning to do." — *Pele*

While hosting a daily sports radio show is a dream job, it can be a grind, especially during summer. Our listeners weren't tuning in to hear us break down box scores for three hours. So, to mix things up, we wondered if we should hold a bikini contest. Our bosses welcomed the idea.

A few weeks later, after securing a diamond pendant necklace from one of our sponsors as a prize, seven beautiful ladies joined us as we moved our broadcast to the conference room, where there was more space than our cramped studio.

Huddling behind a table, we introduced the first contestant. Awkwardly asking the scantily clad cutie about her background, we dove into such lofty topics as her preferred underwear and dating status.

Interviewing each contestant, we did our best play-by-play announcer impersonations. Describing the women to the live audience wasn't easy, though. They were all attractive, When we learned one of the ladies was a wrestler, we wanted to see her in action. The shredded stunner needed a volunteer, so we thrust C.K. into the spotlight. Moments later, our teenage radio prodigy was lifted and body slammed. The room erupted in laughter. While C.K. may have enjoyed snuggling up with the bombshell during the initial hold, his head nearly hit the conference room table as he was thrown to the ground. Disaster was averted by mere inches.

After tallying our scores during the commercial break, we asked the women to take a group shot. The ladies happily obliged. It wouldn't be long until our new website was flooded with listeners checking out the pictures.

Then, as our producer Slow Joe played a drumroll sound effect, our contestants waited anxiously for the announcement. When we declared the winner, our victor jumped with joy while the other contestants clapped enthusiastically. The contest had been a tremendous success.

Moving back to our studio for the remainder of the show, C.K. felt differently. Behind the scenes, he had witnessed drama. Though the ladies sounded like sorority sisters on the air, C.K. noticed sniping and jealousy. Even worse, one contestant had lingered to voice her complaints. A half-hour after the contest was over, she was still wandering our hallways, wondering why she hadn't won.

That's when it dawned on us. We might hold more contests, but we'd never judge them again. We had plenty of idiot friends that wouldn't mind taking the bullets.

★ ★ ★ ★

One year into our stint hosting the night shift on WJFK, we continued to work without a contract. Nevertheless, program director Jeremy Coleman wanted to create a spectacle to commemorate the achievement. After the sales staff secured sponsors and a location, we gave away tickets for our anniversary celebration.

When we arrived at Bridges Billiards and Grill in Fairfax on June 3, 1998, the place was jumping. The bar was packed, including some of our friends and family. Scheduled guests like Washington Redskins general manager Charley Casserly waited in the wings.

Opening the show with a live performance from the local rock band Emmet Swimming, the raucous crowd excitedly greeted us. A few minutes later, Mike O'Meara delivered a hilarious yet touching toast, mocking his occasional golf partner E.B.'s attention deficit syndrome.

Later, some of our favorite guests included Ryan Keuhl and his teammate Shar Pourdanesh. The audience burst into laughter as Ryan lit into Cakes with a classic tale. One afternoon, Ryan had been driving on the Beltway when he noticed Cakes' winter green Saturn putt-putting along in the next lane. Attempting to flag him down by pounding his horn and waving his arms, Ryan had no luck. Cakes remained oblivious. An hour later, Ryan listened to Cakes rip into the crazy driver that he had successfully ignored. That's when Ryan called in to set the record straight. Hearing the story for a second time was still funny and the crowd laughed in approval.

We reminisced with our favorite "SportsCenter" anchor Linda Cohn, who had been our very first guest in the weeknight slot. Redskins quarterback Gus Frerotte offered his congratulations, too. When the show wrapped, it was a relief, but I had a surprise with a 15-minute video montage of our cable access days to share with the audience.

Though most everyone had heard about our BCTV show, nobody had seen the evidence. As the clips played, the crowd howled during a segment featuring a series of our terrible predictions. Later they roared as they heard a classic E.B. rant about his beloved Terps.

It had been just one year of full-time radio, but we had built so many connections with our listeners. We owed them everything. We were living out our dream.

Though we didn't feel worthy, having a successful radio show meant we were invited to various events. Even though I had played golf only a handful of times, I thought I should represent the show when Washington Wizards play-by-play announcer Steve Buckhantz invited us to participate in his charity tournament. Buck frequented "The Sports Junkies" as a guest, and his tournament raised more than $150,000 annually for research and care at St. Jude, the Memphis Children's Hospital. Though I was trepidatious and sucked at golf, Buck assured me that didn't matter. This event was a scramble tournament, and I would be assigned to a group that wouldn't have to use my shots. Lucky them!

Arriving at the course, I waited for Buck's opening remarks. After welcoming the field and thanking sponsors, he began to introduce the cast of celebrities. He started, "Three-time NBA All-Star, NBA champion with the Washington Bullets in 1978, his number 45 hangs from the rafters at the MCI Center, my television partner, Phil Chenier!" Everybody clapped.

As Buck continued, I became increasingly nervous. Then, just before I was set to be introduced, Buck enthusiastically hyped another former champion, "Two-time Pro Bowler, NFL MVP in 1983, and Super Bowl Champion. You know him, you love him, the great Joe Theismann!" The crowd roared. Once a villain during the 1970s Sonny vs. Billy quarterback debate around Washington, Theismann was now a hero.

After the ovation died down, Buck did his best to sell the radio noob. "And from the popular show "The Sports Junkies" on WJFK radio, J.P. Flaim." A polite smattering of applause followed, but it felt embarrassing. I thought my terrible golf game would be the most awkward part of the day. Wrong.

Luckily, the group I was assigned to was extremely friendly. After apologizing for not being a real celebrity *and* being a terrible golfer, we managed to have an enjoyable time. Still, my ego was bruised. It didn't matter that Buck was a friend of the show. It didn't matter if it was for a great cause. I wasn't a golfer. I wasn't a celebrity. What was I thinking?

So when Mike O'Meara asked if we'd play in his charity tournament, I let E.B. take the bullet. Though he loved golf, E.B. was hesitant to participate because he wasn't a fan of the scramble format.

Beyond that, as outgoing and outrageous as he might be on the air, E.B. is more of an introvert in real life. Playing with people he didn't know wasn't inviting. Still, he reluctantly said yes because of his affinity for Mike, with whom he played golf occasionally.

Once the tournament started, E.B.'s discomfort dissipated. His foursome was welcoming, and he began to enjoy the day. But that changed abruptly. Just as E.B. stepped to the tee box for the group's second hole, a golf cart approached. The marshal driving shouted, "Hey, are you the group with no celebrity? I've got former Redskins lineman Ron Saul with me!"

Even though Ron Saul was a fantastic guy with colorful stories of his playing days, it was humiliating for E.B. But it was great material for the show.

★ ★ ★ ★

Behind the scenes, negotiations with WJFK were contentious. Jeremy Coleman, supportive in person, was much more cutthroat with our agent, Uncle Joe Suntum. General manager Ken Stevens demanded that his point man remain thrifty.

Armed with sales sheets that showed advertising rates had quadrupled in our time slot since we took over, Uncle Joe pushed for a significant raise. Unfortunately, Jeremy was resolute, claiming WJFK could bring in a less popular show and still make money. We had no idea if he was bluffing.

Growing weary of the back and forth that lasted for months, we buckled and signed our first employment contract with Infinity Broadcasting, the parent company of 106.7 WJFK, on July 8, 1998. Settling on a 10 percent raise, we'd make $165 per show, roughly $43,000 per year. It wasn't close to what we expected, but at least we had security.

Relieved that we had signed a contract, we continued to experiment on the air. With C.K. on board as a willing crash test dummy, we tried an on-air dating game. Even if it didn't lead to a love connection, we hoped it would be compelling radio.

After the sales department secured a complimentary dinner for two, we pimped out our shy, awkward teenage wunderkind. Though we didn't have a large contingent of women vying to date him—not surprising given how much we razzed him on the air—a few ladies actually showed up for the contest.

Uncomfortable throughout, C.K. awkwardly picked the winner, an older woman in her 30s. We couldn't wait to find out what might happen, considering C.K. wasn't old enough to drink legally. What would the older woman do to our radio prodigy? A few days later, we learned C.K. was alone in the older woman's house after their dinner. But the age gap was too much. C.K. grew scared and left, unaware he could have advanced Cougarism by a decade. Instant classic.

★ ★ ★ ★

As much as we hustled during the infancy of the show, pouring through media guides and making countless calls to book our guests, we also built relationships to make our job easier. Doug Hicks, the public relations director for the Washington Capitals, was an ardent listener in his 20s who knew the key to our hearts. Joining us at a happy hour appearance at Hooters in Fairfax, Doug brought us free schwag, including Capitals jerseys. We had a new best friend.

Later, he would help us book guests he knew to fit the show, such as Capitals enforcer Craig Berube. Joining us in the studio, "Chief" used Cakes as his rag doll as he demonstrated how he took control of fights on the ice. Pulling Cakes' sweatshirt over his head in a nanosecond, Cakes went into an instant panic while the rest of us laughed hysterically.

Beyond working with the local professional sports teams, we connected with Brotman, Winter and Fried, a prominent public relations agency that promoted many big local sporting events, including the Legg Mason Tennis Classic. During his DeMatha High tennis days, E.B. had volunteered as a ball boy for the tournament. In addition, he would occasionally regale us with tales of dealing with obscure tennis stars like Jay Berger. So we obliged when Brotman, Winter and Fried asked if we'd welcome a tennis player to promote the tournament. The only question was: Who would join us in the studio?

On July 21, 1998, Justin Gimelstob, a tall, lanky 21-year-old rising star from California, made his way to our Fairfax studios. We didn't know much about the former All-American from UCLA, but that changed quickly. Gimelstob had played the best players, including Andre Agassi, whom he had beaten the summer before. Gimelstob knew Agassi on a different level than most of his peers and praised his graciousness.

Next, we asked about his mixed doubles partner, Venus Williams. Gimelstob had won the Australian and French opens mixed titles with Venus just as she was becoming one of the top female players. A year earlier and still just 17, Venus had advanced to the U.S. Open finals, losing to Martina Hingis.

In an interesting twist, Gimelstob had dated Hingis. While we hoped he'd be open about the relationship, we didn't expect bombshell revelations. He claimed to be Hingis's first. Our jaws dropped. We couldn't believe what Gimelstob divulged on live radio.

Taking it to another level, we also learned he had just been to hedonism in Jamaica. As Gimelstob painted the picture of "pleasure without pain," we were completely engrossed. We laughed uncontrollably, hearing him confess to throwing out his back during a dalliance.

Just 30 minutes earlier, we had no idea who he was, but now Justin Gimelstob was our favorite tennis player.

★ ★ ★ ★

After hitting No. 1 in our first Fall ratings book in 1997, we were humbled—and confused—when we slipped to No. 5 in the winter book. It didn't make sense, especially when the 1998 spring numbers saw another slight dip. We felt our show was better, we were more experienced, and based on the number of callers and reactions when we made public appearances, it seemed like we had more listeners. Arbitron had to be wrong. The ratings system had to be a joke. We couldn't believe the alternative.

But with the summer season looming and our ratings floundering, I wrote a memo with my thoughts on how we could get back to the top. Undoubtedly, football season would breathe life into the show, but I realized after talking with Jim McClure that we were hurting ourselves by not maintaining focus.

According to Jim, we needed to tighten up things, even if the phone lines were popping on a specific topic. When we went too long, we couldn't hit other subjects, resulting in less variety. We would also be forced into shorter segments later in the program, resulting in almost as many commercials as airtime. That wasn't a recipe for success.

As we got together to discuss a plan for the fall, it was great to hear each other's opinions. Even though we saw each other every night, we rarely talked about the big picture. Since we loved hearing Cakes dabble with impressions, we urged him to do more, whether it was college football announcer Keith Jackson or Dallas Cowboys owner Jerry Jones. Lurch voiced his opinion that we needed more sports content and guests.

Not agreeing, E.B. and I thought what made our show unique was the balance between sports, entertainment, and our personal lives. While Lurch wasn't addressing the problem from a pious standpoint, he wasn't as interested in our more risqué content. Though there wasn't unanimity, we would focus more on sports in the fall. We would try new segments like "Big Man on Campus," highlighting top college football players. We'd debut "Friday Night Fatties," where we'd pick our biggest betting locks with an over-the-top presentation as an homage to the handicapping shows that filled the television airwaves on the weekends.

David Schwab, a local publicist for Brotman, Winter & Fried, was an avid listener who related to our rise just as he was embarking on his public relations career. Schwab understood what worked on "The Sports Junkies."

After helping us book golfers during our broadcast from the Kemper Open earlier that summer, we got to know Schwab even better when he invited us to dinner at Ruth's Chris Steak House in Crystal City, Virginia. As we sat around the table swapping stories, E.B. wondered, "I still don't get what you do for a living."

Schwab looked at E.B. and asked, "Are you having a good time? Do you like the food?" My radio cohort instantly replied, "Are you kidding me? This is incredible."

Following up, Schwab probed, "You think you'll mention it tomorrow?" We snickered as it finally dawned on E.B. "That's what I do for a living," Schwab explained. But, even if we were being played, we didn't mind. The food was fantastic.

On October 14, 1998, Schwab arranged what became one of our most memorable interviews. To promote Fight Night, one of the most significant charity events of the year, the former heavyweight champion Ken Norton, who had beaten Muhammad Ali in 1973, joined us on the phone. Schwab sat in the corner of Norton's hotel suite at the Washington Hilton as the conversation quickly went off the rails.

First, Lurch asked Norton about his son, who played linebacker for the San Francisco 49ers. Then, trying to score points, Lurch mentioned his favorite team's 7-2 record. Without hesitation, Norton quipped, "whoopee-doo." There was something about how he said it that made each of us chuckle. Norton didn't care. It was going to be an unpredictable ride, and we had nothing to lose.

Asking if he would get drunk during the festivities, Norton mumbled, "No, I don't drink beer." While the answer surprised us, it was clear that he was already punch drunk. And even though he wasn't offering cogent answers, we were enjoying the back and forth.

Then we asked the former champ about the myth that women weaken a boxer's legs during training. Norton stammered, "Don't start no stuff, won't be no stuff." While it was hard to discern exactly what he was saying— perhaps 50 professional fights had taken their toll—we had to laugh. Norton was having fun, too, so we pressed forward.

Upping the ante, E.B. asked Norton whether he had reaped the rewards of being the baddest man on the planet and slept with hundreds of women. Not ducking the verbal jab, Norton offered a one-liner that would immediately become a show soundbite for years to come: "Is a pig's butt pork?" Norton's cold deadpan response had us rolling.

Meanwhile, Schwab listened to the off-the-rails interview from a phone in the suite just 10 feet away. As we finished the interview, he prayed Norton would hang up his phone immediately. Schwab knew us too well. There was going to be shrapnel. Much to his dismay, the hulking heavyweight stayed on the line just long enough to hear E.B. proclaim, "If that's not a reason boxing should be banned, I don't know what is."

Finally hanging up his phone, Schwab braced for Norton's reaction. Making a fist, he approached the young publicist, whose stress level had been rising throughout the interview. Luckily, Norton didn't throw a haymaker. Instead, he offered Schwab a fist bump and walked away expressionless and muttering, "good interview." Norton was wrong. It was unforgettable.

★ ★ ★ ★

By the fall of 1998, Slow Joe became our full-time producer. After our anniversary, Brian Cosgrove, who had run our board since the weekends, had pressed management to hire him as a full-time employee. Instead, he was fired. While we didn't support the decision, we were immersed in our own dispute. Even though we had a signed contract, we still weren't receiving the expected health care benefits. Jeremy Coleman dodged the question, saying he didn't know why. A week later, we received a detailed memo explaining the company still classified us as "part-time" employees. We couldn't believe our eyeballs. We felt hoodwinked.

Now with Slow Joe by our side, the frustrated musician began prepping jingles to complement the show, including a ditty for "Bother the Pro," one of our favorite segments. With a Looney Tunes song playing underneath him, Joe crooned…

E.B., J.P., Lurchy and Cakes
Bother athletes asleep or awake.
It may turn out money or turn into a show
It's the crazy segment that's called 'Bother the Pro.'"

While the intro was fun, the chase to connect with our pro targets was a gas. Chatting and flirting with hotel operators as we'd try to reach Miami Dolphins coach Jimmy Johnson or other luminaries built the drama. Then, when the coach would answer only to hang up after our interview request, we still felt successful. But getting an unexpected yes from guys like running back Ricky Watters, outfielder Larry Walker, or NBA baller Greg Ostertag was truly thrilling. Sometimes the subsequent conversations even turned into the best parts of the show.

Similarly, "Friday Night Fatties" evolved into one of our most popular segments. What started as an over-the-top goof with the four of us shouting our picks became so much more. Lurch even began using sound effects. When we heard a door knock, we knew Lurch's alter ego, "the teaser king," would emerge to offer even more big, fat winners. Soon callers were jumping on and using their own sound effects, challenging other callers while touting their picks.

Beyond our signature segments, we welcomed beautiful women to the show as often as possible. Tiffany Taylor, a local student who had graced the pages of *Playboy* magazine, became a friend of the show and popped in occasionally. When it appeared C.K. had formed a bond with Tiffany, we wondered if there was more to the story. Sadly for C.K., there wasn't, but the on-air needling was our pleasure.

When supermodel Cindy Margolis joined us in the studio a few weeks later, we were nearly speechless. Running the board, Slow Joe admitted that he had never been that close to a woman so beautiful. At the time, the 33-year-old bombshell was the "Queen of the Internet." While hearing Cindy talk about her days as a Barker's Beauty on "The Price Is Right" wasn't necessarily gripping, her beauty was mesmerizing, and having her on the show was tremendous. Our male audience knew exactly who she was, and they scoured our website for pictures afterward.

Likewise, they knew Nina Hartley, too. Landing in our Fairfax studios just a few weeks after Cindy's visit, the contrast was stark. The popular 39-year-old porn harlot looked like she had been through the wringer. And she had, having appeared in hundreds of adult movies. Yet amazingly, she was still performing in 2021.

Nevertheless, hearing her lisp through the interview as she talked about being naked on the "Boogie Nights" set was interesting. Nina remains a media pro, having lectured at Ivy League colleges and making the rounds on nationally syndicated shows about the adult film industry's rights. Lurch may not have loved the porn talk, but we thought our audience might. If only these kind of segments would show up where it really mattered.

★ ★ ★ ★

When Arbitron released the 1998 Fall ratings book, we weren't going to act like it wasn't important. *It was.* Sure enough, we scored our highest ratings yet with an 8.5 in men 25-54. We were back in first place, and it wasn't close. The accomplishment was rewarding, our bosses were thrilled, the sales department delighted. Soon they were preparing sales sheets that said, "A strong show continues to grow." The memo pointed out that we had finished No. 1 in a multitude of demographics. Hard work had paid off.

A few weeks later, E.B. offered a suggestion. Why not write a letter with our ratings and recent guests to George Solomon, the assistant managing editor for sports of the *Washington Post*. Sure enough, my phone rang a few days later. Leonard Shapiro was on the line. Quite pleasantly, he began by complimenting our success. He had read my previous letters, and though he admitted we weren't his cup of tea, he uttered the magic words: "So I guess I'll give you a little pop."

Answering questions for nearly an hour, I began to wonder if Shapiro might trash us. Anxiously awaiting the column for days, it finally appeared in

Sunday's edition of the *Post* on February 28, 1999. We were thrilled. Sunday was the most circulated edition of the paper at almost 1.1 million subscribers. Many would see Shapiro's piece.

Shapiro wrote, "They call themselves the 'Sports Junkies' and their swift ascent to the top of the ratings in the Washington market has been one of the more remarkable stories in local broadcasting in recent years." He wasn't lying.

Predictably, Shapiro jabbed us as he explained, "The Junkies appeal is somewhat mystifying to a 50-something fogy." *Maybe?*

"It doesn't seem to matter what they talk about, whether it's the usually sad state of the Washington Wizards or the pitfalls of trying to wallpaper the rec room," he wrote. And even though he scoffed at our "hippy-dippy slang-laced language" and wasn't a fan of the "constant drone of background music," much of the column resembled a press release touting our accolades.

Shapiro mentioned how we led the ratings in 20 demographic categories—lifted straight from my letter—and quoted our 33-year-old program director Jeremy Coleman, who summed up the allure: "They are genuinely entertaining. They come across as very real people. It's not manufactured, and they have a very natural sense of humor."

E.B.'s suggestion had paid huge dividends. The headline alone—"The 'Sports Junkies' Are a Spreading Addiction"—was beyond what we expected. But Shapiro had done so much more. He also teased us with an interesting nugget. "There already is talk about out-of-market syndication."

That was news to us.

★ ★ ★ ★

Each night after we signed off, WJFK turned to nationally syndicated programming. Westwood One carried "Ferrall on the Bench" from 10 p.m. to 1 a.m. Cakes and I listened regularly as we carpooled home. Little did we know the raspy-voiced host Scott Ferrall was poised to leave his national deal to pursue his dream job calling games for the expansion Atlanta Thrashers NHL team, leaving a huge hole in Westwood One's lineup.

Since the CBS-owned Westwood One network already syndicated "The Don and Mike Show," they were familiar with our bosses Ken Stevens and Jeremy Coleman. Hearing about our meteoric rise in the ratings impressed them. Not only did we finish atop the ratings in the fall, but we backed that up with another first-place finish in the winter book. Our ratings ballooned to a 12.1, nearly a 50 percent increase.

Armed with rising ratings, we needed better representation. As much as we liked Uncle Joe, we needed a killer agent. If we were going to be syndicated, we wanted more money and the benefits we deserved. After consulting

Mike O'Meara, we decided to go with his agent, Doug Woloshin, who had represented Hall of Fame Redskins running back John Riggins. That was good enough for us.

With Woloshin beginning to negotiate, we returned from an exciting weekend covering the NFL Draft in New York and were asked to fill in for "Ferrall on the Bench" for two nights. That didn't mean we would replace him permanently, but our new agent was making progress. Westwood One wanted us, but they also wanted us to broadcast until midnight to retain most of the Ferrall affiliates.

We couldn't fathom adding two hours to the show. Five hours of nightly radio seemed daunting. We preferred to stick to three hours starting at 7:30 p.m. since we often started late anyway with "The Don and Mike Show" bleeding into our time. But Jeremy Coleman warned Woloshin that we'd have far fewer affiliates if we didn't agree to go late.

Ultimately, we were presented with two options—start at our regular time with affiliates having the option of joining at 8, 9 or 10 p.m. (WJFK would then refeed the show for later hours to some affiliates), or stay on until midnight.

Though we wanted to strike a deal, we didn't want to roll over this time. We had a list of demands.

1.) We wanted the freedom to run commercial breaks whenever we wanted;
2.) We asked for a full-time guest booker;
3.) We sought to hire another producer to help Slow Joe behind the scenes. Even though he was still in college, we wanted C.K. to take over as executive producer.

Beyond that, we wanted a budget to help us book regular guests, and we hoped to broadcast from more major sporting events, such as the Super Bowl and college basketball's Final Four.

Negotiations moved at a frenetic pace. Stevens had consulted with Coleman and felt this was the "opportunity of a lifetime." But when our new agent asked for $150,000 per man, Ken groaned that he would have to pay four of us and said the show could be done with less than four people.

Trying to divide us wasn't going to work. Our bond was too strong. And Ken's offer, $75,000 per man, was laughable for a nationally syndicated program.

Threatening to let Westwood One know there was no deal and that this would be our last contract with WJFK, Stevens told Woloshin that he would begin looking for a replacement. Doug believed it was a bluff and told us to wait patiently. He was right.

A few days later, Woloshin presented us with an offer sheet: We would broadcast from approximately 7—or whenever Don and Mike finished—until 11 p.m. The 7 o'clock hour would only be heard locally on WJFK, with national affiliates picking us up from 8-11 p.m. While some affiliates would carry all three hours live, others might pick up later and replay earlier portions or replay the entire show.

We would also receive 15 days of vacation, talent fees for commercials and appearances would increase, and we'd be given a budget of $30,000 to hire a producer for the syndicated show. In addition, we would have to agree to three commercial breaks per hour, but we would have the freedom to take our breaks whenever we wanted within those hours.

Then there was the salary. Ken Stevens was now offering us a starting salary of $100,000 each. There was no time to negotiate. Westwood One was scrambling. They needed somebody to fill Ferrall's void quickly and permanently.

Looking back, it was just a few years earlier that we were making $75 a show. Now we were being offered a six-figure salary. Done deal.

On May 17, 1999, we signed our term agreement to start national syndication the very next day. That night, as we closed the show full of adrenaline and anticipation, Lurch belted out our new signature line, "We're the 'Sports Junkies,' the future of sports radio."

9

FRAT PARTY

"I got my hands up. They're playing my song. You know I'm going to be okay. Yeah, it's a party in the USA." — *Miley Cyrus*

Three years earlier, we cut a demo that was described as a train wreck. Now we were about to embark on national syndication. It would be weeks before we ironed out the details in a formal contract, but we knew who we wanted to be part of our team.

While we often razzed Slow Joe for his on-air miscues, we loved him anyhow. He was one of our guys. So was Chris Kinard. Even though he was still a student at American University, we had confidence C.K. could handle full-time producer responsibilities. He would primarily book guests and serve as our liaison with Westwood One.

Before our first national show on May 18, 1999, our signing was announced via news release that described us as "gutsy, honest and spirited." Westwood One added, "the four twenty-something hosts bring a down-at-the-corner-bar-feel to radio." The release also mentioned some of our new affiliates, including WDFN in Detroit and WFAN in New York, the leading sports talk station in the country. We were about to step into the big leagues.

Still, it was business as usual when it came to the show. Our preparation and content weren't much different. We were still "The Sports Junkies" and we would talk about what was interesting to us. Fortunately, we would be able to focus on the Washington teams in the first hour when we were heard locally on WJFK. On our first syndicated night, we started by thanking our home audience that had propelled us to a new career plateau. They had been along for our ride, and this was just the next stop.

Starting the national portion of the show at 8 p.m., C.K. had lined up some great guests that would appeal to our new audience. With the NBA playoffs in full swing, we had Marques Johnson, former NBA player turned Fox Sports commentator who was full of energy and charisma. Before breaking down the playoffs, he spoke about working alongside Wesley Snipes and Woody Harrelson in "White Men Can't Jump."

Later, we connected with one of our favorites, University of Maryland grad Scott Van Pelt from the Golf Channel, offering insight on Tiger Woods and the rest of the PGA Tour. Then, to appeal to our new affiliates, C.K. wisely booked hosts from Detroit's WDFN and WQAM in Miami, the flagship home of the Miami Dolphins. Both hosts welcomed us to their markets. We knew they probably didn't know much about us, but we also knew Westwood One would notice we were reaching out to the affiliates.

Broadcasting until 11 p.m., we didn't feel the weight of the extra hour. It was just another show, even though we were being heard coast to coast.

★ ★ ★ ★

Going national meant more Junkies media attention. First, Jonah Keri from the *Washington Business Journal* wrote, "They get the numbers, plain and simple." While that was true on WJFK, we didn't know how we would be received across the country. "Ferrall on the Bench" had more than 100 affiliates just a year earlier, but after the ratings dipped, many of his affiliates dumped the show. We had to maintain the roughly 50 remaining sites.

One of those affiliates was our sister station in Baltimore. But just a few weeks into the national show, sports media columnist Milton Kent of the *Baltimore Sun* had heard enough and wondered, "After listening to the 'Sports Junkies,' here are three words for WJFK (1300 AM) general manager Ken Stevens: Are you serious?"

But according to *Sports Illustrated*, we were "America's hot new radio show." The three-paragraph item in the Scorecard column spelled our names correctly and mentioned we often went long stretches without talking about sports, referencing our shark versus croc debate.

However, *The Sun*'s feature columnist Kevin Cowherd visited with us during a show in the fall and declared, "Listening to The Junkies' hip, edgy rants on every topic under the sun, one thing becomes abundantly clear: This is not your old man's sports-talk show."

We were "white-hot right now"—Cowherd's words, not mine—and it wasn't because we were talking four hours about the resurgent Redskins or the curiosity of new owner Dan Snyder. And, we had grown tired of provincial sports media critics killing us for being ourselves while beating the crap out of our competition. Five months into our national syndication deal, we were rolling. Locally, we had hit No. 1 in the ratings for the fourth straight quarter.

Media Week highlighted us in a four-page cover article titled "Guy Talk." This exposure was huge within the radio industry, especially national advertisers. Companies like HBO had jumped aboard, sending us to a few boxing matches and booking guests on our show before big fights, and this article could lead to more.

Luckily, Tim Wendel seemed to understand us, writing, "Somewhere between Howard Stern and straight sports talk exists the netherworld of 'The Sports Junkies.' Sitting in with this foursome for a night on the air is akin to witnessing a train wreck. The show can often be spectacular, but beware of flying debris."

We still couldn't escape the train wreck comparison. *Didn't they understand?* The train wreck is why the show works!

But questions remained within the article, which touched on the evolution of sports talk radio and whether "guy talk" would last. Wendel wondered, "In the world of talk radio, nobody is certain if The Junkies, with their offbeat mix of sports and guy talk, are the latest trend, something to be emulated, or simply an airwave aberration."

We didn't have the answer, and didn't care. We were too young, too focused, and possibly too naïve to be supposed visionaries. We only hoped the article would help Westwood One land more advertisers. So we ignored the question next to the picture of us leaning over the sound board. The caption read, "Are the Sports Junkies the future—or just four wacky guys?"

★ ★ ★ ★

Behind the scenes, C.K. worked diligently to book the best guests, which was easier given our national status. Convincing Ravens coach Brian Billick to join us was easier now that we were heard in Baltimore. Similarly, booking Buccaneers Pro Bowl linebacker Derrick Brooks wasn't as daunting since we had an affiliate in Tampa. And because we were on WDFN in Detroit, we'd book Mike Stone, host of the popular "Stoney and Wojo" show, and Michigan basketball coach Brian Ellerbe, who attended Bowie High School. We loved joking with him about Prince George's County hoops.

Meanwhile, we were always on the lookout for new show characters. We stumbled onto a couple of diehard fans during the Redskins postgame coverage hosted from the stadium's club level after home games. Not only did they love the home team, they loved "The Sports Junkies," but not nearly as much as they loved alcohol.

We dubbed our new pals Guy the Drunkard and Drunk Mike. Both were loud and brash. Mike bragged about sneaking beers into the stadium hidden in his pants while Guy would ramble about anything and everything. Though we weren't condoning their behavior, they were funny. They would become regular callers as we heard more of their drunken tales—from walking home on the Beltway to getting into fights with fans.

We also continued to mix things up, like having the game developers from 989 Studios preview the latest sports video games for Sony PlayStation. Even if those segments were more suited for television, we did our best to describe the action and gave away copies on the air. Our audience loved those freebies. Plus, we got copies for ourselves. We loved that more so.

But hosting a nationally syndicated show had its share of pitfalls. Keeping the affiliates happy was a chore, but sometimes we'd find guys that understood the vibe of our show. Steve Politziner and Craig Karmazin hosted "The Steve and Craig Show" on WTLX in Madison, Wisconsin, and were even younger than us. They were also fans of "The Sports Junkies," and we became fans of theirs. That was probably a good thing. Craig's father was Mel Karmazin, chairman and CEO of CBS Radio. If Craig liked us, maybe his dad would, too. Beyond that, Craig owned our affiliate in Madison, so he was actually one of our many affiliate bosses. We wanted him on our side.

Luckily, we had a lot of people like Howard Skall as fans. He lived just a few miles from Cakes in Olney, Maryland. He also happened to be the vice president of NFL Players Inc., the licensing and marketing arm of the NFL Players Association.

When we became nationally syndicated, we knew there would be more opportunities to travel. Now Skall was offering us the chance to broadcast from their players party in Atlanta just a few days before the Super Bowl. This was a no-brainer partnership.

In the days leading up to our trip, E.B.'s neuroticism made for great radio. He worried about everything, from getting to the airport on time to what type of plane we were boarding. Cakes was his partner in whine. Both vowed to get loaded before takeoff, which made for a delightful start to the trip. Then, Lurch bemoaned the airplane seating. It was too small for his 6-foot-6 frame.

Though we hoped for warmer temperatures when we flew south, an ice storm had struck Atlanta the week of the Super Bowl XXXIV game between the Tennessee Titans and St. Louis Rams. When we arrived on Thursday, January 27, 2000, rain and freezing temperatures greeted us.

After settling in our hotel, we headed to the players party, where Skall welcomed us. We were excited to be in the middle of the action, but we didn't know what to expect. As we kicked off our show by discussing our travel, hotel accommodations, and what would become a thriller between the Rams and Titans, the party started filling up, and the buzz grew.

Sneaking a few cocktails as we finished the local portion of the show, the next three hours were a cavalcade of guests with some of the biggest names in the NFL. We conducted 12 interviews, including former Heisman Trophy winner Herschel Walker, who was still shredded at age 38. But that was just the start.

With the show behind us, we hit the bars and hooked up with our old pal Ryan Keuhl, now with the Cleveland Browns. As we slugged beers scouting some of the celebrities partying among us, Keuhl called us a "bunch of donkey dicks." We couldn't stop laughing. Soon "donkeys" would become part of the show's lexicon with a weekly "Donkeys of the Week" segment.

The next day, after sleeping off our hangovers, we prepped for what we hoped would be another high-energy four hours of radio. It was the polar opposite. Radio row was dead and so were we. Instead of 12 interviews, we had none. Fortunately, we still had the Super Bowl to preview.

As fun as our two days in Atlanta had been, the weather was about to worsen. Our flights back home weren't until Saturday night. We hoped to beat the incoming storm.

Before leaving for the airport, we dropped by media headquarters for free food. While beginning to feast, a crowd developed. Muhammad Ali had sat down to watch Mike Tyson's fight in Manchester, England, against Julian Francis. We had never felt anything like being in the presence of "The Greatest of All Time."

Awkwardly, I snapped a few pictures with my buddies standing behind Ali. Eventually, Cakes stood in line and took a personal photo with the champ. Lurch, E.B and I wondered why we hadn't followed suit.

Returning to the hotel to pack, we noticed Jerry Rice hanging out near the hotel lobby. Since I had mostly been taking pictures of my boys the entire trip, I asked Cakes to grab the camera as I posed with the future Hall of Famer for a photo. Just as I made my move, a bellhop approached the legendary receiver. We took the picture together.

Nevertheless, we were able to get out of Dodge just in time. As we boarded the plane, E.B. and Cakes listened to the pilot explain the de-icing procedure we'd have to sit through before takeoff. As we looked out our windows, a chemical was sprayed on the wings, and later a crew member gave the pilot a big thumbs up. Cakes's defensive mechanism kicked in and he began to chuckle nervously as we joked this could be our demise.

Of course, it wasn't. Landing safely in Washington, our first Super Bowl trip had been a success. Not only had we hit a home run with the show from the NFL players party, but we had so many great stories. And personally, I had my picture with Jerry Rice. Alas, Tony Chica the bellhop, was in the frame, too. That was also part of "The Sports Junkies" story.

Months earlier, an 18-old freshman at George Mason University approached me and Lurch during a happy hour bar appearance just a few miles away from our Fairfax studios. Bret Oliverio, a recent graduate from Lake Braddock High School, was an avid fan of the show after hearing a screaming match between me and E.B. The subject of the fight was irrelevant. Bret had never heard anything like that exchange on the radio and was instantly hooked.

Hoping to work on the show, Bret struck a conversation, and, almost immediately, his easy-going demeanor and charisma captured our attention. Like Lurch, Bret had played high school hoops. His dad, a high school basketball coach, also listened to the show. So, when Bret finally worked up the courage to ask about working on "The Sports Junkies," we figured he would be a great fit.

After clearings things with C.K., Bret began volunteering once a week by answering phones. Though he wasn't being paid, he was having a great time and learning the nuts and bolts of radio. As time progressed, he began to run the board on weekends and filled in more during our show.

He quickly became our new target for on-air ridicule. From his limited palette—he had never eaten fish!—to his "meaty thighs," we busted his balls like jai alai. While he could have become defensive, Bret took the punches. Off the air, I started playing pickup basketball with Bret and his high school pals. At 29, I was the oldest guy in the gym, but it was still amusing to hear Bret and his boys drop show lingo.

Somehow, our pickup games led to a $100 bet as Bret and I battled one-on-one live on the air in the radio station's parking lot. In the end, the young gun beat the old head by a point, but it wasn't without controversy. Bret's dad had called a dubious timeout as Bret was on the ropes and gasping for air. Who knew there were timeouts in one-on-one?

Ultimately, Bret proved to be an increasingly valuable part of "The Sports Junkies." Alongside fellow intern David Bernad, a collegiate basketball player at McGill University in Canada, we had formed the most cohesive production team yet.

But David wasn't fond of his nickname. Struggling with his perimeter shooting the first time he played with us, we dubbed the college player "Clank David." Though he wanted to prove us wrong the next time we played, he was just an intern. He would have to live with the harassment.

In August 1999, Cakes had beaten me in a golf challenge. I was still stewing over the bitter defeat almost a year later. The competition had sprouted from an on-air grilling. While E.B. and Lurch were improving their games, they chastised Cakes because he wasn't making progress. When I stupidly opened my mouth and jumped on the pile, Cakes didn't appreciate the needling. It was one thing if the guys he was playing with ripped his ineptitude, but he didn't understand my taunt, given I didn't play the game.

Before I knew it, money was on the line, and the "Cakes vs. J.P. Golf Challenge" was born. Cakes would spot me 15 strokes, and he vowed to retire if he lost; I offered to swim across the lake at Pleasant Valley Golf Club in Chantilly, Virginia, if I lost.

It didn't take long to realize I didn't stand a chance. There were no mulligans. There were no gimmies. So, on the second hole, each of my strokes counted when I hit a shot deep into the woods and stupidly tried to get it out. Scoring an 11, I mentally prepared to jump into the lake.

As we were playing, I mingled with the listeners who had come to see the putrid display. Cakes, however, remained deadly serious. E.B., serving as his caddy, helped Cakes line up his putts. When all was said and done, he managed to shoot a 106. Not pretty. But my 134 wasn't close. I was $50 lighter in the wallet and about to get wet.

As Slow Joe left for the station to edit the highlights of our outing—he had been recording the shenanigans for all 18 holes—I took off my socks, shoes, and shirt and dove into the lake. At least the gallery would have something they wouldn't forget.

The following weekend, when I joined E.B. and some of our soccer friends for dinner, he revealed something that got under my skin. Informant E.B. claimed Cakes had been less than sportsmanlike. It struck a nerve that he was "acting like a dick," yelling "get in the water" and "go out of bounds" after some of my shots. I wouldn't forget.

One year later, I was ready to pounce. A local golf pro had given me his card during an appearance. Though he knew I didn't play golf, he offered lessons if I changed my mind. I had. When spring arrived, I began taking weekly lessons. By summer, I was hitting balls twice a week and working on my short game at a par-3 course near the station. Then I started testing my skills on real courses. I had improved quickly, from shooting a 134 to the low 90s. I was confident I would smoke Cakes this time.

To add spice to a potential rematch, I connected with Guy the Drunkard, who had talked smack with E.B. on the air about who was the better golfer. I thought having two matches would be better than one. I didn't need to ask. After lining things up with Westfields Golf Club in Clifton, Virginia, I sprung the rematch on the air. Nobody saw it coming.

Cakes was initially reluctant to defend his crown. But after Guy the Drunkard cajoled E.B. into playing, Cakes had to say yes for the two individual matches, aka "The War at Westfields." Fessing up to practicing, I would play Cakes straight up this time. No strokes. But there was $100 on the line.

In the end, I got revenge and E.B. fended off Guy, who kept things surprisingly competitive. But I turned down the prize money from Cakes. He was still my boy, and the rematch was never about the money. I wanted to win and send a message. Revenge is a dish best served cold.

★ ★ ★ ★

One year into our national syndication deal, we still rarely heard from any of our affiliates across the country. We figured that was a good thing.

Every few months, we would bring in three or four married couples and play the "Junkiewed Game." Embarrassing the newlyweds about their sex lives made for fun but awkward radio, but that wasn't nearly as daring as holding a live nipple piercing in the studio. We cringed at the sight.

Our annual bikini contest had become a tradition like few others (say, The Masters golf tournament). Procuring better prizes meant a bigger and more competitive field of beautiful women. But, to us, that wasn't so important as having our friends and favorite callers join the festivities. We decided against being judges, so we handed out VIP judging seats like Halloween candy.

Even though it was a visual event, we needed Blind Mookie to join us. Mookie had lost his eyesight after being shot by one of his brothers. We had never heard a story like his and were amazed by his positive attitude. So, we were happy when one of Mookie's older brothers accompanied him to the station. We were also wowed by his muscular physique. Instantly, "Cock Diesel" Tony became a new show character.

Joining them were two white rappers; Styles from the Under, who had crafted a show intro for us; along with Guy the Drunkard, Derek from Logan Circle, and Sactown Mike. Sactown, who longed for the days of Chris Webber in a Washington Wizards uniform, had grown to legendary status. His calls into the show always made us laugh, but his stories often left us speechless. For example, his fiancé threw her engagement ring out the window as they argued while driving. No surprise, they never married.

To say the bikini contest was chaotic would be an understatement. Our luminaries were half-loaded and battled for the microphone throughout the competition. Offering brutal assessments of the competitors, the judges didn't show any tactful judgment. They nitpicked each contestant, from the fit of their bikinis to flaws in their physiques, as if they were 10s. But not all their criticism was directed at the ladies. Sactown Mike made fun of Derek's breath relentlessly.

For the better part of two hours, the hilarious vibe continued. With almost a dozen guys pounding drinks and talking over one another while gawking at half-naked women in tiny bikinis, the show had the feel of a college frat party. Of course, that was exactly what we wanted.

10

THE HOMIES

"True friends stab you in the front." — *Oscar Wilde*

Perhaps it started the night we held our "Homies Fantasy Football Draft" live on the air. Pouring into our Fairfax studios with a cooler full of beer, many of our best friends made their on-air debuts, leading to them being a significant part of Junkies lore.

Our listeners would know them as Horsey, Crickety, Squirrel, Pastry, and Bucky—all nicknames, some with more originality than others. Horsey's last name was Horstkamp; Pastry worked at a pastry shop; and Bucky shared the same nickname as his father. Others dated to their childhood. Craig Walden had been dubbed "Crickety" Craig because he was always bee-bopping around his neighborhood. But Glen Hardesty had been called "Squirrel" since elementary school days, when a friend said he ran like one.

Boys and men will always find better-fitting names for their friends, especially in sports. Somehow, the monikers had stuck with them through college, when we'd all connect and become a tight-knit group of friends.

Our audience would get to know this band of like-minded brothers who talked the same vocabulary as us. From the beginning, listeners latched onto our slang using words like "silly," which means something was great, and "hurting," the exact opposite. Soon silly evolved into "Silly Bazilly."

Listeners constantly asked about the origins. Did we lift "money" from the movie "Swingers?" No, it was just the sophomoric way we talked to our friends. Maybe we picked it up during our days playing pickup hoops in Prince George's County. When you swished a jumper, you'd shout "money!"

The terminologies weren't concocted when Horsey said he got "cised" after picking Jerome Bettis in his fantasy draft, or when Crickety dropped "it's a show" as E.B. selected Redskins running back Terry Allen just ahead of him. We all spoke in the same unsophisticated manner.

So, opening the phone lines that night of the draft, we loved hearing callers shred the Homies for botching their picks. We were used to being grilled by our listeners, but it was the Homies' baptism. For half the show, we ridiculed each other and laughed. We thought it was great radio. Either that, or we had pounded too many beers to notice otherwise.

Moving forward, we wondered if there might be a way to incorporate the Homies more into the show, particularly Tommy "Horsey" Horstkamp and Craig "Crickety" Walden. Horsey had been a frequent target of our scorn as we mocked everything from his last name to the oversized trash can that sat in the middle of his kitchen. Horsey was an easy target. But so was Crickety. The only difference was, our annoying friend, who oozed personality and charisma, fired back more often. We didn't mind. In fact, we fed off the counter-punching.

Recognizing their appearances were always entertaining, we asked them to consider doing movie reviews. Without hesitation, they obliged.

They launched the "Homies Movie Review" with their own ratings scale. This wasn't the stuff of Siskel and Ebert, but that's not what we wanted. If they loved a flick, they gave it a "Silly Bazilly" rating. If they hated a movie, it was "Butt Doo Doo Trifling." As ridiculous as this sounded, their reviews worked. But equally funny was hearing them bicker like an old married couple over sharing popcorn and buying just one drink to save money.

There may have been times when Horsey and Crickety confused us with their movie plot descriptions—we often wondered if they actually saw the films—but that didn't matter. They made us laugh and we figured our audience was laughing, too.

★ ★ ★ ★

Throughout our radio tenure, one of our biggest strengths was building great relationships with our sponsors. One of the best was with HBO. Not only would the network help us book many of the biggest names in boxing, such as world champions Oscar De La Hoya and "Sugar" Shane Mosley, but they would send us to their mega fights to help with the promotion. Cakes flew to Las Vegas on HBO's dime. Then E.B. and I landed in New York to watch Felix "Tito" Trinidad beat Pernell "Sweat Pea" Whitaker at Madison Square Garden.

There is nothing like the scene surrounding a big boxing match. We were thrilled to catch a glimpse of the celebrities arriving on the red carpet, including Jay-Z, the cast of "The Sopranos," and Whitney Houston. The fight was exhilarating, as well. I never felt more like a Boricua than when Tito made his ring entrance with hundreds of Puerto Rican flags waving in the air. Then he dominated Whitaker for 12 rounds.

HBO offered to send us to London to see boxing phenom Prince Naseem Hamed defend his world featherweight title in 2000. Since we wanted to keep the free trips coming, we automatically said yes. Unfortunately, none of us could go. Westwood One and WJFK wouldn't allow us to take time off, so we wondered if we could send Horsey and Crickety as our correspondents.

Sure enough, the Homies headed to London. After settling into their hotel rooms, they met up with a friend who worked at a nearby pub. Trying a trendy drink, the boys pounded Red Bull and vodkas and caught a quick buzz. Returning to the hotel to call into the show, we quickly became disappointed. We wanted the Homies to paint the town. Instead, they were ready to retire. That was unacceptable.

We began fielding calls with suggestions. Within minutes, the Homies were heading to Piccadilly Circus at our listeners' behest. The pair, who had never traveled overseas, needed to experience more culture. Drinking Red Bulls and vodka at a pub wasn't going to cut the expense check.

Arriving at Piccadilly Circus, Horsey and Crickety marveled at the bright lights and packed streets. Walking among the crowd, the clueless Americans noticed a commotion. "There are some sillies up there," Crickety declared. But when our two idiot representatives got a closer look, it was a bunch of men dressed in drag.

Dismayed, our boys watched the spectacle until a man promoting a nearby strip club asked if they were interested. When they arrived at the club, the promoter walked inside and emerged with a curious request. The club had room for just one of them. The Homies weren't about to split up. Instead, they walked away and ended up at Cheers in London. Typical Americans.

While things may not have gone smoothly, listening to their tribulations had us captivated. Hearing their misadventures left us laughing. We hoped HBO would be happy. We were pumping the hell out of the fight.

The next day, Horsey and Crickety ran into an HBO executive on the elevator as they were headed to the pre-fight party. When asked who they were with, our intrepid reporters dug our grave. "We're here for the Sports Junkies," Horsey answered. The exec asked, "So none of the guys came?" Crickety responded foolishly, "No. They couldn't come. We just do movie reviews for them once a week." The disappointment on the executive's face was apparent right away.

Oblivious, Horsey and Crickety proceeded to the HBO party and feasted on the free food and drinks. Later, as they found their way to their seats, famed ring announcer Michael Buffer introduced the champion. As Puff Daddy's "I'll Do This For You" blasted throughout the arena, Prince Naseem Hamed, the ultimate showman, entered on a flying magic carpet a la Arabian Nights. Then Puff Daddy emerged to greet the champion. Horsey and Crickety couldn't believe the spectacle. The crowd exploded.

Then, a few rounds into the championship bout, Prince Naseem spectacularly closed the show with a straight left that flattened his opponent, Vuyani

Bungu. Horsey and Crickety couldn't have asked for more. Unfortunately, HBO didn't feel the same way. The Homies had left our relationship with the network on the ropes. As much as we tried to make things right, HBO never sent us on another free trip. We were KOed.

Despite the setback, the Homies weaved themselves into the fabric of "The Sports Junkies." Whether they were joining us during our conference room bikini contests or being part of our live fantasy drafts, they added flavor to the show.

Off the air, golf was becoming a bigger passion for many of the Homies. Not surprisingly, smack talk ensued as the Homies claimed they could beat the four of us. Though Cakes and I stunk, how could we lose to a team that included Horsey and Crickety? Plus, E.B. and Lurch were using their free golf hookups and playing all the time.

Deciding to hold a Ryder Cup-style competition, we just needed to find a willing location. That's when our friend Tom Healy stepped up, offering his new golf course, Blue Mash, located just a few miles from Cakes' home in Olney.

A few years earlier, Tom had discovered the show as he was opening Waverly Woods in Marriottsville, Maryland. We couldn't make it to their media day, but that didn't stop Cakes from calling Healy a few days later to score a free round on the Fourth of July. Tom was stunned by the audacity. He had never met Cakes, and now he was asking for a freebie on one of the busiest days of the golf season? Denied.

Still, Tom would invite us to play at Waverly again, and eventually, E.B. and Cakes would join him for a round. Having a great time, things took a wide turn when E.B. heard thunder. Tom couldn't believe how quickly E.B.'s mind turned to doom and gloom, so they played it safe and cut the round short, retreating to the clubhouse for beers. This was the beginning of a true friendship. Tom would become an honorary Homie. E.B. pressured him to participate in a radio version of "Who Wants to Marry a Millionaire?" Tom passed, but now he was offering his new golf course for our grudge match.

As we built drama for "The Clash at Blue Mash," smack talk grew as the match date approached. Whether it was Crickety ripping into Cakes or Lurch saying he couldn't lose to Pastry, we *could not lose* to the Homies. Feeling confident, I upped the ante by offering to swim across the lake at Blue Mash if we lost. With E.B. and Lurch being strong golfers, I didn't see how we could lose.

Arriving at his new course that summer Saturday morning in 2001, Tom was pleasantly surprised to see fans there to witness our match. Among the gallery, our pals Sactown Mike and Chad the Stalker were ready to provide commentary, along with our new intern Omar, a socially awkward kid. With the help of C.K. and Slow Joe, we would grab audio throughout the competition and play it back on Monday to reveal the winners.

During the first nine holes, we fell behind quickly. Squirrel was the best golfer among the group and defeated E.B. Meanwhile, Lurch lost to Pastry, and Cakes was upset by Crickety, though he did manage a highlight. With a group of listeners watching, Cakes's nerves got the best of him and he whiffed on a tee shot. He wouldn't hear the end of that epic fail.

Sadly, when the match-play portion of the competition was over after nine holes, we found ourselves down 3 and 1. On the back nine, we'd play alternating shot with each match worth two points. We had to win both matches. As E.B. and Cakes cruised to a win over Pastry and Crickety in just six holes, it all came down to me and Lurch.

We were entrenched in a battle with Squirrel and Horsey. Down one when we reached the 17th tee, a par-3 water hole, it felt like thousands of eyes were upon me. As E.B. and Cakes watched anxiously, I took out my 5-iron and prayed I would find the green. Somehow, I did, and our match was even. Everything was riding on the last hole.

When Squirrel ripped his drive down the middle of the par-5 18th hole, Lurch and I knew we were in trouble. As listeners rooted us on, we flailed. I couldn't keep the ball straight, and neither could Lurch. Incredulously, the Homies had done the unthinkable. They had taken us down, and we knew they would brag loudly on Monday's show.

As the Homies celebrated, we worked our way to the lake. A smattering of listeners who endured the entire match deserved a payoff. After taking my shirt off, Sactown Mike grilled my physique. I didn't care. I was more concerned about the lake snakes. Sucking up my pride, I dove into the chilly water. It was a fitting end to a sad misfortune.

Regardless of how successful we were or whether our ratings were sky high, we never wanted to play if safe. So it came as no surprise when C.K. booked Dennis Hof, the owner of the Bunny Ranch brothel in Nevada, which had been featured on HBO's new series called "Cathouse."

Hof was a great radio guest. The charismatic smut peddler told countless stories of celebrities partying at his brothel. Sounding like a seedy salesman, he invited us to join him for a weekend. Since our wives wouldn't appreciate the gimmick, we had to pass, but the invitation was open-ended. We could visit anytime or send a correspondent—so we did.

While we had done our fair share of shock jock radio before, we dove deeper into the cesspool of radio stunts as we held a contest to send one of our listeners to the Bunny Ranch. During our "Biggest Loser" contest, we heard from Steve, who had walked in on his wife cheating on him with his boss. As the two began yelling at each other, she threw her high heel at Steve and knocked out a tooth. Though it sounded implausible, Steve convinced us otherwise. He was indeed a huge loser.

But sending Steve to the Bunny Rach alone wasn't good enough for us. We needed chaperones to keep us updated on the chaos of the trip. We selected our pals Drunk Mike and Bucky, one of our Homies, who jumped at the opportunity. A few days later, our rag-tag trio arrived at the Bunny Ranch ready to party.

While some radio shows may have highlighted love and romance on Valentine's Day, we were getting updates from a brothel. Not disappointing us, we learned Steve the loser had already blown through all of his money. Spending time with one harlot wasn't good enough for Steve. He wanted a threesome and went out with a literal bang.

Bucky loved every minute of his first night, finding his own floozy to party with, at least for a few hours. Then his need for weed led him on an ill-fated search. Listening to his desperate tale of driving hundreds of miles looking for a dealer had us in disbelief. None of us smoked, so maybe we couldn't relate. We could only laugh hearing the anguish in Bucky's voice.

Then there was Drunk Mike, who was barely coherent. He was having the time of his life. Rambling incessantly, Mike had partied all night with the Bunny Ranch bimbos, though he reportedly had some performance issues. Given how much he drank—Mike had downed over a dozen beers and almost a fifth of vodka—we weren't shocked.

When Dennis Hof joined the conversation, the legend of Drunk Mike reached new heights. The gregarious Hof, who had owned the Bunny Ranch for over a decade, marveled at Mike's boundless binge, having only seen rock stars such as Vince Neil and Tommy Lee party as hard. That's respect. Our well-chosen motley crew had delivered.

11

MO MONEY, MO PROBLEMS

"It's like the more money we come across, the more problems we see."
– *Puff Daddy*

National syndication carries a certain amount of gravitas. Friends, family or listeners who departed highly transient Washington could now hear us on radio stations coast to coast. This was exciting and meaningful in great part because we were being heard in New York on WFAN.

In 1987, "The Fan" became the first full-time sports talk radio station in the country. A few years after launching, they hit gold by pairing Mike Francesa with Chris "Mad Dog" Russo and quickly became a New York institution with national recognition. Both made regular appearances on David Letterman's late-night TV show.

The rise and popularity of WFAN led to an explosion of sports talk with radio stations trying to mimic their success. In 1992, 570 WTEM became the first all-sports station in Washington and emulated "The Fan" right down to its programming and jingles.

Even though we landed on a hot talk station and not an all-sports format, we hoped to quickly build an audience in New York and keep WFAN's management happy. Unfortunately, we started with our feet in quicksand.

Before our syndication, WFAN had been running Scott Ferrall live from 10 p.m. to 1 a.m. Though Ferrall's show was often preempted for New York Mets baseball, Ferrall went live when their coverage concluded. If fans in New York wanted to talk about Mets after the game, Ferrall was the natural outlet for their calls. Since we were off the air at 11 p.m., we rarely were live in New York. Instead of a rabid live audience, "The Fan" would get a replay of "The Sports Junkies" until 1 a.m. Less than ideal.

Predictably, WFAN management wasn't thrilled. They wanted live programming. Soon the most powerful sports talk radio station in the country threatened to drop us. Our new bosses at Westwood One panicked. If we weren't able to hold New York, was it worth syndicating us at all?

Initially, Westwood One asked if we could broadcast live until 1 a.m. There was no way. We felt confident we could do four hours of entertaining radio, but how would we fill six hours without repeating ourselves and growing bored?

Recognizing syndication was a terrific opportunity, we decided to appease WFAN and host a separate hour of live radio for them from midnight to 1 a.m. The agreement would be temporary. We hoped to win over management and the New York audience quickly. We hoped they would listen to us whether we were live or not. Maybe this was a dream?

At first, the extra hour of radio wasn't a problem. We would rehash the top stories of the day, update listeners with scores from other games in progress, interact with callers from New York, New Jersey, and Connecticut. That was fun because their accents and sports passion were unmistakable.

However, after several months, we grew increasingly wary. While it was nice to hear from new callers, they were rarely interested in anything beyond the New York teams. They didn't seem to care about Tiger Woods winning another major golf tournament or Brandi Chastain ripping off her jersey as the U.S. women won the World Cup. Instead, it was a constant flurry of Brooklyn and Long Island calls asking about the Yankees and Mets. Maybe we could have tolerated it more if we didn't have to wait an hour before jumping on the airwaves, but we weren't going to bow at the altar of WFAN forever.

Though it may not have been wise, we informed WFAN that we couldn't continue after months of hosting the midnight hour. They would either have to take the show being aired to the rest of the country or not run us.

Since being in New York meant nothing to our bottom line—we were paid the same regardless of the number of affiliates—we didn't care. So when WFAN decided to drop us, we were at peace. The juice wasn't worth the squeeze, but our syndication headaches were just beginning.

★ ★ ★ ★

Shortly into our three-year national deal with Westwood One, we didn't have a firm grasp on how many stations were carrying us live or how many people were listening. The only feedback we received was during weekly conference calls. Though we wanted Chris Kinard to oversee these duties solely, Westwood One wasn't sure if a college student could handle the full-time producer responsibilities. To appease them, I was dubbed the producer and had to join the calls. Westwood One didn't need to know the arrangement was just a formality.

In only a few months, we realized Westwood One was disorganized. All we wanted was an updated and accurate affiliate list, but the information remained elusive. Regrettably, we never were sure who was carrying the show. The list always seemed to be changing.

Beyond that, we never had a grasp on which affiliates were carrying us live. Occasionally, we would glean information from callers. Carmen in Detroit became a regular, but it was always after 10 p.m. As it turned out, WDFN was running the final hour of our show live, followed by a replay of our first two national hours. Good to know.

But that wasn't the only hurdle for gaining a national audience. Unlike WJFK, which had a booming 50,000-watt signal, many of our new affiliates broadcast on the AM dial with much less power and range. Our Miami affiliate, WQAM, was only a 5,000-watt station, but that was during the day. At night, they powered down to a feeble 1,000 watts.

Another obstacle was the schedule. At WJFK, we were on every night. But WJFK was a hot talk station and most of our new affiliates were sports talk stations that carried live games at night. We might not be heard live in some cities where we had affiliates unless there was a rainout for a baseball game. How were we expected to gain listeners if we were barely on the air?

The truth was many affiliates viewed our show as late-night filler. They didn't care about our content, parodies, music, and things that made us popular. The reality was money—they didn't want to blow out their budgets by hiring local hosts. Instead, they could run a replay of the Westwood One feed of our show into the wee hours of the night at a much cheaper cost. They weren't invested in "The Sports Junkies."

★ ★ ★ ★

Unfortunately, we were dealing with more bullshit than ever before. When we signed our term agreement in May 1999, we couldn't imagine how long it would take to enforce everything. We intended to have Slow Joe and C.K. compensated fairly. In fact, our agreement called for Westwood One to provide $30,000 for a production fund.

Since WJFK was already paying Slow Joe, we figured to bump his pay after using most of the production fund to compensate C.K. WJFK didn't see it the same way. According to them, we couldn't allocate $25,000 to C.K. and $5,000 to Slow Joe. The station argued that our agreement wasn't clear and some of the production funds must be used to pay Slow Joe's underlying salary.

Whether they were right or wrong, our lawyer Doug Woloshin's billable hours began to climb as the back and forth continued for months. Eventually, we relented, and C.K. and Slow Joe had to settle for $20,000 salaries each. It wasn't the outcome that we had hoped, but we couldn't afford to keep fighting a cheap-ass wrong.

The production fund battle was only one front in our war with management. Following our lawyer and agent's advice, we had formed a corporation. While that seemed wise, things that should have been easy became highly challenging. Namely, benefits. Seven months into our syndication deal, bennies were still unsettled. In fact, Woloshin received a letter stating we weren't eligible to participate because we weren't considered employees.

We were livid. The agreement specified we should be considered full-time status "entitling participation in all employee benefit plans including health insurance." How could this be an issue?

With the dispute dragging into the spring, there was more urgency than ever for a resolution. E.B. and I had pregnant wives at home and we couldn't believe the uncertainty with our health insurance.

Eventually resolving the issue with temporary and expensive COBRA coverage almost one year after signing our national deal, we realized forming the corporation may have been a mistake. From fighting for our producers to monetizing employment taxes and receiving benefits, we had aggravations and struggles at every turn. Meanwhile, our lawyer had been charging billable hours all along. We even got a bill for his time during a round of golf with E.B. and Lurch.

Management may have been jerking us around, but resolving the terms of our contract never should have been an endless dispute. Huge lesson learned. Even though we liked Woloshin, he wasn't a radio insider. We would hire one to negotiate our next contract.

Despite the headaches, our national syndication deal had successes. When we hosted the weekend show, we were heard in Baltimore on WJFK's sister station, 1300 AM. Now we were back every night with an audience that was already familiar with us. Similarly, we built a following in Blacksburg, Virginia, home of the Virginia Tech Hokies. Since many of the Tech kids were from the Washington area, we had a start on building a following in the Blue Ridge.

Having Westwood One behind us, we were also able to travel more. Road trips were always fun. Though there was predictable complaining beforehand, our adventures, or misadventures, always made for excellent show fodder.

Walking the grounds in Flushing Meadows, New York, for the U.S. Open tennis tournament, we witnessed the phenomenon of Anna Kournikova. The teenage sensation known more for her beauty than her play had hundreds of people peering into her practice court as she warmed up before a match. We couldn't believe how many fans gathered just to catch a glimpse. But then, we were right in the middle of the mindless mob.

Spotting New York Knicks coach Jeff Van Gundy, we couldn't leave without attempting to get him on the national show. Taking a bullet for the team, Cakes bravely approached the diminutive and fiery basketball coach. Though Van Gundy took his business card, we knew getting him was a longshot. Plus, the card read "Cakes" instead of John's real name. Could it be less professional?

Leaving the tournament, sales rep Jeff, who had accompanied us after landing Heineken as the trip sponsor, flagged down a limousine. We were flattered. After piling into the limo, we began to sweat in the miserable late-summer heat. Asking our Latvian driver to turn up the air conditioning, he delivered the bad news. The a/c wasn't working. Just our luck. Even though it wasn't his fault, we lit into Jeff on the air that night. It was all in good fun.

Our trip home was not without another memorable moment. On the Acela train to Washington, Lurch noticed someone familiar sitting just a few rows away from us. Staring at the woman and trying to figure out who she was, Lurch realized it was Bebe Neuwirth, the Tony Award-winning actress who played Dr. Frasier Crane's wife Lilith on "Cheers." When we stared at the Broadway star, we received the evil eye in return. Bebe wanted to remain incognito. We couldn't care less. And we couldn't wait to rip her on the air.

Well into our second year of national syndication, our focus remained on staying atop the ratings in Washington. Since the fall of 1998, we hit No. 1 nine times. We couldn't control what was going on with the syndication mess, but if Jim McClure and Jeremy Coleman were happy with us, we felt like we had job security.

One of our most popular segments emerged from an on-air friendship with Jim Koch, the founder of Sam Adams beer who invited us to broadcast from his brewery in Boston. We jumped at the opportunity. While we had fun on the air and partied in Boston, the highlight was winning free beer for a year by besting the radio competition in a Wiffle ball home run derby.

When we returned home, we began to receive cases of Sam Adams beer every few weeks. We reveled in the spoils of victory, including Slow Joe, who never even swung the Wiffle ball bat. Sometimes we opened beers during the show. That led to a brainstorm. Let's have a drinking competition on the air!

Once we arranged rides home, we received a thumbs up from our bosses. The on-air shenanigans were worth the next day hangovers. Our listeners loved hearing us slur our words and get silly as we got hammered. Though we always razzed each other, adding alcohol meant even more verbal jabs. Plus, our listeners wanted to find out who would get the most drunk. The drinking show was so popular that it became a Junkies tradition.

A few weeks later, Washington headed to Green Bay for a Monday night matchup. Since WJFK was the team's rights holder, we'd be preempted locally, but we were still responsible for doing a show for our affiliates. Broadcasting from the Westwood One studios in nearby Crystal City,

Virginia, on Monday night, September 24, 2001, we began the show by recapping Week 2 in the NFL. Later, as Brett Favre began to shred the Redskins' defense during a 37-0 shellacking, we were suddenly bitch-slapped like Jack Sparrow. We hadn't taken one phone call. Westwood One was the radio home of "Monday Night Football." All of our affiliates were carrying the game. We were broadcasting to no one.

★ ★ ★ ★

It shouldn't have been a complete surprise. While we enjoyed the spoils of a national show—we were making good money and traveling to more major events—there were always syndication issues. Over two-plus years, we lost some affiliates and gained some, too. One of them was KILT 610 AM in Houston, a top 10 market. KILT revamped its lineup and added "The Sports Junkies" to its evening programming. But when the *Houston Chronicle* mentioned the lineup change, station operations manager Bill Van Rysdam said, "I'm not a fan of guy talk."

Nevertheless, Westwood One convinced him to give us a shot since their ratings had been sliding. A few weeks into the agreement, things appeared to be running smoothly. Connecting with our old friend Charley Casserly, by then the Houston Texans general manager, we figured KILT management would be happy with our close relationship. But that changed September 25, 2001, just one month into our stint. Michael Jordan issued a one-line statement through his management agency:

"I am returning as a player to the game I love."

This news was monumental and led every sportscast in the country. The greatest player in basketball history was making another comeback. But this time, at age 38, he would wear a Washington Wizards uniform.

Not surprisingly, our show centered on Jordan's return. Would he regain his MVP form? Would the Wizards become a contender? Or would Jordan taint his legacy? The phone lines exploded. Four hours flew by. We knew it was a great show.

The next morning, C.K. heard differently. Our Houston affiliate wasn't happy. Their management wondered why we didn't talk about the playoff-contending Houston Astros. Were they serious?

Bill Van Rysdam felt like we focused on Jordan's return too much. He would have preferred if we broke down Jeff Bagwell's plate appearances against St. Louis Cardinals pitcher Woody Williams. We were dumbfounded and disheartened. We knew we couldn't do a show that catered to every market. That was never going to make us happy. We wanted to talk about what was interesting to us. If that wasn't good enough for Houston, *c'est la vie.*

12

THE UNTOUCHABLES

"It's not what you achieve, it's what you overcome. That's what defines your career." – *Carlton Fisk*

Watching Michael Jordan don a Washington Wizards uniform was great for sports talk radio in Washington, D.C., but when it came to watching the legend play night in and night out, he would never live up to old expectations. Though he did have his share of highlights, like the game he scored 51 points, the hype of Jordan's two-year comeback exceeded the reality.

The same was true about our national syndication deal. We loved making more money, but our experiences with WFAN in New York and KILT in Houston soured our enthusiasm. Unlike our first few years on WJFK, when we had full management support regarding our content, syndication meant outside voices constantly offering their opinions. Maybe we would have felt differently if we received bonuses for adding affiliates, but more affiliates just meant more bosses. Entering the third and final year of our national deal, we wanted a new, true radio agent plugged into the industry, someone to help us avoid the headaches.

A few months earlier, Gregg "Opie" Hughes and Anthony Cumia, who climbed to the top of the afternoon drive ratings in New York, signed a national syndication deal. That created shockwaves in the industry, including at WJFK. To make room for the two raunchy shock jocks, G. Gordon Liddy, who had hosted middays for nine years, was canceled. The ripple effects were huge as "The Don and Mike Show" moved to middays so WJFK could carry "Opie and Anthony" in the afternoon.

Since the fast-rising duo was making millions, we began our search with their agent, meeting Bob Eatman for lunch in downtown Washington. Described as a killer when it came to negotiations, we were surprised the super agent based in Pacific Palisades, California, was much different than expected. Eatman was a diminutive, kind and gentle soul who spoke with immense pride about his family. He played the French horn with his brother Ross, an agent in New York City. Bob's calm demeanor was appealing, though likability wasn't a requirement and personal feelings wouldn't cloud our judgment. We needed somebody well-connected, and nobody knew the radio industry better than Bob. His client list was impressive, including other radio stars like Kidd Kraddick and Dr. Drew. He also had experience dealing with TV superstars such as Jimmy Kimmel, and Ryan Seacrest, who also has a big radio imprint. But what attracted us was Eatman's relationships with all the major players in the industry, including our general manager, Ken Stevens.

Leaving the meeting, we were confident Bob could advance our careers. But would he take us as clients? We were small fish compared to most of his clientele. Fortunately, Bob liked us, too, and by January 2002, we had signed a three-year agreement with Robert Eatman Enterprises. For his services, Bob would take 10 percent of our pay. We hoped he would be worth that kind of coin.

We couldn't have asked for a better lead-in since our first radiocast in the nighttime slot on WJFK. "The Don and Mike Show" dominated afternoon drive, leaving a huge carryover audience for us. More than four years later, WJFK's lineup change meant we wouldn't see Don Geronimo and Mike O'Meara daily anymore. While we'd miss seeing Mike—he was always supportive and joked around with us—we couldn't say the same about Don. Our relationship wasn't so simple. Though he seemed to support us, his personality was mercurial, and our interactions were limited. He was always hyper-focused on his show, so he had less time to chew the fat with us.

Beyond that, Don seemed annoyed, particularly with me, that we had expressed our frustration for starting late due to their show bleeding over with commercial breaks. I wondered how we'd be able to get ratings during the 7 o'clock hour when we were routinely starting at 7:30 or later with their commercials bleeding deep into our time. Though management agreed we were being screwed, they weren't going to upset the Don and Mike money apple cart. Geronimo wielded too much power.

Now that "Opie and Anthony" had taken over the afternoon shift on WJFK, we figured to seldom deal with Geronimo again. But many dominoes fell after the lineup change. First, our biggest advocate, Jim McClure, who had risen to operations manager, moved to Los Angeles to pursue a better opportunity. He would be sorely missed personally and professionally. And Geronimo became our new boss when he was installed as creative program director at WJFK.

We didn't know what to expect. Would Don start interfering with our content or would he be hands-off? It didn't take long for us to learn. In a conference room meeting, he prefaced unilateral changes by saying he was a fan of our show. Then he told us we were spending too much time beating up Slow Joe. So, without any consultation, he moved Slow Joe to his show and installed Cameron Gray as our producer.

While we respected and liked Cameron—he had worked for G. Gordon Liddy for years—we had grown to love Joe. Admittedly, we picked on him a lot, but that was just a function of his role. Whoever filled the position would become a punching bag. The troubling thing was we didn't have a say in the decision.

Later, as we discussed content, Don offered a few suggestions. Recognizing we prepared diligently with a show outline, Don suggested we try more spontaneous segments. He felt our tangents were often the best parts of the show. We agreed. Advising us to spring topics on our partners wasn't a bad idea. Don described it as "planned spontaneity," but truthfully, we had been using some of this approach for years.

Regardless of our icy relationship, we couldn't disrespect Don's radio acumen and accomplishments. He knew what worked. So, it made sense when he suggested dropping our background music. Hearing the music behind us was our comfort zone, but we didn't need it anymore. It was distracting to some listeners, especially with so many voices on the air. Dropping the music wasn't going to make or break us anyway.

As the meeting ended, Lurch announced he didn't want to deal with the pressure of taking us in and out of commercial breaks anymore. He wanted to step aside as the show's unofficial bus driver. Don didn't object. Besides, I was leading us into discussions as often as Lurch, so it wasn't a seismic shift. But Don looming over the show might be.

★ ★ ★ ★

The Washington Redskins got off to an anemic start to the 2001 season, losing their first five games under new coach Marty Schottenheimer. That made for easy sports talk radio. Had owner Dan Snyder hired the right guy for the job? Was Schottenheimer too old school to succeed? Lucky for us, the narrative changed when the Redskins ripped off five straight wins, leading us to a new show character.

Todd from Stephens City, Virginia, called to predict a Redskins victory over the Cowboys in Week 5. Full of confidence and a thick country accent, Todd said we could shave his head if the Redskins lost. After an ugly 9-7 defeat in Dallas, he joined us to pay his penance in the studio. Todd relished the attention and became an instant favorite by letting us shave a Tic-Tac-Toe board into his head. He'd be known to our audience as Cowboy Todd.

By then, Sactown Mike was already a favorite. Building upon his popularity, we asked him to hit the streets and hear what people had to say about some of the biggest topics of the day. Sactown usually leaned on his friend Gelly as they covered everything from Michael Jordan to Osama Bin Laden. Regardless of the subject, Sactown's contributions made us laugh.

Later we'd pair Sactown with Cowboy Todd and Drunk Mike for a game we called "Movie Mania." Listeners would have to identify the movie as the trio stumbled their way through famous dialogue.

One of our regular callers, Chad the Stalker, known as Chad Dukes when he called, worked his way into our inner circle. Hired to intern for us by C.K., Chad was warned not to enter our studio unless asked. C.K. feared E.B. would attack Chad if he appeared too eager. Luckily, Chad restrained himself just enough and proved to be invaluable. Eventually, we leaned on him as an on-air correspondent during our "Not So Amazing Race." When given a chance, Chad shined. It was clear he would be an on-air star before long.

With C.K. and Cameron producing the show, we attended our third Super Bowl, being held in New Orleans. Once again, the highlight was the star-studded lineup from the NFL Players party and hanging out afterward. Now that we were all family men—Jason and I had married in the early days of the nighttime show—being out together didn't happen as often.

Still, our travel and accommodations always made for entertaining radio. After the 9/11 tragedy the previous September and an airliner crashing into a New York City neighborhood on November 12, E.B., Cakes, and I opted to drive to the Super Bowl. As Lurch flew without a hitch, we realized we had made a gigantic mistake. The drive to and from New Orleans was interminable.

Heading home, we stopped in Albertville, Alabama, to say hello to Cakes's mom. As we pulled onto her driveway, Cakes pointed to the imaginary watch on his wrist and adamantly told us we'd be there no longer than an hour. Then, while Paulette gave E.B. and I a tour of her home, Cakes grew impatient. When his mom offered us food, we could see his frustration, but we weren't going to be disrespectful. We had known Paulette for 30 years. So the trip home would eventually resume, and we'd have plenty of time to rip into Cakes on the air— at least an hour's worth.

Our national syndication deal was just a few months from expiring. While we hadn't loved our tenure with Westwood One, six-figure salaries had put us in a position to buy our first homes and start families. But, hearing whispers that we might not be renewed, our new agent had diligent work to do.

When Bob Eatman connected with WJFK general manager Ken Stevens, he learned the rumors were true. Despite hitting No. 1 for the 11th time in Washington, our national deal was unlikely to be renewed. Westwood One had wanted live programming from 10 p.m. to 1 a.m. and had grown weary of our 7-11 shift. Many of their affiliates couldn't carry us live.

Reporting back, Eatman informed us Stevens said we should be prepared for a pay cut. While Bob shared the details, he knew Ken from previous deals and confidently predicted the blowing of smoke.

Reassuring us WJFK couldn't afford to lose "The Sports Junkies," Bob pointed to our ratings, which were now the highest at the station. While Howard Stern was grabbing a 9.4 in the mornings and "The Don and Mike Show" followed with a 9.6, we had a 12.5 in men 25-54. That was nearly six full points higher than "Opie and Anthony," who finished with a 6.8 as our lead-in.

A few weeks later, Bob arranged a meeting with a rival. Bennett Zier, a vice president at Clear Channel, ran the popular rock station DC101. Bob asked us to meet with Bennett for an initial introduction. Sitting down with the confident and brash executive at the Silver Diner in Rockville, Maryland, we heard countless radio war stories over breakfast, including how Bennett helped build the "Elliot in the Morning" show into one of the most successful drive shows in Washington. Bennett felt he could do the same with us in the afternoons.

Since Bob advised us just to listen, we didn't commit to anything. Then, the next morning, Bob received a call. Ken Stevens asked, "What the fuck are you doing with my boys?" Our general manager had caught wind of our clandestine meeting. When Bob told Ken he wasn't hired to negotiate a pay cut, Ken interjected, "I never said that."

We had leverage.

Losing our national deal could have been a devastating blow to our collective confidence, but it was also a relief. Growing up in the Washington area had always been one of our advantages. Now we wouldn't have to worry about relating to a national audience.

An expert storyteller, E.B. would share anecdotes of his childhood more often. Though we were neighbors in Bowie, Maryland, and lived similar middle-class lifestyles, you wouldn't know that if you listened to E.B. as he poor-mouthed his upbringing. For example, he relished the tale of having to share one Roy Rogers hamburger with his three younger siblings. He claimed that's why he loved the fixin's bar so much. He could load his quarter of a burger with unlimited pickles.

Although I wasn't sure if the story was true, I knew he wasn't lying about the terrible clothes he wore as a kid. Though I had my share of clothes from Sears, I never had to wear the Maypops shoes like E.B. Despite knowing what happened, it's still hilarious to hear him tell the story of going with his dad to Kmart for his first pair of Nikes. E.B. was on top of the world... until his mom learned they had spent more than $10 on new shoes. E.B. had to return his fresh kicks. Instead of the Nike swoosh, he wore sneakers with a whale.

He finally saved enough money to buy his first pair of Nike Air Force Ones during high school. Proudly wearing them to Wild World, a theme park just down the road from us, E.B. and I put our shoes in a cubby as we got in line for a water slide. When we got off the ride, the Air Force Ones were gone. With his shoes stolen, we headed home on the Metrobus with E.B. barefoot. As E.B. weaved the classic yarn for our audience, you could still hear the pain in his voice.

E.B.'s manic and neurotic nature was a constant drumbeat on the show. Whether he was playing free golf or shopping at T.J. Maxx, E.B. always found a way to complain. While airing his grievances often made us scratch our heads, hearing about his misery was entertaining and left us in stitches.

His passion for the home teams, especially the Redskins, was genuine and palpable. When Washington would inevitably flounder, we knew what was coming—a must-hear E.B. rant. Though we would have preferred to cover a winner, hearing him lose his mind about a favorite team was always a grand consolation prize.

Meanwhile, he spoke with reverence about his dad, who held multiple master's degrees and a doctorate in philosophy. During the early days of the radio show, the Reverend Dr. Carl O. Bickel would record our shows for posterity. Though the shelves in his home office were crammed mostly with religious books, he also had boxes filled with tapes of "The Sports Junkies." E.B. loved taking his dad to Redskins games, one of the benefits of working for the home team's official radio network.

Providing a stark contrast to her son, E.B.'s mom Shirley would join us occasionally on "The Sports Junkies." The piano teacher who studied drama in college didn't mind being our moral compass. She would cry, "*Eric,*" when her shameless son would raise topics ranging from sex to religion. Awkward embarrassment was a natural fit for our show.

Despite the fun and rating success we were having, Don Geronimo was becoming a headache. Unbeknownst to the four of us, C.K. and Cameron were forced to report to him regularly as Don was discouraging our producers from booking too many guests. This directly conflicted with our wishes, especially Lurch, who liked having at least two or three guests per show.

Things came to a head when Lurch asked C.K. to book Baltimore Orioles outfielder Jay Gibbons. When Don heard the interview, he became incensed. Don believed we shouldn't have any baseball players on the show, even if they were from the home team unless they were superstars like Cal Ripken Jr. So, he berated C.K. and Cameron, and called a show meeting.

Lounging in our small, shabby office on the second floor, we anxiously awaited Don's arrival. Since Cameron and C.K. had clued us in beforehand, we readied ourselves for a fight. Regardless of whether Don was right or wrong about our audience liking our interviews, it was our show. Why was he messing with us?

As Don walked into our office, we were taken aback by his dramatic entrance. Wielding a baseball bat, he appeared to be trying to intimidate us a la Al Capone in "The Untouchables." We couldn't believe what we were seeing. Did he think he was going to strike fear in us? He wasn't a physically imposing figure. We laughed at his attempt to show us who was boss.

Then, Don fired the first salvo, attacking our inexperience. "You guys think you know everything." We didn't, but that wasn't the point. We were producing a successful and money-making show by talking about things that were interesting to us. Throughout our radio careers, we had been afforded that editorial freedom. So, why was Don poking his nose in our business when we were delivering first-place numbers?

No matter what he said, we weren't going to bow down. Maybe if he hadn't entered hot with the baseball bat, we might have listened, but nothing Don said was going to change the way we felt. It was our show.

After some yelling back and forth, nothing was resolved. We were going to book whoever we wanted. Don insisted otherwise. Forcefully saying he had the final say, we rolled our eyes as he left our office. Whatever respect we held for him was gone. He had approached this meeting entirely the wrong way. Unfortunately, our producers were caught in the middle.

Still heated, E.B. and I asked Cameron to join us for a quick chat. Driving to the Ruby Tuesday parking lot just minutes from the studio, we lit into Cameron. "Why were you so quiet?" I asked. "It's our show, not Don's show. What the fuck?" Cameron's discomfort was apparent. Don had put him into a bind. "You work for us," E.B. continued, "and it's your show, too! If Jason wants to book a stupid guest, it's your job to book him. If Don bitches at you, deal with it. That's part of the job."

Continuing for several minutes, it finally dawned on Cameron, who relented. "You're totally fucking right." Cameron was on our team now. Nobody was going to divide us.

The baseball bat incident unified us. We had built "The Sports Junkies" into a success on our terms and didn't need Don Geronimo telling us what to do. As we informed our new powerhouse agent about the crazy clash, Eatman assured us he would handle the problem.

A few weeks later, on May 15, 2002, he proved his worth in spades as we signed a new, guaranteed three-year contract at WJFK. Even though we lost our national syndication deal, Bob secured a $25,000 raise for each of us. Moreover, since we weren't making the money as most of his high-powered clientele, Bob agreed to take an agent fee of just 5 percent. If we made more in the future, he reserved the right for a bigger cut. We were okay with that arrangement.

Also, Bob assured us Don Geronimo wouldn't be hovering over our show anymore. He was "voluntarily" stepping down as WJFK's creative program director. Bob Eatman carried a big stick.

During the summer of 2002, we celebrated five years in the nighttime slot on WJFK. The talent lineup was different, but the powerhouse addition of "Opie and Anthony" had proven to be a boon. But all things come to an end.

That August, the two syndicated shock jocks from New York held their third annual "Sex for Sam" contest, where couples scored points for having sex in public. Describing a simulated sex act at St. Patrick's Cathedral sparked public and media outrage. William Donohue, Catholic League for Religious and Civil Rights president, organized protests, and the situation became untenable for our parent company Infinity Broadcasting, which owned 180 stations across the country. Gregg "Opie" Hughes and Anthony Cumia were fired, leaving a hole in WJFK's lineup.

The fallout was massive. Our general manager Ken Stevens and program director Jeremy Coleman, who were also running WNEW in New York, home of the "Opie and Anthony" show, were collateral damage. Both were suspended.

Meanwhile, Eatman was in the middle of everything as he represented the fired Opie and Anthony. Though we knew he would have his hands full dealing with the wreckage, there was a new opportunity for us. Expecting "The Don and Mike Show" to return to afternoon drive on WJFK, we wondered if we might be able to move to middays.

While we continued to work at night, Eatman convinced WJFK to replay our show in the midday slot. If the audience responded well, we might take over the time slot. That was the plan, but then life threw us a curveball. Eatman called me and said eight words that would change our lives forever:

"WHFS in the mornings, what do you think?"

Morning radio had never entered our minds, but it was the prime-time of radio and paid the most. So, when the four of us discussed our options, it was an easy decision. Though we were nervous about leaving our comfort zone and competing against the likes of Howard Stern, we couldn't pass up the opportunity.

Giving Eatman the green light to move forward with negotiations, we pressed on in the nighttime slot at WJFK, but it wasn't long until we had an offer. Bob had secured a new three-year deal. In year one, our salaries would jump to $205,000 a man. By year three, "The Sports Junkies" would become a $1 million show. Bob would increase his commissions to 7.5 percent. He was worth the raise.

Leaving WJFK wasn't going to be easy. We had met so many listeners who were devoted to the radio station and "The Sports Junkies." Without them, we were nothing. Announcing our departure, countless callers offered their congratulations. They understood it was a huge opportunity and were excited for us. Still, others lamented the move. They wouldn't be able to listen to us in the mornings. They were saddened by the news.

Truthfully, we were torn. We didn't want to turn our backs on loyal listeners. But our audience didn't realize everything that had happened behind the scenes. They didn't know we faced a pay cut. They didn't know Don Geronimo had become a major pain in the ass. And they didn't know we received an offer we couldn't refuse.

Even though it was hard to say goodbye, at least we had the chance. After more than 1,300 shows, we signed off from WJFK on Wednesday, October 2, 2002. We didn't know what the future would bring us, but we were ready for the new challenge.

Happy 6th birthday John-Paul! J.P. blowing out the candles, Cakes to his right in dark shirt, E.B. in the white vest, 1976.

E.B.'s parents 25th wedding anniversary. Cakes on far left, J.P. on far right. E.B. in back, 1985.

Jason Bishop, aka Lurch, knocking down a 3-pointer for DeMatha against Cardinal Gibbons, March 1988.

Lurch in the front row wearing number 31 during his freshman season at the University of Richmond, September 1988.

This is where it all started—Bowie Community Television, summer 1995.

Our first guest on BCTV, former Washington Bullets general manager Bob Ferry, spring 1996.

The article that changes our lives. Thank you, Dick Heller.

Our first intern, Thomas Block, paying his penance on the air during our "Torture the Blocker" segment, 1997.

Pioneer adult film star Jenna Jameson joins "The Sports Junkies," 1997.

First publicity photo of "The Sports Junkies," fall 1997.

Lurch with MTV's "Downtown" Julie Brown, 2000 Super Bowl in Atlanta.

Cal and Billy Ripken join us in studio, 2004.

At the 2004 HFStival, hanging out with Redskins players LaVar Arrington, Rod Gardner and Darnerien McCants.

Backstage with Jay-Z before the HFStival, 2004.

Magic Johnson in the studio, 2004.

J.P. gives a stiff arm to a member of the D.C. Divas during the Junkies Turkey Bowl, 2004.

Professor Cakes doling out fantasy football advice to Junkette Lindsay on "JunksTV," 2004.

13

STEPPIN' TO THE A.M.

"I love sleep. I need sleep. We all do, of course. There are those people that don't need sleep. I think they are called 'successful.'" — *Jim Gaffigan*

Walking into the Lanham, Maryland, office building that housed 99.1 WHFS, we couldn't anticipate how we would be received. We only knew the station was struggling and its rival, DC101, was kicking their ass. But, after running a focus group, the brass at WHFS was convinced there was one way to boost their ratings: Hire "The Sports Junkies."

Immediately, we noticed how different our new home was compared to the dumpy offices at WJFK. Everything was bright and shiny. Lights flashed incessantly behind a glass wall with all the radio equipment in a room directly across from the 4th-floor elevators.

Strolling through the main lobby with gold records lining the hallways, we were escorted to the 95.5 WPGC side of CBS Radio. We would meet the general manager of WHFS and WPGC, Sam Rogers. Unlike WJFK's Ken Stevens, who was aloof, Rogers had a commanding presence and gregarious personality. The Penn State fanatic knew sports, but his background was in sales. He could see ratings and revenue increasing and WHFS returning to its booming heyday with our show leading the way.

Introducing us to Jay Stevens, WPGC's program director, Rogers talked about the hip hop station's track record of success. Though Robert Benjamin would be our new program director, Stevens would be working with us, too. It was clear management would be more involved with our show than we were accustomed.

Nonetheless, we were excited. There would be concerts and promotions, and we'd have a studio specifically built for the four of us. Management would help us achieve our goals. Rogers, Stevens, and Benjamin were fans of the show. Though we never liked anybody interfering with our content, we could deal with a bit of meddling so long as they were paying us the big bucks.

Taking us on a tour of the WHFS side of the floor next, Benjamin introduced us to some of our new colleagues. Bob Waugh was a grizzled deejay who helped grow the annual HFStival to one of the largest outdoor concerts in the country. Pat Ferrise served as a deejay and music director, helping guide the sound of the alternative rock station. Both were cordial and pleasant, but I wondered if they felt like we were infringing on their music turf.

Then, just as our tour was ending, two guys burst through the hallway door to greet us. Oscar Zeballos, an aspiring deejay whose radio name was "The Big O," gushed with compliments. Equally eager was another part-time deejay, "Spam," who sported a Scottish kilt. Both asked us about fantasy football and were genuinely excited about our arrival.

Then, just as we were about to leave, Spam blurted out, "Let me show you something, so you don't forget my name." Lifting his shirt as he turned around, we saw in big block letters his radio name, SPAM. Our new colleague had a target tattoo on his lower back. WHFS was going to be a wild ride.

Leading up to our first show, we quickly learned music would be front and center. Though we were hired to boost the station's dwindling ratings—the *Washington Times* reported revenue at WHFS had dropped from $16 million in 2000 to $12.2 million in 2001—Robert Benjamin said we would have to feature some of the music played throughout the day.

Our new program director envisioned as many as eight songs per hour. We couldn't believe it. How could we realistically make a ratings impact if we had to play so many songs? Had the new boss seen our ratings? While the WHFS morning show was getting crushed by the competition with a paltry 1.9 rating in men 18-34, we had a 19.5 in the same category.

Arguing that WHFS wasn't going to turn the tide by playing more music, we settled on four songs per hour. Chris Kinard would serve as our executive producer and work hand-in-hand with Benjamin. C.K. would also book guests and deal with the sales staff and promotions department.

Unfortunately, Cameron Gray had decided not to join us. Cameron was comfortable in his new position as WJFK's operations manager and didn't want to wake up at the crack of dawn. So Benjamin had an experienced producer and board op in mind. Though we hadn't met Tim Reid yet, it seemed a minor detail since he would work alongside C.K. anyway.

Our new show format did worry us, though. There would be four commercial breaks per hour. We wondered if that would disrupt our flow. Four songs. Four breaks. It was a week before the first show at our new home and the question was already there…

Was this going to work?

★ ★ ★ ★

With our first show fast approaching, there wasn't much time to consider what we were leaving behind. Though WJFK and WHFS were owned by CBS Radio, we wouldn't be able to bring our library of sound drops over to the new job. Our rap intros wouldn't make it to Lanham, either. So it was time to start anew in many ways.

To generate buzz for our first morning show on Monday, October 14, 2002, Benjamin suggested starting at 5 a.m. Though we would be fighting for an audience against many established morning shows, WHFS was fixated on Elliot Segal at DC101. Since his show started at 5:45 a.m., Benjamin wanted us to grab as many listeners as possible before Elliot went live. While we were contractually obligated from 6-10 a.m., we wanted to be team players, so we grudgingly agreed.

Waking up that early proved to be a chore. Instead of sleeping in after the nighttime show, we had to set our alarm clocks. Luckily, there was no Beltway traffic to battle at the ungodly hour, but it was painfully obvious the 4 a.m. wake-up call had shocked our systems. We felt like zombies. Still, we had to get ready.

Meeting Tim Reid for the first time, we had a friendly exchange—he preferred to be called Reid—but there was no time to waste. We had to get comfortable in our new surroundings. While Reid moved to an adjoining studio to run the board, we sat down in our new studio. Since there hadn't been time to build the console yet, we sat around a folding table with microphones clamped to the edges.

So when Reid pointed at us and our microphones were hot, we did what we had always done. After a brief introduction, we lit into the Washington Redskins, who had fallen to New Orleans 43-27 the day before. There had been tremendous preseason hype over the Redskins after owner Dan Snyder hired Steve Spurrier from the University of Florida. Spurrier had unleashed the new offense for 38 points in Osaka, Japan, during their first preseason game, which was fool's gold as the ol' ball coach mindlessly bragged about the result against second- and third-stringers. But now reality had struck, the Redskins were 2-4, and it was clear they weren't very good. Quarterback Patrick Ramsey was sacked seven times and threw four interceptions against the Saints. We suspected Spurrier's Fun 'n Gun offense was going to be a bust in the NFL.

Despite our logger-headedness, we powered through the show. It wasn't hard. Football season was our cake and ice cream. Five hours flew by and the commercial breaks and music didn't kill the show. In fact, we liked the music. But what stood out was the callers. The phone lines popped all morning.

While some congratulated us on the new gig, others vented about the

Redskins. Disgruntled fans were starting to see where the season was heading, and they weren't happy. Regardless, our new bosses had to be pleased. WHFS may have been a music station, but many sports fans were already tuned to 99.1 FM.

Legendary WPGC host Donnie Simpson walked down the hallway to wish us luck. Doused in cologne, the 48-year-old radio and BET icon smelled and looked like a million bucks. Known to arrive in a Ferrari just minutes before his morning show went live, Donnie flashed his bright smile and asked how we felt. He could see the early-morning wake-up had kicked our asses.

"Don't worry. I don't even set an alarm clock. You'll get used to it!" he claimed. We hoped the "Green-Eyed Bandit" wasn't lying.

Soon we were back to the daily grind, offering our unfiltered, unscripted, and often immature takes while laughing four hours every day. But life wasn't all rainbows and unicorns. We had lost many of our listeners. Though we knew that was inevitable, it still pained us. Emails were pouring in, damning our move and wishing we would return to WJFK so they could listen to us at night.

While some couldn't tune in because they were working, others had to make a choice. Though we would pick off some of Howard Stern's massive audience, many weren't willing to give us a chance. Instead, they were loyal to Stern.

Still, none of those issues could touch our new fear about the WHFS reach. While WJFK had a 50,000-watt signal that boomed in Virginia, WHFS's signal was weaker in our wheelhouse. Northern Virginia had been our home base for five years with our largest audience. Now our signal couldn't reach many of the listeners who helped build our careers.

On the bright side, WHFS's signal extended north to Baltimore. But management didn't care. Maybe he was exaggerating, but Sam Rogers said WHFS didn't make any money off Baltimore. Advertising rates were lower. Revenue was lower. "The Sports Junkies" were hired to boost the ratings in the Washington market. Rogers, Jay Stevens, and Robert Benjamin all knew the WHFS signal couldn't compare to DC101's in the District, but there was no quarter for excuses. We had to move the needle in Washington.

Talking football was always a big part of the show, but music was part of our conversations, too. But now, instead of arguing about old school rap versus the new school, we were promoting songs by bands like New Found

Glory and Good Charlotte. Of course, some rap music was universal and had such mass appeal that it crossed genres. For example, Eminem's first album, "The Marshall Mathers LP," was released in May 2000 and became one of the best-selling albums of all time.

So, with Eminem's first movie, "Eight Mile," having a D.C. premiere in November, WHFS wanted a big promotion on its new signature morning show. After a brainstorming session with Benjamin, we held a "Cracker Rap" contest with aspiring white rappers.

We had no clue if we'd have many entrants, but management was true to their words regarding promotional support. Not only did we have an Xbox console to give away, we also had tickets to the D.C. "Eight Mile" premiere. Perhaps even more enticing, the winner would head to the premiere in a limousine full of strippers from Nexus, a gentleman's club in the District.

Our phone lines were jammed with wannabe rappers. Aaron Schwartz didn't have the same fluff as most contestants who went by their rapper names, such as Fuzzy Byskitz and JabbaJaw. When we began speculating what the contest might be like, Cakes argued that a guy named *Schwartz* didn't stand a chance. He mockingly called him "Schwartzy" to belittle the hopeful contestant.

A few days later, the show moved to the conference room to accommodate 16 contestants and a small audience of listeners and station employees. A table was set for The Junkies to judge the performances. WPGC personality Shack would serve as emcee, adding flavor to the show. This was going to be a goof anyway.

We were wrong. Whether the aspiring rappers were teachers or worked in the corporate world, they sounded great, at least to us. That included M.C. Melba Toast with an over-the-top costume featuring fur and a fedora.

But two acts stood above the rest. Seez Mics was a tested battle rapper who also was a fan of our show. Little did we know, the University of Maryland student whose real name is Cole Policy had been part of our first talent show in 1997 while performing in a group called Educated Consumers. Years later, he was making a name for himself in the underground world of battle rap. He had won the weekly rap battle at 93.9 WKYS eight Fridays in a row. Thinking our contest might turn into a joke, Seez Mics was reluctant to enter.

He sounded polished and reminiscent of the hip hop group Gang Starr, but Schwartzy stunned us with his charisma and performance. The former Marine had been rapping since he first heard LL Cool J as a kid. Now he was jumping on stage with an up-and-coming band from Northern Virginia called Sev, which had just signed with Geffen Records. Though Schwartzy wasn't an avid radio listener, many of his friends, including his boys from

Sev, urged him to enter.

Sounding more like Limp Bizkit or Linkin Park, the short Jewish rapper had the audience in his hands as his beat kicked in and he began to rhyme:

Hey yo, what's up?
My weakest rhymes shut you schmucks up
So pick your guts up. After these words cut ya
I'll slice your appendix
And watch it hemorrhage
And drink your blood like it's an alcoholic beverage.

It was a strong start, but it was his clever lines like, "*I'm on the Sports Junkies. When I'm done, I'm changing the show to Schwartz Junkies*" that separated him from the pack. Always bet against Cakes. Schwartzy was declared the winner.

But we weren't done and wanted to have our own rap battle like Rabbit and Papa Doc in the movie. So while Schwartzy made us laugh, Seez Mics's lines seemed more spontaneous. Targeting the newly crowned champ, who had asked to play his own beat, Seez Mics fired:

I can rhyme over any beat, so what are you gonna say?
Change it to mine, so I can win
Son you're cheating
I grab the microphone like your neck and you're not breathing.

Not only had we pulled off a successful promotion, but there was actual talent in the room. We also discovered new characters like Schwartzy, who would be riding high in a limo full of strippers to the "Eight Mile" premiere.

Two months in, one thing was crystal clear. Donnie Simpson was either lying or so rich that sleep deprivation didn't affect him. For us, it was soul-crushing and we couldn't stop whining. Eventually, we realized complaining wouldn't help us win any listeners, especially those waking up just as early and driving to their jobs. All we had to do was talk for four hours. We vowed to stop whimpering. Easier said than done.

Being the top dogs at WHFS was nice. Everything ran through us, including live musical performances. Regrettably, our first was nearly a disaster, thanks to me. The Donnas were an up-and-coming alternative rock band comprised of four women from Palo Alto, California. Setting up their equipment in the conference room to accommodate the band and a small audience, we interviewed them briefly before performing their new single, "Take It Off." When the lead singer's microphone appeared to crap out, I tried to fix the issue, approaching the microphone stand. Instead, I threw off the band, which didn't know what was happening. Though it was just a few seconds of awkwardness, my boys grilled me relentlessly.

With Christmas approaching, WHFS held its annual Nutcracker concert. For weeks we sampled the music and gave away tickets. We were excited to attend and be part of the spectacle. We couldn't wait to see Chris Martin and Coldplay perform. We also wondered how the rabid alternative rock audience would react to the musical twist, James Brown.

Arriving together that Friday evening, December 13, 2002, in a promotional van that took us from a nearby hotel to the MCI Center, our excitement couldn't be contained. Thousands filled the arena. The energy was through the roof.

After program director Robert Benjamin gave us some instructions, we started to pound drinks to calm our nerves. We didn't know how the rock audience would react to the four sports guys who had taken over in the mornings on their favorite music station.

Fortunately, the crowd's energy had grown to a fever pitch when we stepped on stage to introduce the first live act. We had been to the MCI Center for Wizards games, Capitals games, and concerts, but now we were on the stage and the place was packed. After a brief introduction, the crowd roared approval. Even though we knew they weren't cheering for "The Sports Junkies"—they just wanted the concert to begin—the moment was intoxicating. We returned to the backstage bar and grabbed a fresh round of drinks as the music started to boom. Even the bands that we weren't familiar with, like Box Car Racer with Tom DeLonge and Travis Barker from blink-182, had the crowd jumping.

Privy to backstage drama, we witnessed former Smashing Pumpkins lead singer Billy Corgan act like a punk as his handlers ordered everybody to clear the hallways before his side project Zwan took the stage. We couldn't believe our eyes. This was Zwan, not The Rolling Stones.

Impressed by our "Cracker Rap" contest, Robert Benjamin suggested holding a live rap battle with some standouts, including Schwartzy and Seez Mics. The crowd wasn't feeling it. Some booed while others threw coins.

Several cocktails into his evening, Lurch was incensed. As he gave the double-barrel middle fingers salute, he challenged the crowd, "*Anybody. Anywhere. Anytime.*" While we laughed—we knew Lurch was hammered—Jay Stevens was livid. But what was he going to do? The show must go on.

We returned to the stage and introduced James Brown. Despite Benjamin's desire for the four of us to promote the morning show as much as possible, Brown's manager had a different agenda. He claimed only a handful of people had ever introduced the "Godfather of Soul," so after some negotiating, E.B. and Cakes were given the honor. But they were also given a specific set of instructions. After reading the notecard given to them verbatim, the curtain opened, and the diminutive 69-year-old legend began to belt out, "I Feel Good." The crowd went wild.

While the Rock & Roll Hall of Famer was great, Chris Martin and Coldplay took it to another level. Playing the piano as he belted out hits like "The Scientist," the crowd was awed by the British superstar. And so were we. Though Coldplay had released just two studio albums to date, it was easy to see they were on a different level.

Trying to come down from the incredible rush, the four of us jumped into different station vehicles and returned to the hotel headquarters. As luck would have it, Lurch shared a van with three members of Coldplay. Still drunk and not exercising much judgment, he began to whistle the band's biggest hit, "Clocks." What a night. Unforgettable.

★ ★ ★ ★

Entering 2003, WHFS management delivered on its promise to build a new studio specifically designed for "The Sports Junkies" with a new console. Looking through a glass partition separating us from the adjoining production studio, we could see our new producer and board operator Reid, who had become our latest target.

While Reid was skilled at running the board, we wondered why he constantly looked disheveled and exhausted. We learned he was sleeping in his car. His home was in New York, and he was driving back and forth on the weekends, occasionally driving in the middle of the night. That wasn't sustainable, but we grilled him about the sacrifices and poked fun at his unkempt appearance. Taking the beating was just part of the producer's job.

Having graduated from American University in 2001, C.K. was now fully running the show behind the scenes as our executive producer. Working at a music station proved challenging. There were constant promotions, so C.K. continually had to deal with the sales staff, promotions department, and programming.

To appease our new bosses, who were fixated on the music, we debuted a new segment called "Hit or Hurting." We would bet on whether songs were destined to be smash hits by playing them before hitting the WHFS rotation. Though we didn't always love the music, we loved the game. Occasionally we'd whiff on a sure thing like "Hey Ya" by Outkast, but that was fine. We've never minded embarrassing ourselves.

Capitalizing on the popularity of ABC's hit show "The Bachelor," we asked our pal Doug Hicks, vice president of communications for D.C. United, if there might be a pro soccer player we could use. Hicks recommended Ryan Nelsen, a 25-year-old defender from New Zealand. When we announced "Nelly the Bachelor," hundreds of emails poured in from women seeking to date the soccer star.

A few days later, Nelsen was in the studio with 10 ladies vying for his affection. Setting Nelly and the bevy of beauties up for an introductory breakfast in the conference room, we leaned on Chad Dukes, who had come over to intern at WHFS, and the Big O, for updates. Not surprisingly, the women thought Nelly was hot and his Kiwi accent was charming.

But Nelly couldn't date all the contestants. We arranged three dates with chaperones, so he was forced to cut seven of the ladies that stood next to him. Hearing Nelly's anguish as he dropped the hammer was curious theatre. While seven contestants left disappointed, we couldn't wait to discover what happened during his three dates. "Nelly the Bachelor" was off to a super start.

Then, Nelly went out with a cute deejay who spun records at various clubs in D.C. The Big O served as their chaperone and drove them in the station van to a World Wrestling Entertainment show at MCI Center. Pounding drinks and holding hands from their front row seats, the couple wanted to hang out afterward, so they headed to a nearby club. While the Big O went to the bathroom, Nelly and his date ditched him. Oscar panicked. He didn't want to fail as our intrepid reporter/gossip.

Heading back to the van deflated and bewildered, he was relieved to see the windows were steamed and the van was rocking. It wasn't tough to figure out what was happening.

Though the soccer stud didn't kiss and tell, we had a pretty good idea what happened. And so the contest continued for the better part of two weeks, concluding with the three finalists back in the studio with jewelry going to the winner. While they continued to fawn over Nelly, we put him on the spot again. Nelly picked the deejay. Big surprise? Not at all.

★ ★ ★ ★

On Sunday, February 23, 2003, we landed at Madison Square Garden in New York for The Grammys. Trying to spot celebrities, we managed to catch a glimpse of the most infamous intern in our nation's history, Monica Lewinsky. Instant show material.

Later we witnessed more history as Paul Simon and Art Garfunkel opened the show, performing together for the first time in a decade. Even though we didn't have great seats, the nonstop musical performances were fantastic.

Incredibly we watched Bruce Springsteen and the E Street Band perform "The Rising," Springsteen's response to the 9/11 trauma. The band hadn't recorded a studio album for 18 years, so it was great to see them together again. Later, Lurch's friends from Coldplay collaborated with the New York Philharmonic with a rousing version of "Politik." This time there would be no whistling.

Slugging beers at a nearby bar after the show, we reveled in how lucky we were to have these work perks. Then we noticed a superstar, at least to us, holding court at a nearby booth. It was Q-Tip from A Tribe Called Quest. We were excited. We had listened to so much Tribe during our college years and beyond. Now we were partying with him! At least, that's how we tell the story. As Q-Tip would rap, "We on an award tour with Muhammad my man. Going each and every place with the mic in their hand." We were, too.

★ ★ ★ ★

Hosting a morning show paid dividends, especially with guests. Bands such as Papa Roach and Toad the Wet Sprocket joined us in the studio every few weeks. Hearing them perform was always a treat, even if the artists weren't at their best so early in the morning.

We also were landing interviews with bigger names, including actors like Ben Affleck and Ashton Kutcher promoting their new movies. But there was nothing like getting to know one of my childhood heroes, Cal Ripken Jr.

With the help of John Maroon, one of our public relations buddies, the Baltimore Orioles icon joined us in the studio with his brother, Billy, to promote their new venture, Ripken Baseball. The two told interesting stories of playing for their dad in the major leagues. Cal and Billy were charismatic and personable and seemed to like us. The brothers joked throughout the segment. Cal revealed he had called pitches one season from his shortstop position as the inexperienced catchers and pitchers leaned on the future Hall of Famer. We couldn't have felt better when the interview wrapped, and we had struck a new friendship.

Later, Lurch would cash in on the budding relationship and play basketball with the hyper-competitive Cal. We wondered what the games were like since it was an invite-only game, commonly with former college hoopsters. Hearing Lurch describe Cal's compound and gym was fascinating, but he took the pickup game to another level, providing jerseys for all players. Lurch proved himself worthy, more than holding his own on Cal's court. He would be invited back, and Cal has an open invitation on "The Sports Junkies."

★ ★ ★ ★

The HFStival, launched in 1990, was the station's signature event. By 2003, it had grown into one of the largest all-day concerts in the country with some of the biggest rock bands gracing the stage at RFK Stadium.

In the weeks leading up to the massive event, our job was to help sell tickets. To do so, we announced the lineup, sampled some of the music, and gave away tickets. Then, continuing to push the boundaries of morning shock jock radio, we held a panty raid for all-access passes. Listeners who brought the most female lingerie to our studios would win the tickets. Maybe we shouldn't have been surprised, but our favorite rapper Schwartzy lapped the field.

On the day of the HFStival, Saturday, May 24, 2003, Schwartzy arrived in style. Bringing two strippers to the show, he enjoyed his backstage passes to the fullest. While we could only live vicariously through our new friend, we loved his stories, and he had a humdinger for us. While hooking up in Green Day's locker room, one of the strippers told Schwartzy to open his mouth. Complying instantly, Schwartzy was given an ecstasy pill. His HFStival experience was about to get crazier.

Our responsibilities left us running around throughout the concert. Jumping on the main stage in front of thousands of rabid rock fans, we introduced some of the biggest acts in the alternative rock industry, like Good Charlotte and Jane's Addiction. Then we introduced some of the lesser-known acts such as Switchfoot on the side stage. Rushing, Cakes and I decided to climb an 8-foot-high chain link fence en route. While I didn't have a problem, Cakes wasn't so lucky. One of the links ripped his shorts.

Despite the hiccups, Robert Benjamin, Bob Waugh, and Pat Ferrise knew how to put on a hell of a show. There were bands we loved, such as Audioslave, and others we didn't know as well that surprised us, like The Roots. There weren't any duds.

As darkness fell and exhaustion set in, we jumped on stage one last time. We thanked the crowd and introduced the closing act, Godsmack. When their compact lead singer Sully began to belt out "I Stand Alone," he had the entire audience transfixed. Watching thousands of revelers on the now-muddied field continue to rock out after standing in the hot sun for hours was an up-close confirmation that nothing compares to being a rock star.

Heading into the summer, we began to lean on the Big O and Chad Dukes more often. When Lurch bragged about returning clothes to Nordstrom without receipts, we decided to see how far we could take the premise. Listening to the Big O and Dukes attempt to return a golf club at a nearby Office Depot was stupid but funny. Stupidity always thrived on "The Sports Junkies."

Arguments, complaints, and personal challenges also fared well with our audience. When I jabbed Dukes about his portly frame, the aspiring deejay raged and challenged me to a fight. Accepting immediately, I wasn't allowing Dukes to retreat. Our verbal warfare would turn into real punches, and we hyped the hell out of the grudge match. The buzz grew, and we offered listeners to watch the action in person.

On the morning of the bout, Dukes entered our studio with a bang. Since we had been giving away Hulk hands on the air to promote the upcoming movie "Hulk," Dukes painted himself green. Then, stunning us when he walked into our studio, Dukes poured it on like a WWE wrestler cutting a promo, vowing to destroy me.

Dukes was having fun as a consummate showman, but I wasn't taking our fight lightly. After some verbal sparring, I exited the studio to get ready. I didn't want to walk into the fight cold, so I went for a quick jog to break a sweat.

A half-hour later, with mats covering the floor of the crowded conference room, Dukes made his ring entrance, sans the green paint, with shorts and a tank top. Next, I walked in with basketball shorts and a cut-off towel draping me like Mike Tyson. Trying to look menacing, I scowled at my fellow combatant before going nose to nose during our final stare-down.

As my radio partners described the scene, station employees poured into the conference room for a glimpse. Robert Benjamin couldn't believe this moment was truly happening. He had grown increasingly nervous for liability reasons but couldn't convince us to call off the fight. The buildup had been too much fun. There had to be a payoff, so fight on!

When the bell rang, real punches started flying. We were scheduled for three rounds at two minutes each. While Dukes had a size advantage, I was in better shape. If I could withstand his frantic initial flurry, I would land more punches later in the round.

Sure enough, Dukes began by bull-rushing me and throwing haymakers. While a few shots rang my bell, I also managed to connect. As the round progressed and Dukes wore down, I started finding my range. Landing a solid left-right combination to the top of his head, Dukes looked dazed and confused. Since I wasn't sure if he was playing possum, I didn't go in for the kill. Instead, I approached him cautiously as I began to fire off another jab. Before I could do any more damage, the bell rang, and the first round was over.

Gathering myself during our one-minute break, I was incredibly winded, but gazing at Dukes, I could see he was gassed.

Still, Chad mustered enough energy to charge at me when the bell rang for the second round. As he fired off another flurry, I managed to block most of the punches. Then I found my range. Connecting with a left jab to Dukes's nose, I followed up with a right cross. He was hurt, and this time the bell wouldn't save him. I fired off another left jab that landed flush on his jaw and then cocked my right hand to throw the hardest punch of my life. Landing square between his eyes, Dukes dropped like a sack of potatoes.

The crowd was in disbelief.

As Dukes was sprawled in pain on the mat, I showed no mercy and flung my gloves at him. With my hand raised in victory, I started to feel guilty for what I had done to my friend. We liked each other and were on the same team. He would be fine. Still, as great as our fight was for the show, like Apollo Creed said in "Rocky" after his victory, "Ain't gonna be no rematch."

★ ★ ★ ★

Change was in the air that summer. Robert Benjamin, who had proven to be our ally, was out as program director. Sam Rogers had recruited Lisa Worden from the popular rock station KROQ in Los Angeles, where she served as the music director for eight years. Lisa's mission was to change the station's sound and get listeners to stay tuned to WHFS's alternative rock music that filled the airwaves after we signed off at 10 a.m.

Our producer Reid was also leaving. We knew it was only a matter of time. How could he keep driving back and forth from New York?

With Reid's job open, we met with our new boss to discuss the options. While Lurch and I lobbied to bring Bret Oliverio back into the fold—he had since graduated from James Madison University—Worden and Stevens insisted a female voice would be smarter. Lee Anne Smith, a young and attractive part-timer who worked in the promotions department, would take over the position.

Even though we didn't know her well, she fit in seamlessly. Instead of making fun of Reid, we could dive into Lee Anne's dating life and all the guys who were pursuing her.

Unfortunately, we now had to deal with weekly meetings. Worden wanted to kick around ideas and discuss upcoming promotions. It didn't take long for us to realize she wasn't a big fan of "The Sports Junkies." Even though she liked us personally, Lisa felt our show sounded too much like a locker room. In an immature response to the perceived dig, we added lockers to our studio a few weeks later.

Jay Stevens also began poking into our business more often. The WPGC program director, whose personalized license plates said "10 Share" for the hip hop station's ratings, had been a supporter of ours when we launched, but now we weren't so sure.

Bursting into our studio to chide us about our content, Stevens asked, "How could you guys not talk about "2 Fast 2 Furious?" It hit number one at the box office." We didn't care. While Jay may have been used to fake radio where hosts feigned interest in pop culture, that would never be us.

Since there was little we could do about the anemic broadcast signal, we trained our guns on the competition. When we learned Lance Armstrong's publicist was trying to book interviews with morning shows across the country, we hatched a plan. We would reach out to producers for "Elliot in the Morning" and book Armstrong on their show. If we played it right, the prank would embarrass our rival and possibly bring over some of his audience to WHFS.

Sure enough, DC101 began to promote their upcoming interview with the legendary cyclist who had won four straight Tour de France titles. Little did they know our protégé Chad Dukes would be playing the role of Armstrong. When Dukes called in for the interview, we wondered how long it would take Elliot to figure out he was talking to an impostor.

While Dukes didn't sound remotely like the famous Texan, Elliot and his crew were clueless. Dukes duped them for seven minutes. Then, he dramatically flipped the switch when Elliot asked about the greatest moment in his career. Dukes proclaimed, "When The Junkies moved to HFS in the mornings, you jack-tool. I can't believe you thought this was Lance Armstrong." Elliot was speechless. Then, after a few seconds passed, he did the only thing he could do. He cackled and went to break. Dukes had delivered a masterpiece.

As good as we felt about the show's direction, we would be judged by the ratings. Before we took over in the mornings, WHFS ranked No. 14 in its target demo, persons 18-34. Howard Stern maintained a 9.5-point lead while the "Elliot in the Morning" show held an 8-point advantage.

There was a lot on the line by the time the 2003 Summer ratings book was released in mid-October. If our ratings stunk, Lisa Worden and Jay Stevens would interfere more. On the other hand, if they were strong, we could fend off unwelcome suggestions.

Exceeding expectations, we were in a dead heat with Howard Stern. Our bosses were ecstatic. We closed the nearly 10-point advantage in less than a year and were tied with the "King of All Media" in fourth place.

Though DC101 was still ahead of us in third, the top two spots were held by two urban stations, including our pal Donnie Simpson at WPGC, and Russ Parr on WKYS. But the rebranded "Junkies in the Morning" were officially in the hunt.

The sales staff furiously prepared sheets touting our growth. In persons 18-34, WHFS's morning numbers had increased by 167 percent. The numbers were even more dramatic in men 18-34, where the station was up 184 percent. More listeners were changing their morning routines and listening to us.

Noticing our gains, Jennifer Frey of the *Washington Post* wrote a column titled, "Young Adult Listeners Make 'Junkies' a Habit." The opening line read, "Look out, donkeys, The Junkies are on your tail."

14

HEARTBREAK

"Death ends a life, not a relationship." – *Jack Lemon*

The truth about all-important radio and TV ratings is they can be very fickle. Fluctuations sometimes happen that make no sense. We saw that years earlier with Howard Stern. In one quarter, his ratings dropped by 50 percent. Impossible. So it wasn't surprising when his astronomical numbers returned the next quarter. Stern was a ratings juggernaut.

Despite the flaws that everyone in the industry cusses, ratings can show trends. It was becoming clear more of the WJFK and DC101 audience was flocking to "The Junkies in the Morning" show on 99.1 WHFS. The shift from "The Sports Junkies" branding may have seemed like a big deal to some, but it wasn't for us. Listeners had been calling us "The Junkies" or "The Junks" for years. Since our show was about much more than sports, dropping it from our title made sense. We didn't want to scare off any potential listeners, especially the diehard WHFS music crowd. Slowly but surely, we were winning them over. The key was to keep having fun.

New program director Lisa Worden wasn't a fan of our jock banter, but ratings confirmed we had a winning formula. She just needed to stay out of the way (which bosses do not concede readily). Unfortunately, we would have to deal with weekly meetings. Lisa wanted to kick around ideas and discuss upcoming promotions. It didn't take long to realize she wasn't a huge fan of our show. Lisa was a music person, and even though she seemed to like us personally, she felt our show sounded like a locker room, so we added lockers to our studio as a childish response.

Earlier in the fall, the Washington Redskins gave us ample material. The passionate fanbase was beyond frustrated as coach Steve Spurrier's second season collapsed, losing 10 of their final 12 games. Then, a few days after the season, Spurrier called owner Dan Snyder from a golf course and quit, walking away from $15 million after winning just 12 games in two years.

By then, we were veterans of the home teams disappointing. We couldn't fathom witnessing a championship parade in downtown Washington, so we pressed on like we always had. Though we had dropped sports from our title, our phone lines were constantly flooded with fans longing for the days of Joe

Gibbs, when the Redskins were winning Super Bowls and RFK Stadium was *the place* to be.

While talking sports was our specialty, Worden majored in music. So despite butting heads occasionally about our content, the marriage was working. Lisa focused on the station's sound and concerts, and occasionally brought rock stars to the studio. It also meant we were the lead hype men when it came to the station producing a big show or event.

When we announced the 2003 WHFS Nutcracker, we were pumped as the lineup included some great bands, such as blink-182, Hoobastank, Staind, and Korn. This time we wouldn't make the mistake of bringing our rapper buddies to the stage. Instead, we'd get on and off the stage swiftly and try not to fight with the audience.

Arriving at the Patriot Center in Fairfax, Virginia, Lisa staged us in the concourse to conduct interviews and help build the excitement. While we weren't thrilled to do the extra work, it was the right thing for us to be in the middle of the action as thousands of fans poured into the building. Some of the music fans still might not know who we were.

Interviewing the bands worked out fine, too. Most of the artists were pretty down to earth, including Doug Robb, the lead singer of Hoobastank. Worden had Grade A intuition the band was about to explode. A few months later, their power ballad "The Reason" climbed up to No. 2 on the U.S. Billboard Hot 100. Later, they would fetch a Grammy nomination for song of the year.

Once we were done with our pre-show responsibilities, we were able to enjoy the concerts. Though we rarely reflected on our careers, being part of the spectacle reminded us how lucky we were, even though we still didn't like waking up early.

In mid-January 2004, just a month after the concert, we received our latest ratings. We had done the unthinkable. We beat Howard Stern in WHFS's target demographic of persons 18-34. While we held no ill will for WJFK, the results justified our decision to leave. Not only were we making more money, but nobody could say we were riding the coattails of a stacked lineup anymore. We were carrying WHFS.

More young men like us were listening to 99.1 in morning drive than before. In the male ages 25-34 demographic, we finished No. 1. And that was despite our broke-dick signal. We could only imagine how high our ratings would climb if we had DC101's booming stick.

The Washington Times noted our ascension, pointing out we had become one of the top-rated morning drive programs among men. But that didn't tell half the story. WHFS's numbers in men 25-34 had climbed from a 2.6 to a 10.3, a 296 percent increase in one year. In the coveted adults 18-34 category, WHFS had increased by 85 percent. Not bad for four regular guys talking primarily sports.

A few weeks earlier, our assistant producer Lee Anne Smith informed us she was moving and leaving the show. We wanted our former intern Bret Olivero to rejoin us. Since his days as our intern, Bret had run the board at WJFK whenever he had the chance and produced Redskins radio. He also hosted his own show, "The Sports Phenoms," with two of his buddies on Saturday nights.

Regardless of the fun he was having, Bret wanted to come back, and we knew he'd fit in seamlessly. We just had to convince Lisa Worden. This reunion wasn't a problem since Bret now had the requisite experience, and we had the ratings.

With Bret joining us, we had our most cohesive team yet. Though we had fun with Lee Anne, our chemistry with Bret was undeniable. He knew exactly when to chime in and always amused us. Hearing about his hookups was great. Bret claimed he wrote "business meeting at 9:00 am" on a whiteboard in his dorm room to shoo his conquests early the next morning. Whether we heard about his dating misadventures or poked fun at his ignorance when we played "Bet on Bret," he quickly became an audience favorite.

Meanwhile, we stumbled onto two new show regulars. There's something about radio that attracts wildly unique characters. Larry was an excitable teenager who was obsessed with two things: porn and "The Sports Junkies." His voice alone made us laugh. Then there was Bruce the Hugger. For years, we had known of Bruce as a Bowie legend, of sorts, renown for walking around town seeking hugs. Now he was frequently calling into our show. Though he never had much to say, it made him happy to connect with us. In turn, we were delighted to oblige and hear that he was still collecting hugs.

Holding contests also remained a big part of our show. When we learned about cougars—older women who chase younger men—we launched a "Sexy Mama" contest. Now that we were on WHFS in the mornings, more women were listening, which meant more ladies were lining up for our competitions. After posting photos of nearly 40 contestants online, our male audience flooded our website. Later, when we would bring the finalists to our studios to pick the winner, we knew men would be listening.

While we continued to have fun on the air, the promotions at WHFS kept coming. Hosting a Super Bowl party at a downtown club, the popular rock band Incubus jumped on stage at halftime and blew away our audience. We also hosted a March Madness party with Cakes living out his dream as a rock star when he went on stage with New Found Glory. We were having the time of our lives.

★ ★ ★ ★

Thursday, April 22, 2004

The calls started pouring in toward the end of the show. Gathering information, C.K. refused to put them through live on the air. Informing Bret first, our producers weren't sure how to handle the situation. Then, as the show closed, C.K. delivered the devastating news. Our dear friend Craig "Crickety" Walden had been in a severe car accident. The details were sketchy, but apparently, Crickety and his beautiful wife Shannon drifted off Route 2 in Calvert County and smashed into a tree earlier that morning. Both were airlifted via helicopter to Prince George's Hospital in Cheverly.

Bracing ourselves for potentially tragic news, the four of us raced to the hospital. While Shannon was in critical condition, Craig was dead. We couldn't believe it. Our 32-year-old friend, who was so full of life and beloved by so many, was gone.

As we gathered with friends and family at the hospital, tears streamed as we stood dumbfounded. We couldn't comprehend that Crickety was no longer with us. How did this happen? Why did it happen? Why Crickety? It made no sense.

Over the years, Crickety had been part of so many great moments in the show's history. The most memorable came when he provided an unintentional drama that unfolded on the air. Holding our Homies fantasy baseball draft during the show, Crickety was desperate to select pitcher Pedro Martinez, who had won the Cy Young Award during three of the previous four seasons. He was so desperate that he attempted to bribe our intern Erin, who was pulling names for the draft order from a hat.

When Erin told us about his plans, "CricketyGate" was born. We had to uncover the truth. Though Crickety played coy when confronted about his devious plan, we had a smoking gun. He made the mistake of mailing a $50 bribery check to Erin. Busted! Even so, Crickety was loved by us and the audience, whether it was his movie reviews or jawing back and forth with the four of us.

Though Crickety was a huge part of "The Sports Junkies," Craig Walden was so much more. He was a devoted husband and family man who lit up a room instantly, a true friend who kept us laughing and held a substantial piece of our hearts.

At E.B.'s wedding in 1996, Craig "Crickety" Walden styling in the vest (front row, far left). Jason and I are in the back row.

In his honor, the Craig Walden Foundation was established with an annual charity golf tournament that generated hundreds of thousands of dollars for the Children's National Medical Center. Luminaries such as Maryland Gov. Bob Ehrlich and Cal Ripken Jr. joined us as we broadcast before the tournament and honored our dear friend.

Craig "Crickety" Walden will never be forgotten by "The Sports Junkies." We loved him like a brother.

15

NEVER ASK FOR DOUBLE

"What's money? A man is a success if he gets up in the morning and goes to bed at night and in between does what he wants to do."
— Bob Dylan

The one question we continued to field more than any other, even after taking over in the mornings on WHFS, remained, "Is that all you do?" People couldn't comprehend that we didn't have second jobs. How could we talk for four hours and make a living?

While we weren't seeking more work, we always listened to other opportunities. In the fall of 1999, there was a brief flirtation with Buena Vista Television, which syndicated shows like "Who Wants to Be a Millionaire" for ABC. Executive Eliot Goldberg said they were looking for young, fresh talent and were intrigued. After receiving audio highlights and a montage of our BCTV days, Goldberg called back impressed.

"You guys are really good," he started. Then, likening us to "The X Show," a guy-themed program that aired on the FX network, the executive said, "you would be great in late night." Nonetheless, Goldberg felt we were best-suited on a network like ESPN2. The glowing reviews stroked our egos, but Buena Vista ultimately passed. It was just a tease.

A few months later, in April 2000, Fox Sports called. They were looking for a younger, hipper version of "The Sports Reporters," ESPN's Sunday morning show featuring some of the top sportswriters in the country. After receiving a package of photos, articles, ratings, and demo tapes that I prepared, the director of program development, Peter Sussman, called back with promising news. David Hill, the president of Fox Sports, loved our name and went so far as to say, "these are our guys."

The talks intensified quickly as Fox was looking to produce a one-hour show that would precede their Sunday morning NFL programming hosted by Chris Myers on Fox Sports Net. The idea had sprouted from Hill, who helped launch Fox Sports more than a decade earlier. Now he was looking for four Jimmy Kimmels to complement their game day coverage. According to Sussman, the programming guys were behind us. Still, we'd have to shoot a pilot before receiving an actual offer.

By May, we had a test option agreement. Each of us would make $500 per show for the first 26 episodes. Then we'd make $750 per episode for the following 26 weeks. Finally, if we made it to year two, we'd make $1,000 per show, which would increase to $1,500 if we continued into a third season. But that was just the opening salvo.

Meanwhile, Sussman had us scrambling to shoot a pilot. By June, he had arranged a three-camera shoot with a technical director and an audio technician at the nearby studios of Comcast SportsNet in Bethesda, Maryland. When I asked how we should dress, he recommended that we go casual. Sussman claimed his bosses were more concerned about what the show might look like than our individual appearances. He also suggested one guest interview and developing branded segments.

Creating content was never our problem. So we were ready to go after asking our pal Ryan Keuhl, now with the Cleveland Browns, to join us for a segment. Opening with our "Junkies Sports Page," we ripped through a range of topics from the NBA Finals to the latest NFL news at a furious pace. Next, we dove into our "Bad Boy of the Week," grilling hothead Atlanta Braves pitcher John Rocker, who had threatened a reporter. Later we'd joke with Ryan, who shared some hilarious stories of his playing days.

We brought back "Give It Up" during our fourth and final segment, where we lauded tennis star Mary Pierce and joked about how impressive her sports bra had been. Sussman had warned us not to be too provocative, but we couldn't play it completely safe. Wasn't this for Fox Sports anyway? After making predictions during a high-energy "Fast Forward" segment, I closed the show, "We're the Sports Junkies, we hope to see you in September."

Ten days later, Sussman called back to say they liked us, that we knew sports, and had great chemistry. I could feel the "but" coming. Then he added, "We want to push some other buttons and see what comes of it."

Taking the blame for misdirecting us, Sussman said Fox Sports looked for "more edge and attitude." That contradicted our prior conversations. Adding that David Hill saw potential in the four of us, they wanted a looser format. That was ironic since *looseness* was our specialty.

There was one issue we probably weren't going to overcome anyway. Since Fox was looking for the anti-"Sports Reporters," they didn't want four "whitebread" guys who looked the same and dressed the same. My frustration grew. Sussman had explicitly told me that it didn't matter how we looked.

But it wasn't just our wardrobe that bothered Fox Sports. We didn't have a person of color or a female. While Sussman said that wasn't a prerequisite, he claimed to hammer home the point that we came off too similar. My ire grew even more. *They knew who we were before we shot the pilot!*

Later, Sussman offered some suggestions should we get a second chance. Maybe one of us could wear a fedora while somebody else could smoke a stogie. As silly as it sounded, Fox Sports wanted characters. Joking, I offered, "Maybe I could get a neck tattoo?" But I wasn't serious, and I wasn't happy. We had been misled.

Before hanging up, Sussman said the executives loved our colorful take on Mary Pierce's sports bra. More irony. I had presented the entire pilot outline to Sussman before the audition, and he had warned me several times that we shouldn't be too controversial. Oh well. Live and learn.

★ ★ ★ ★

By the time Carey Smith, a former producer at ESPN, called to pitch a television show in the summer of 2003, we were jaded. We had met with a so-called producer who seemed more interested in showing off his luxury car. But, when I asked for his business card, he couldn't produce one. We quickly realized he was full of shit.

For some reason, we attracted these types of losers. Years earlier, a caller had convinced E.B. and Lurch he would fly us to Augusta in his private jet to attend The Masters. Maybe their judgment was clouded by their love of golf, but alarm bells sounded when we were asked for some of our private information. Soon it became apparent we were dealing with a phony. Luckily, we never shared our social security numbers.

Smith seemed legit. He had an actual resume, plan, and a team in place that would secure sponsors and handle everything on the production side. We did, however, have to film another pilot. This time there wouldn't be any executives telling us that we weren't edgy enough. "JunksTV" was an extension of the radio show, and we were going to be ourselves.

Opening with the "Junkies Jump-Off," we blitzed through the top stories of the day. Then, sitting down with Chris Samuels, star offensive lineman for the Washington Redskins, we crushed the interview as the crowded audience at the RFD Washington bar laughed throughout. Then we closed the show with our "Donkeys of the Week." If this demo wasn't good enough, so be it.

After editing the pilot, Carey Smith met the decision-makers at Fox 5 and Comcast SportsNet in Washington to make a pitch. While everybody claimed to love the show, he was rebuffed. They either didn't have enough money in their budgets or were concerned about some of our racy material. Now we were too edgy.

After several months, Smith found our landing spot, WUSA-Channel 9, the local CBS affiliate. We would air late at night, Saturdays at 2 a.m. While that may not have been prime time, we didn't care. Smith would pay us $750 per episode and assume all the risk. Besides booking guests, he would secure the sponsors, the location, set up the camera crews, produce and edit the show. We just had to show up and do our thing.

In September 2004, Channel 9 aired the first of our 13-episode season with a slick cartoon intro featuring the four of us racing in a cab throughout downtown D.C. The inaugural "JunksTV" episode garnered some surprisingly high ratings. But why was Channel 9 surprised? We had started by producing entertaining television, albeit on cable access. Now we were just a little more polished.

As we began filming weekly episodes of "JunksTV," another opportunity emerged. Josh Shalov and Stephen Palgon, producers for Star Crossed Pictures, were developing a show for ESPN Classic that they described as "Pardon the Interruption" with a twist. ESPN's popular debate show featured two of our favorite writers from the *Washington Post*, Tony Kornheiser and Michael Wilbon. We watched them frequently. Now ESPN Classic was looking to replicate PTI's success by developing a signature show complementing their lineup featuring classic games and documentaries. Shalov and Palgon had listened to us on WHFS.com and grew intrigued. They felt we would be the perfect fit, but we'd have to convince ESPN.

The next few weeks were frenetic. First, we shipped a CD with show highlights, including a recent debate where we argued whether Kobe Bryant could ever surpass Michael Jordan as the greatest NBA player of all time. We included newspaper articles, ratings, and highlights from our BCTV days and waited to hear from the network.

Within days, Crowley Sullivan, ESPN Classic's program director, reached out to discuss the possibilities. Although he expressed trepidation about some of our raunchy material, he loved the tapes. Our next step was meeting Sullivan in person at Rip's Country Inn in Bowie. Sullivan grilled us like we were taking a test, peppering us with questions ranging from our backgrounds to sports knowledge. When a nearby table became too loud, he asked the table to quiet down. Crowley Sullivan wasn't playing games.

For nearly four hours, we discussed everything from the show's concept to how we would become the faces of ESPN Classic. But Sullivan also wondered what our commitment level might be. Would we be willing to drop radio? Would we move to Orlando to join the ESPN family? ESPN is owned by Disney and has studios there. Sullivan felt it would be far easier to land superstar guests if Florida was our home base.

The next stage in the process was a meeting with Mark Shapiro, ESPN's executive vice president for programming and production. During a conference call to prep us for meeting Shapiro, Sullivan told us not to hold back from his high-powered, Emmy Award-winning boss. He advised us to wear suits and ties and show we could play by their rules. ESPN was concerned we might be too wild. We could assuage Shapiro's fears by showing we were family men with children who grew up together.

The talks with ESPN intensified so fast that we had to get our agent involved. Bob Eatman was plugged into the radio industry, but he wasn't a TV agent. But his brother Ross worked with television clients, handling a range of TV personalities, from meteorologists to news anchors, and would oversee any future negotiations.

By the following Monday, we had received a run-down for our tryout, which would occur that Friday. Preparing on the phone was intense and unlike anything we had done before. While we had always been a free-wheeling show, we had to lay out everything so the ESPN cameras could follow quickly. Instead of just opening up the discussion, the producers demanded I let them know exactly how I would introduce each topic and who would jump in first. Then they wanted to know who would follow and how I'd transition to the next topic. Each segment was meticulously prepared.

ESPN flew us to its New York City headquarters two days later, a Wednesday, where Sullivan introduced us to the great Mark Shapiro. While Shapiro intimidated some, we weren't scared. What did we have to lose? Advising us not to be a predictable point-counterpoint list show, Shapiro urged us to be smarter. As we flew back to D.C. that evening, we weren't exactly sure what he meant. Hearing positive feedback from Josh Shalov, who had spoken to Sullivan, we learned the Shapiro meeting had been a success. He liked us. There were other ESPN shows in development, but we were very much in the running. Now we had to deliver.

Two days later, Sept. 24, 2004, we returned to New York City, fully prepared and ready to roll. Sitting in the makeup chairs of their morning sports talk show "Cold Pizza," we never looked better. Then, moments before we would start shooting, calamity struck. I tripped on the staircase leading to the studio and fell. My ankle swelled to the size of a softball. Fight or flight kicked in, and I started sweating profusely. I had prepared harder for this moment than any previous audition, but now it was quickly becoming a disaster.

Finding a nearby bathroom, I stripped down to my boxer briefs to cool off. After a few minutes, I managed to calm myself and stop sweating. I dried off using paper towels and put my suit and tie back on while grimacing in pain. My boys were already seated when I limped into the studio. Marveling at how quickly my ankle had ballooned, they wondered if I could proceed.

I had no choice. More than a dozen crew members were waiting, including camera operators, audio technicians, and board operators.

A few minutes later, the floor director pointed at me, and it was go-time. We found our rhythm with ease. While I set the table, E.B., Cakes and Lurch were on fire. Not only was it a mixture of great sports content and laughs, but we also hit all the marks. We crushed the audition. When we closed the "Same As It Ever Was" pilot, the entire crew gave us a standing ovation.

Taking us to a nearby steakhouse afterward, Ross Eatman was blown away and convinced we'd receive an offer. Raising a toast, we were able to relax and reflect on the whirlwind. We had come so far. In 1995, we started a goofy cable access TV show on a whim with friends and family running our cameras. Now we had just shot a pilot for ESPN and nailed the audition.

★ ★ ★ ★

Returning home, we were confident we had done everything in our power to show ESPN we were worthy. Frustratingly, we didn't hear anything for weeks. *Maybe we weren't as good as we thought?* But we finally received word. ESPN's executives loved the pilot and wanted to move forward. Sullivan would pass the baton to Al Jaffe, ESPN's vice president of talent, to negotiate.

As contract talks heated, Cakes started perusing properties in Orlando. Though we had told Ross we didn't want to leave Washington, Cakes wasn't going to be unprepared. Even if that made sense, we grilled him anyway. There was a long road of negotiations ahead, and Cakes was putting the cart way before the horse.

Two weeks later, we were back in New York for a meeting with more executives and producers. Greeting us when we arrived, Ross warned us that he might have to leave early because it was his wedding anniversary. His wife was throwing a party later that evening.

Sitting around a huge conference room table, they showered us with compliments after the initial introductions. Everybody loved the pilot, and now they were sharing ideas on how they could make the show look amazing, from graphics to set design and wardrobe. Halfway through, Ross stood up and explained he had to leave. As soon as he exited the room, one of the ESPN executives asked, "Did your agent just walk out of the biggest fucking meeting of your lives?" The room erupted in laughter. We could only shake our heads in disbelief.

Connecting with Ross a few weeks later, Jaffe began to dive deeper into contract negotiations. Expressing ESPN's preference for us to leave radio and focus on the new show, Jaffe wondered if we'd be willing to move to Orlando or New York. That wasn't going to happen unless their offer blew us away.

Ross explained that we preferred to continue with the morning radio show and shoot the daily TV program in Washington.

While Ross dealt with contract negotiations, we still had to convince one more powerful executive. John Walsh was best known for shaping ESPN's "SportsCenter" and contributed to countless shows on the network. We met at the Cheesecake Factory in D.C., where we were pleasantly surprised by his genial and non-confrontational personality. We enjoyed our lunch immensely and left feeling like we had the blessing of ESPN's godfather.

Before long, we received our first offer. By then, ESPN had begrudgingly acquiesced to Ross's request to continue with our radio show and shoot the TV show in the District. Our salaries would start at $100,000 each per year.

Since this was just the initial offer, we didn't know what to think. We figured hosting a national TV show for ESPN would be in the same stratosphere as our radio contract, especially since they had mentioned us possibly quitting radio so many times.

Talking it through with Ross, we mentioned how much work it would take to put on the nightly program. Instead of heading home from Lanham at 10 a.m., we'd have to drive into Washington and prep for hours before shooting in the early evening. There would be no more afternoon golf for E.B. and Lurch. There would be no lunchtime hoops for me. And we'd all be missing dinner with our families. Was making an extra $100,000 a year worth giving up our freedom and disrupting our routines when we were already earning a great living?

Understanding our misgivings, Ross assured us that this was just the opening round. Ross felt the offer was light, especially for a nightly show that would air nationally. Telling us to wait patiently, Ross prepared a counteroffer. He would ask for double.

Regrettably, silence followed again until Ross finally heard back from Jaffe. ESPN Classic had decided to go in a different direction. However, Jaffe left the door open to work with us on future segments. It sounded a lot like "let's still be friends" after a devastating breakup.

Months later, in August of 2005, ESPN Classic would launch "Classic Now" hosted by *Sports Illustrated* writer Josh Elliott. Instead of paying the four of us, ESPN decided to pay for just one, although it wouldn't be for very long. "Classic Now" was canceled after just seven months.

We'll always wonder what might have happened if we accepted the first offer. Could we have tanked on ESPN? It's hard to fathom. They loved our pilot and twice flew us to New York. But there is one hard, lasting lesson from this experience: Man, never ask for double.

16

ADIOS MEANS WELCOME BACK

"In this business, if you lose, you're gonna get fired. Now, if you win, you still may get fired." — Stan Van Gundy

After our dear friend Crickety died, getting back to the show seemed trivial. One of our brothers was gone and we couldn't come to grips with the loss.

Unfortunately, the world didn't stop moving. For WHFS, the biggest event of the year was looming, and we were the station's chief promotional arm. Leading up to the 2004 HFStival, we announced the stacked lineup and began to build the excitement.

Infuriating some of the hardcore alternative rock music fans, the most famous rapper on the planet, Jay-Z, would be part of the momentous event. We couldn't wait to see how the crowd would react. Would they *really* be upset, or would they love him? We also wondered if Beyonce might join him. Maybe we would get to hear a live version of "03 Bonnie and Clyde?" The power couple was "the new Bobby and Whitney."

Leading up to the concert, C.K. booked an interview with Jay-Z, who said he was looking forward to performing before thousands of rock fans. But my radio partners presented an important question: They had started wearing NFL and NBA jerseys regularly, and they wondered if one of the coolest people on the planet would give his stamp of approval.

Awkwardly, E.B. asked, "You think it's still cool for white guys in their 30s to wear jerseys?" Chuckling, Jay-Z crushed my boys' spirits. "Nah. I don't wear jerseys anymore. It's all about the button-downs." Regrettably, Jay-Z's response wasn't going to change anything. My unstylish partners had a hookup that was offering them jerseys at a deep discount.

Beyond interviewing Jay-Z, we were fortunate to strike a friendship with an up-and-coming band, O.A.R. The group, like us, included four friends that grew up together, attending Wootton High School in Rockville, Maryland. The bandmates decided to attend Ohio State University, where they sought to build a following. Figuring they had a better chance to get signed by a record label if they became popular at one of the largest universities in the country, their strategy was beginning to bear fruit.

We didn't know what to expect when O.A.R. joined us live. We had met our share of demanding musicians. Ryan Key, lead singer of Yellowcard, seemed annoyed when we had interviewed him months earlier. While we were promoting his band, he acted as though he was doing us a favor when we asked him to perform their smash hit "Ocean Avenue." Was Key afraid he wouldn't sound great that early in the morning? Well, he didn't.

Conversely, the five friends from O.A.R. were enthusiastic and appreciative. They happily obliged when we asked them to play their hit single "Hey Girl" that had peaked as high as No. 26 on the Billboard 200. Though we were impressed by their musicality and how great they sounded, we also connected with them personally.

The boys from O.A.R. had grown up listening to "The Sports Junkies." Now their lead singer, Marc Roberge, was calling us "legends." A little flattery goes a long way. O.A.R. was our new favorite band.

★ ★ ★ ★

By the time we hit the stage at the 2004 HFStival, we knew the deal. While management wanted us to be front and center introducing bands, the thousands of fans standing on the RFK Stadium field didn't care about us. They were there for the music. So when we jumped on stage, we kept it short and sweet. We were just as eager to watch the bands in action.

Our first HFStival was great, but the 2004 lineup blew it away. Our new best friends from O.A.R. got the crowd going early with fans cheering like maniacs for the local boys done good. Closing the set with their signature "Crazy Game of Poker," they had achieved one of their dreams. They had graced the main stage at the HFStival, playing in front of their hometown. But this was just the beginning for them.

We heard Ryan Key and Yellowcard belt out "Ocean Avenue" with the crowd singing along. Though Key had been a diva in the studio, Yellowcard sounded great, and he was a legit rock star.

The lineup was so good that popular acts like Fall Out Boy and Lit didn't make it to the main stage. Instead, they were on the so-called street stage while our old friends from Jimmy's Chicken Shack appeared on the locals-only stage. During the day, we bounced around handling our responsibilities but mostly enjoyed the music.

On the main stage, acts like The Offspring, P.O.D., and Papa Roach had the crowd rocking. Then, Cypress Hill brought something different as the hip hop group gave the crowd their first taste of rap at the festival. But as good as they were, Jay-Z was waiting to appear, and the buzz through the stadium was growing. We were lucky to interview him backstage for a few minutes and take pictures. The vibe felt eerily similar to when we ran into

Muhammad Ali at the Super Bowl. Jay-Z had a powerful presence.

Before he would perform, the crowd backstage grew. We were joined by Washington Redskins linebacker LaVar Arrington and receivers Rod Gardner and Darnerien McCants, our 2004 Junkies Bachelor. Then we took to the stage and quickly introduced the greatest rapper alive.

Retreating to our perch just a few yards to the side of the stage, we were awestruck as the crowd erupted when Jay-Z emerged. Any thoughts the diehard rock fans would revolt were erased immediately. Rapping "Izzo (H.O.V.A.)," Jay-Z sang, "that's the anthem, get your damn hands up," and the crowd did. Nonstop.

While all of the bands that day were impressive, Jay-Z was on another level and transcendent. Fifty-thousand fans were delirious as he belted some of his smash hits like "Dirt Off Your Shoulder" and "99 Problems." We loved it, and so did Beyonce, who was just a few feet away from us. As enthralled as we were by Jay-Z's set, Beyonce was mesmerizing. We had never seen anyone that beautiful, not even Cindy Margolis.

So when Jay-Z finished his set, it was almost a disappointment The Cure would close the show. Lurch had played many of the legendary English band's songs during his deejay days at Salisbury. Now thousands of fans were leaving as The Cure went through their catalog of hits. Jay-Z was an impossible act to follow.

Back at the hotel for the afterparty, we mingled with some WHFS staff and our new friends from O.A.R., plus other musicians. It felt like a frat party. But we never partied in college with rock legends like Robert Smith, the eclectic lead singer from The Cure. Noticing that he was standing alone, Cakes and Lurch approached the ghoulish star to ask for a picture. He agreed, reluctantly.

They say a picture is worth a thousand words, but we'll never know. Cakes never developed the film from his archaic camera.

The summer of 2004 was an amazing time for us on and off the air. Celebrating eight years on the radio, we held a special invite-only show at the 9:30 Club in D.C. We had already hosted anniversary shows with big audiences, but we leaned on local bands or even our white rapper pals for musical entertainment. Now we had the two brothers from Good Charlotte, Joel and Benji Madden, who grew up in nearby Waldorf, Maryland, performing a special acoustic set just for us. It was truly crazy. Good Charlotte had sold over 2 million copies of their latest album, "The Young and the Hopeless."

Later that summer, we found ourselves on stage introducing the Beastie Boys. But, the ballyhooed return of the rap trio to the 9:30 Club after a five-year hiatus did not go off without a hitch. We expected to introduce the band before 9 p.m., instead we were apologizing as the Beastie Boys' flight was delayed. A thunderstorm had ruined their travel plans, and now they were on a train heading to D.C. The show wouldn't start until 11:15 p.m.

After Beastie Boys management had pizzas delivered to quell the agitated audience, the legendary rap band made up for delay when they finally hit the stage. Belting out their hits like "Sure Shot," the crowd was not disappointed. It was an unforgettable performance. Closing the show with "So What'cha' Want," there was just one thing, and we weren't going to get much of it. Sleep.

Our summers at WHFS also meant an annual trek to Dewey Beach, Delaware, to host The Starboard's "Running of the Bull" event. Steve "Monty" Montgomery had built an institution, including a tradition that coincided with Pamplona, Spain's Festival of San Fermin.

Though Monty didn't need The Junkies to host the festivities, he liked the attention. Not only were we climbing the ratings in Washington, but we were killing it in the Baltimore market, too, finishing second in adults 18-34 in the most recent Spring book. That audience included a ton of drunkards that wanted to party with us at The Starboard, so Monty invited us out for the second year in a row.

Unbelievably, Monty paid us handsomely even though he didn't ask us to do much. Beyond jumping on rickety scaffolding to make announcements alongside an Elvis impersonator, we were paid mostly to pound beers. Monty would take us inside The Starboard's cooler to down shots. Then we'd watch an excited crowd follow a fake bull onto the beach and return to the venue and drink even more.

The event was a smashing success. Literally. Cakes got so trashed that he threw a glass against a wall for no reason. The simple answer was our binge drinking days from college were well behind us. We couldn't hang anymore. Luckily, after Cakes was escorted out of the bar, we were able to get him back inside. Maybe that wasn't the wisest play, but he was being paid for his drunken stupor.

Besides our Dewey Beach shenanigans, we continued to have fun on the air. For years we had said the winners of our annual bikini contests were always the prettiest contestants. Sometimes the winners didn't have the best bodies. So this time we wanted to eliminate that possibility. Returning to the HFS conference room, we held our first "Daisy Dukes" contest. In front of another esteemed panel of judges, including Drunk Mike and Sactown, the contestants flaunted their figures with paper bags over their heads.

While that may have been degrading, eight willing participants showed off their assets in the shortest shorts to compete for the grand prize as our judges scrutinized their curvy bodies. When we announced the winner, nobody complained. Then each of the contestants finally revealed their faces. Sure enough, we were vindicated. Our winner had a fantastic physique, but she was far from the prettiest. Not even close.

Equally exciting was an in-studio visit from Magic Johnson. Now an accomplished businessperson, Magic joined us to promote his Hoops for the Homeless 3-on-3 basketball tournament. While we tried to discuss everything from his battles with Michael Jordan to the current state of the NBA, it was impossible. Nevertheless, his magnetic personality and charm shined brightly throughout. There was just something about the way Magic told stories that made us all feel warm inside.

Wrapping the visit, each of us lined up for pictures with the Hall of Famer flashing his signature smile. This time, there was no chance that I wasn't going to print the picture. Magic Johnson would find his way inside a frame.

Entering our third year at WHFS, we began to prep our agent for what we hoped would be an even more lucrative contract due to our updated ratings. In the most recent Summer ratings book, we finished fifth in adults 18-34 with a 5.7 share. That nearly tripled the numbers from two years earlier, when Howard Stern and the "Elliot in the Morning" show held a combined 17.3-point advantage on WHFS. Now their collective lead was down to just 1.4 points. Management could not say we hadn't delivered.

Meanwhile, our Baltimore ratings soared even higher. We had beaten perennial power 98 Rock in the ratings twice and hit No. 1 in men 18-34 with a 14.0. Unfortunately, management still claimed our Baltimore numbers weren't important.

Despite our success, program director Lisa Worden demanded weekly meetings. Lurch would remind us about his "no small talk" rule before entering her office every Friday. We didn't want the brainstorming sessions to last any longer than necessary.

Nevertheless, there were times when we stumbled onto worthy ideas. For example, a women's football team, the D.C. Divas, had been asking to come on the show for months. We had never considered the request. Redskins players such as running back Clinton Portis and cornerback Fred Smoot joined us regularly. Why would we have members of the Divas on the show when few had heard of them?

That's when I pitched a crazy idea. What if we challenged them to a game? We'd play them in tackle football. As we began to kick around the possibilities—could we put together a team, where would we play?—we realized none of it mattered if the Divas didn't accept our challenge.

Fortunately, they did. Maybe it wasn't as monumental as Billie Jean King versus Bobby Riggs, but the "2004 Junkies Turkey Bowl" was set. The D.C. Divas would take on the boys from WHFS.

First, we had to build a roster. That didn't take long. Besides our producers Bret and C.K. and intern Justin, we leaned on the Homies by adding Squirrel, Bucky, Horsey, and his brother Johnny to our squad. We also added E.B.'s brother Matt, Drunk Mike, and Guy the Drunkard. Finally, the roster was filled out with WHFS staff members like deejay Tim Virgin and our buddy Spam, giving us 22 men ready to take on the women.

One problem: Only a few of our players had organized football experience.

Lucky for us, Chris Montanez was a veteran football coach who listened to the show regularly. He volunteered to coach and assemble a six-member coaching staff, including two former NFL players, Tyronne Drakeford and Ratcliff Thomas.

Assigning positions during the first of our three practices, coach Montanez named Lurch quarterback. Cakes would play inside linebacker; E.B. would handle tight end, defensive end, and kicker duties; while I would play running back and safety.

Practices were intense. Going through the Oklahoma Drill, we ran into each other like battering rams. Though most of our players weren't heavyweights, we did have a couple of monsters. Kari, a sales associate, played offensive line in college. Jim Jester, a part-time producer and board op, also had college football experience. Squaring up against them was terrifying.

As we readied ourselves for the big game, the hype train rolled every morning. Responding to a poll on our website, most of our audience believed we would lose. The Divas were organized while we were a rag tag group. But public opinion began to shift as listeners could hear how seriously we were taking the game. Still, nobody knew what to expect, certainly not us.

Joining us in the studio the week before our mega matchup, Divas star running back Donna "The Animal" Wilkinson beamed with confidence. Her team was finally getting the attention she always wanted, and Donna believed they would win.

Arriving at the Prince George's Sports and Learning Complex in Landover, Maryland, on Monday, November 22, 2004, just outside FedExField, a drizzle began to fall. Our "JunksTV" crew was there to capture over 8,000 fans pouring into the stands despite the cold and rainy weather. Putting on new uniforms in the locker room, our coaches gave us some final instructions. Finally, we were ready to knock heads with the Divas.

Reaching the field just before kickoff, we were thrilled by the turnout. Fans were sporting signs and banging thundersticks. There was a full complement of referees and a band to entertain the crowd at halftime. Now we just had to play the game.

On our first possession, Lurch hit Dirty Steve from the promotions staff on a wide receiver screen that he took to the house, but there was a flag on the play. The referees called a dubious illegal block and our first drive stalled.

Then, after stopping the Divas on the ensuing drive, we got things going on the ground. Horsey, who played at DeMatha, ripped off a long run. Then I scored the game's first touchdown following Horsey and Bret in the wishbone formation. After E.B. flipped off his right cleat to connect on a bare-footed extra point, we held a 7-0 lead.

Showing heart, the Divas responded. Our intern Justin misheard our defensive call leaving a wide receiver open. The Divas were on the board.

Though the score was 7-6 after their missed extra point, our physical advantage began to wear on the ladies. Marching us down the field, Lurch hit E.B. in the flat; he promptly ran through three Divas tacklers for a 40-yard gain. Then, our running game took over as Kari and Jim Jester led a dominant offensive line that began to knock down our female opponents like bowling pins. Culminating a long drive, Lurch scored on a quarterback sneak as we seized a 14-6 advantage just before halftime.

Things got worse for the Divas in the second half. E.B. forced a fumble with a strip-sack that Drunk Mike recovered. After Horsey had a 21-yard gain, our producer Bret, aka "Meaty Thighs" for his mammoth legs, rumbled into the end zone on a fullback dive. Our lead ballooned to 21-6.

Our dominant defense took over from that point. Guy the Drunkard looked like Lawrence Taylor as he came off the edge for a sack and tackle for a loss. Then Horsey crushed Donna "The Animal" Wilkinson on a run up the middle, making linebackers coach Ratcliff Thomas proud. If anybody thought we'd hold back, they were dead wrong.

Sealing the game in the fourth quarter, Horsey intercepted the Divas quarterback and found the end zone on a pick six. After E.B. connected on his fourth extra point, the clock ran out and we had won the momentous matchup.

Junkies 28, Divas 6.

Winning the game was exhilarating, but we had gained a tremendous amount of respect for our female opponents. Though the Divas were disappointed by the outcome, they proved themselves as athletes and held the realization our silly fracas had outdrawn the Temple-Georgetown basketball game at the Verizon Center, just 11 miles away.

★ ★ ★ ★

In 2001, HBO launched the reality sports documentary series "Hard Knocks." Never had we seen the inner workings of an NFL team as it went through training camp. Along the way, we fell in love with underdogs scratching and clawing to make their teams. We also witnessed dreams being crushed as "the turk" tracked down players and asked for their playbooks before being released.

On January 12, 2005, we met with radio's version of the turk. On Wednesdays, we usually left our Lanham studios fast as possible. Our weekly meetings weren't until Friday. So when C.K. told us Sam Rogers wanted to meet right after the show, we knew something was amiss.

Walking into our general manager's office, we were greeted by two nattily attired men in suits that we didn't recognize. The two executives from Infinity Broadcasting had come down from New York and stood by Sam's desk as he delivered the fateful news.

"Fellas," Rogers started, "WHFS is going to flip formats to Spanish music starting at noon."

Say what?!?!

We hadn't processed the smallest magnitude of that news before the suits said how much they loved us. Their compliments rang hollow. If we were doing so great, why were they flipping formats?

The simple answer was money.

While we were helping them hit revenue goals in the mornings, more than half the WHFS listeners were flipping to other stations once we signed off. With the Hispanic population booming 25 percent to over 400,000 the previous four years in D.C., Baltimore, and Annapolis, Infinity Broadcasting saw an opportunity to stake a claim on the burgeoning audience with a Spanish-language and music format.

Blindsided, we didn't know what this seismic move meant for "The Sports Junkies." But with Howard Stern moving to satellite radio the following year, the executives said we would be the frontrunners to replace him on WJFK in the morning slot. In the meantime, they'd like us to return to our old radio home and work the middays.

In an instant, our world had been turned upside down. We were being asked to leave the building without whispering a word. Since we hadn't been able to discuss the news among ourselves or talk with our agent, the four of us headed to the Pizzeria Uno in Bowie. After talking with Bob Eatman, who reminded us we had a guaranteed contract, we discussed our options.

We could have opted to take the year off and collect our checks. That was enticing. But we worried Infinity Broadcasting wouldn't hand over the keys to the morning slot on WJFK if we didn't play ball with them now. Beyond that, we didn't want to fade into obscurity. Our listeners might move on if we pulled the pay-but-no-play power move. We didn't have any viable options. We would take the rest of the week off and start in WJFK's midday slot the next Monday.

By noon, we finished our lunches and hurried to our cars. We were eager to hear how WHFS would handle the format switch. Still in disbelief, we listened intently to our car stereos as 99.1 FM played Jeff Buckley's 1995 hit, "Last Goodbye." Then, the entire listening audience was stunned to hear, "Esta! Es! Tu! Nueva! Radio!"

Just like that, the legendary rock station that debuted in 1961 was gone. Instead, it was now "siempre de fiesta" on "El Zol."

Adios, WHFS. We were coming home.

17

MONSTERS OF THE MIDDAY

"I'm ready to accept the challenge. I'm coming home." — *LeBron James*

Hundreds of emails poured in after the format flip. Listeners thought it was a joke or an elaborate publicity stunt but reality set in after a few days. The rabid WHFS fanbase was outraged their treasured alternative rock music station had vanished.

Before long, an angry mob, including our pal Schwartzy, was organizing protests and petitions. Infinity Broadcasting's headquarters in New York was flooded with a deluge of calls. Months later, the company would resurrect WHFS on the weekends and in the evenings on 105.7 FM in Baltimore. The HFStival would return too, this time at M&T Stadium with another epic lineup, including the Foo Fighters and Billy Idol. But that wasn't going to change the trajectory of our careers.

Though we couldn't tell anyone yet, we were in line to take over the coveted morning drive slot at WJFK that Howard Stern had occupied since 1988. If we didn't tank in the middays, we'd also likely land our most significant contract. We didn't know precisely how lucrative that might be, but we knew we had the right agent. Now we just had to kick ass in the middays.

Returning to WJFK felt strange. All of the key players in charge before we left— Jeremy Coleman, Jim McClure, and Ken Stevens—were now gone. The lineup was different, too. WJFK had dropped G. Gordon Liddy years earlier, and the "Opie and Anthony" show landed on satellite radio. With "The Don and Mike Show" back in afternoon drive, we would be wedged between Howard Stern and Bill O'Reilly's "The Radio Factor" from 10 a.m. to 1 p.m.

Regardless of the lineup, a slew of shows would be gunning for Stern's slot. We knew there would be much speculation, but we believed we had earned the shot. In the meantime, we would bask in the glory of sleeping in and hosting a three-hour show.

★ ★ ★ ★

The feeling of driving back to the studios in Fairfax, Virginia, was eerie. While the suits had all but promised us Howard Stern's morning slot, we didn't have a contract specifying that commitment. They could change their minds and we could be stuck working middays.

Just a few years earlier, we coveted the midday time slot. Now it felt like a demotion. But we weren't complaining. We could finally sleep in, plus we had not taken a pay cut. Bob Eatman had worked his magic. Guaranteed contracts are a beautiful thing.

Arriving at WJFK on January 17, 2005, we saw familiar faces, including many of our friends from the sales department. First, we met new general manager Michael Hughes, a tall, welcoming man who greeted us enthusiastically. Then we reunited with our former producer Cameron Gray, who was serving as WJFK's operations manager. Cameron was thrilled we were part of the lineup again, and we were happy to see him.

After chatting awhile, we prepared for our first show and walked into our old studio, a noticeable step down from our accommodations at WHFS. The studio was dingy and not as spacious, but it was business as usual once the microphones cracked.

Tearing into the disappointing Indianapolis Colts, who had lost 20-3 to the New England Patriots in a blinding snowstorm, we wondered if Peyton Manning would ever get over the hump and reach the Super Bowl. Patriots coach Bill Belichick and star quarterback Tom Brady had Peyton's number, especially at Foxborough Stadium, where Peyton suffered his seventh career loss.

While talking about the NFL playoffs was fun, the Washington Wizards were starting to make things interesting. Gilbert Arenas was becoming a star and helped the Wizards win their seventh straight game over the weekend. E.B. and Cakes were thrilled as the Wizards seemed poised for their first playoff run since 1997.

Though the Redskins foundered during the fall and missed the playoffs again, at least we'd have Arenas and the Wizards to root for until summer. Unfortunately, the NHL was in the middle of a lockout. We would have to wait and see if the Washington Capitals' top draft choice from 2004, Alexander Ovechkin, was as good as advertised.

It didn't take long for us to fall in love with middays. With Howard Stern as our lead-in, we had a captive audience when we signed on every morning. We were also well-rested. Staying up late to watch games had destroyed us in the morning shift, but now we could stay up late and sleep well, too. It was glorious.

The three-hour show felt like a breeze. Though we never had a problem filling four hours of air time, doing 25 percent less made the show that much easier. In fact, it felt so easy that the boys started playing hands of poker during the show.

By then, poker's popularity had exploded. After qualifying online, Chris Moneymaker's win at the 2003 World Series of Poker revolutionized the game when he became a world champion. One year later, Greg "Fossilman" Raymer emerged as the champion, with more viewers watching poker on ESPN than before. "Fossilman" sat down for an episode of "JunksTV," where we played cards with the champ who had just won $5 million.

While our dalliance with ESPN didn't work out, Carey Smith had managed to produce two seasons of "JunksTV." Along the way, we booked great guests, ranging from Maryland basketball coach Gary Williams, who led the Terps to the NCAA Tournament championship in 2002, to former Redskin greats Brian Mitchell and Gary Clark.

Striking a relationship with Terrapins stud linebacker Shawne Merriman, our camera crew filmed the shredded superstar during his workouts leading up to the NFL Draft. Then we followed him on draft day to his party before the San Diego Chargers selected him with the 12th overall pick.

We also filmed some fun segments. E.B. went rim shopping with Wizards guard Larry Hughes for a "JunksTV" rendition of "Pimp My Ride." Then E.B. got his new Chrysler 200 C "pimped out" with shiny, new rims of his own. While he was bursting with pride, we mocked his "Fentley," which stood for fake Bentley. We had to joan.

★ ★ ★ ★

In Dick Heller's 1996 *Washington Times* column about "The Sports Junkies," E.B. described himself, Lurch, and me as "very opinionated." Then he said Cakes "has a little quieter personality—he provides a good blend with the rest of us."

That is still true. The four of us have such distinct personalities, but one of Cakes's greatest strengths is his ability to shrug things off and go along with the joke, even when he's the target. Maybe it started as a defense mechanism during his childhood, but Cakes's laugh is infectious and can often lower the temperature in the room. Cakes's ability to roll with the punches is most definitely a valuable and welcome trait when working with three powder kegs.

Managing to stay clear of most controversies and on-air fights, Cakes has weaved countless tales that have left us, and the audience, rolling. For example, the father of three revealed that his youngest son, Brendan, born just a year earlier in June of 2004, was a happy accident. We laughed as he recapped living in the moment and forgetting that his wife was not on birth control. Though it was a blessing—Cakes and Amy were devoted to their three children: Kurt, Juliet, and Brendan—hearing his naked confession made for great radio.

Often Cakes would expose his most humbling experiences and poor decisions. Over time, our audience would learn about Cakes maximizing profits with questionable accounting during his days selling cotton candy at Six Flags in Houston. He fessed up to stealing an adult movie when the cashier behind the counter wasn't looking. And he admitted using one ticket repeatedly during his time as a waiter to pocket more cash. Of course, this was all alleged. Maybe it didn't happen.

Cakes often finds himself the target of our ridicule because he rarely gets defensive. Maybe we are asshats, but we love teasing Cakes about crushing on his second-grade teacher and embarrassingly leaving her a note. We love making fun of him for running palms up while sprinting. But we wouldn't be able to do that if Cakes wasn't a willing participant. His affable nature generally remains intact even when he is getting roasted.

Cakes is undeniably lovable, funny, creative, and talented. Gaining confidence with his impersonation skills over the years, he would quickly master Washington Capitals star Alexander Ovechkin's Russian accent. Then he created a game, NHLer or Russian politician, where he could show off his impersonation chops.

Somehow, even when Cakes's impressions aren't particularly close, a la Mike Tyson, he still makes us laugh. His timing is impeccable. While E.B., Lurch, and I jabber away, Cakes often pounces like a cheetah with one-line zingers that leave us rolling.

At appearances, Cakes is far less of an introvert than some of his alpha partners. Our audience loves him. How could they not? Besides his uncanny ability to pick the wrong side of games—a listener even started an "Always Bet Against Cakes" website to track his misses—he is an all-around good guy.

A thoughtful husband, Cakes would occasionally surprise his school teacher wife with coffee and bagels and help her arrange the classroom furniture. He also coached his son's flag football team and was a loyal son to both of his parents even after they divorced in 1995. Visiting them in Alabama and Pennsylvania after they relocated, Cakes never picked a side. That is not who John "Cakes" Auville is.

Before "The Sports Junkies" moved back to mornings, we wanted to revive movie reviews on the show. Though it would never be the same without Crickety, we desired to press forward nonetheless. So Bret and C.K. began booking critics to see if we would have any chemistry. After a few mediocre appearances, we stumbled onto a potential replacement working just down the hallway.

Kevin McCarthy was a 21-year-old intern studying communications at George Mason University. The lanky youngster with a face full of acne manned the front desk and greeted us each morning with an enthusiastic smile. We learned he suffered from severe obsessive-compulsive disorder. Asked to drive the station's promotional vehicle, Kevin declined. Running over potholes left him paralyzed by fear. Irrational or not, Kevin would take repeated U-turns and pictures of the scene to ensure he hadn't killed anybody. The last thing he wanted was more driving.

Despite his anxiety, Kevin seized the opportunity to become our movie reviewer. Approaching me before the show, the student boldly claimed to be the right man for the job. Kevin was a movie aficionado who kept the ticket stubs of every flick he had attended, another symptom of OCD. Not knowing whether he would be good on the air, I could only promise he would be considered. After impressing our producers, he would get his shot.

Entering our studio for the first time, we pounced on him quickly. Before he could mutter one word about his love of movies, he was forced to defend himself on a range of topics—from his OCD to his nickname, Big Daddy Kev. Though he didn't seem comfortable with the trial-by-fire approach, he didn't duck our questions, either.

"Have you ever been laid?" E.B. wondered. Begrudgingly Kevin nodded yes. We didn't know if he was telling the truth, but we appreciated he didn't run out of the studio crying.

Next, Kevin offered his review of "Just Friends," a romantic comedy starring Ryan Reynolds and Amy Smart. Though his plot synopsis and presentation were solid, we weren't sure about his scoring system. Kevin's scale distinguished movies that were worthy of rentals, matinees, or full-priced viewings. If a film received a perfect score, we were urged to drop everything and see it immediately.

Whether or not we liked Kevin, we wanted to add drama. So, leaving his future to our listeners, we opened the phone lines and asked callers to decide Kevin's fate. With the votes deadlocked at four, the ninth caller put him over the top. Kevin was ecstatic, and we were happy, too.

Not only did we have a new movie reviewer, but we had a new show punching bag. BDK was born.

During presidential election years like 2004, politically oriented talk radio stations such as 630 WMAL, home of Rush Limbaugh and Sean Hannity, dominated the airwaves and ratings in Washington, D.C. But that spring, we received our first ratings in the new midday slot, and our impact was significant. Before we returned to WJFK, the station had finished sixth with a

4.8 share in the middays with their target demographic of men 25-54. Now WJFK was in first place with a 10.5.

Paul Farhi of the *Washington Post* called us the big winner in the ratings.

"Those numbers could be a prelude to a fat payday for the four lads, if not a wholesale realignment of Washington's morning radio market," Farhi wrote. "The Junkies' contract with Infinity-owned WJFK is up in October, just a few months before Infinity will be stuck with a huge hole in its morning drivetime lineup with the scheduled defection of ever-popular Howard Stern to satellite radio. Can you say *Junkies* in the early a.m.?"

Farhi was connecting the dots. We were crushing the ratings, but didn't have a new deal in a place, and nothing was guaranteed. Still, a "fat payday" sounded pretty sweet.

Our confidence couldn't be higher about taking over in the middays on WJFK. We knew agent Bob Eatman was already working on a deal with Infinity Broadcasting despite rampant speculation of potential Stern successors.

By the fall, the discussions intensified. Reaching an agreement was only a matter of time. We finished No. 1 in every quarter, and the race wasn't particularly close. Now we just had to plan our return to morning drive.

Fortunately, management at WJFK was behind us. Michael Hughes and Cameron Gray were going to do everything in their power to ensure our success. So, we were in a position to ask for almost anything.

After holding a meeting together, I prepared an email for our new bosses outlining everything we wanted—from the show format to promotions. We asked about a "Junkies Breakfast Club" where listeners could meet at a local coffee shop or Dunkin Donuts to drum up interest. If management wanted us to thrive, they would have to fork over some cake to promote our show.

We also wanted to spice up things by forming a "Junkette" squad. Months earlier, we held on-air tryouts to add an attractive female to our "JunksTV" cast. Ultimately, Lindsay Williams and Shelly Zemrose joined our crew. Our male-dominated audience loved them, from providing sideline reports during the Turkey Bowl to exciting the crowd as we taped the show. So did our new character, Professor Cakes, who doled out fantasy football advice to his pupil Lindsay dressed in a Catholic schoolgirl outfit like Britney Spears in her video "Baby One More Time."

Our demands weren't unreasonable. If management could spend some money upfront on promoting "The Sports Junkies," we could hit the ground running before Howard Stern vacated that coveted morning slot.

★ ★ ★ ★

Losing Stern was a colossal blow to Infinity Broadcasting. He made millions for the company while dominating terrestrial radio ratings from New York to Los Angeles. With his imminent departure to satellite, Infinity Broadcasting had a plan.

In January, they would launch "Free FM." Trying to drive home that listeners wouldn't have to pay for listening to the radio, Infinity attacked the loss of Stern regionally. Comedian Adam Corolla, who hosted "Loveline" for years with Dr. Drew Pinsky, would inherit Stern's west coast affiliates; Rover, host of a highly rated morning show in Cleveland, would take over the midwest affiliates; former Van Halen rock star David Lee Roth would debut in New York and replace Stern on his northeast affiliates; and we would host mornings for their stations in Washington and Baltimore.

Returning to the Baltimore airwaves was a blessing. We had flourished in the market despite the disinterest from WHFS's management. The WJFK signal didn't reach Baltimore during the middays, so it was rewarding to know we would be heard there once again, pending contract negotiations.

Still, before things became official, we met with general manager Bob Philips of 105.7 at Ferrari's restaurant in Laurel, Maryland. A radio lifer, Philips exuded confidence, but listening to him talk about his success selling radio, we began to wonder if he truly wanted us to be part of his lineup. He was saying the right things, but it oozed fake enthusiasm.

Even though we were just a corner piece of the puzzle replacing Stern nationally, Infinity asked us to be part of a photoshoot in downtown D.C. We sat on park benches, played with origami, stood outside a nearby government building, and tugged on a giant-sized check. The photoshoot was goofy, but we appreciated the company's support even though we still didn't know what that meant for our bottom line. We would soon find out.

One year earlier, Stern signed a five-year, $500 million deal to leave for satellite radio. The numbers were astronomical, but Stern had built a radio empire with a massive audience of fans across the country. It would be our job to keep as many of them as possible in Washington and Baltimore.

We knew some of our listeners would join Stern on satellite, and we didn't have his audience reach coast to coast, but we had built a loyal following, as well. Many had listened since we were radio neophytes figuring things out on the weekends. Others jumped aboard when we moved to the nighttime slot. Our audience grew even larger during our three-year stint as a nationally syndicated program. Then we grew into one of the most popular morning drive shows in the mid-Atlantic.

So after months of negotiations, Bob Eatman finalized a deal with Infinity on October 24, 2005, that would keep us with the company for at least three years. In Washington, WJFK could exercise an option and retain us through

2009. We loved the security, but our new salaries blew us away.

Starting January 1, 2006, we'd each earn a raise of nearly $60,000 each and be eligible for bonuses. If we hit No. 1 in the middays in our final quarter, we'd reach a $15,000 bonus. That was already fait accompli.

Beyond the salary increase, we received more vacation days, and our fees for commercial reads and appearances would increase. We would also earn more money in Baltimore, though there was a red flag—we were only guaranteed one year at Bob Philips's 105.7. Our read on Philips was correct. He wasn't in love with us, but he'd still have to pay us for at least a year.

We would make more money than we imagined. The Washington Post noted that WJFK had generated $26.7 million the previous year, with the Stern show accounting for almost 25 percent of the revenue. Our job was to keep the advertisers happy and money flowing. Infinity Broadcasting was placing a big bet on "The Sports Junkies."

★ ★ ★ ★

Leading up to our return to morning drive, we began to receive more media attention. First, the *Washington Post* featured an article with the headline, "Local 'Junkies' Set to Take Over Stern's Morning Radio Turf." Then *Advertising Age*, an industry trade magazine, featured Infinity's Free FM campaign, including two full-page ads of The Junkies. *Fortune* magazine wondered if "The Sports Junkies" might be the next Howard Stern, quoting E.B., "We're low on talent but high on chemistry." Added Cakes: "He's low-balling us. We're scary talented."

Questions remained, nonetheless. *Fortune* asked, "Now in their mid-thirties, can they still rope in the frat crowd?" We thought so.

That's because we knew what to expect. We had hosted a successful morning drive show at WHFS and owned big plans for promotions, plus a new movie reviewer who would become a new show character. We also had an enormous regional population in their cars for an average of 43 minutes commuting to work five days a week. Most of all, we had a 50,000-watt signal that boomed across the District, Maryland, and Virginia.

Waking up before sunrise again wasn't going to be easy. That never felt natural. Maybe we should have stayed where we were, being monsters of the middays. Then again, our new paychecks were bazilly.

Time to set our alarm clocks.

18

GIBBS 2.0

"I don't know if God is a sports fan or not, but I do know this: He loves a good comeback." — *Lane Kiffin*

It only took five years for Washington Redskins owner Dan Snyder to destroy over 65 years of fan equity. Having cycled through four head coaches and a bevy of free-agent busts, Snyder became the favorite target of the vast and angry base as the losses mounted. His name elicited disdain on almost every level—from fans, season-ticket and luxury box holders, local media, fellow NFL owners, and employees. "Trade Snyder" signs began popping up more frequently during home games, and countless callers expressed their wish for Snyder to sell the team. The narrative hasn't changed over the years.

But in the first week of January 2004, all was forgiven. Astonishingly, Snyder convinced Joe Gibbs to return as Redskins coach once again. Of all the scenarios everyone considered for the immediate future of the team, nobody envisioned Gibbs 2.0.

The Hall of Fame coach had retired in 1992 after winning 16 playoff games and collecting those three Lombardi trophies. To call him a legend in Washington is underselling Gibbs. He's a godly figure as a person and coach, so when news broke on the morning of January 7, dreams did not strictly come true because who in their right mind could have dreamed Gibbs would work for Snyder?

The return of the coaching messiah was a boon for sports talk radio. While the Redskins' ineptitude had generated persistent frustration and discontent that filled our phone lines, the return of Gibbs flipped the script. He walked on water in Redskins Nation and NFL circles. His success in the world of NASCAR only increased his mythical status. Whatever he touched turned to gold, so fans and "The Sports Junkies" couldn't wait to see him back on the sidelines. What could possibly go wrong?

★ ★ ★ ★

On the day of Joe Gibbs's homecoming, WUSA-Channel 9 asked us to be part of their coverage. By then, we were regulars on the station's "Sports Plus" program on Sunday nights. E.B., Cakes, and I would jump on the live show, sometimes as late as midnight, to break down Redskins games and the rest of the NFL slate. Lurch would never join for two simple reasons: Appearing was unpaid and destroyed our sleep.

Still, we felt the relationship was mutually beneficial. We were Channel 9's clowns that wore bags over our heads when the season tanked, and in return, they would promote our morning show. Sleep be damned, this was a good arrangement.

Gibbs's return was so momentous that even Lurch agreed to be part of the coverage. He lived in Ashburn, Virginia, just a few miles from Redskins Park. As Lurch and Cakes waited for Gibbs's arrival with a throng of reporters and camera crews huddled in the cold, E.B. and I sat comfortably inside the cozy confines of Channel 9 in northwest Washington. We wondered if we were missing history by not being at the scene.

In the decade since he left the Redskins, Gibbs had become an incredibly successful NASCAR owner and a Pro Football Hall of Famer. On this day, everyone seemed to have the same thought: "Thank you, Joe, for saving this franchise." But we also wondered why one of the greatest football coaches of all time would risk his legacy by returning to the messiness created by Dan Snyder?

The anticipation for Gibbs's arrival at Redskins Park was insane. A delay added to the drama. While E.B. and I helped Channel 9 pad the air time until Gibbs's entrance, our buddies were freezing. Finally, the legendary coach's limo arrived, and a surreal scene developed around Gibbs as he quickly shook a few hands while smiling big. Then, speaking with his subtle Southern twang, Gibbs said, "Thanks for coming out in the cold like this."

That was it. The next thing we knew, the new old coach of the Redskins was inside, ready to make his formal address with the media, team, and employees.

Since everything had been pushed back by Gibbs's late arrival, Channel 9 was left scrambling. Instead of going to Lurch and Cakes live at the scene, the station went to break and bumped them. They had stood in the brutal cold for nothing. 'Em's the breaks. Show business.

Maybe it wasn't fair, but everybody figured Joe Gibbs would have the Redskins in playoff contention right away. Cleaning up the wreckage left behind from Steve Spurrier's final season wasn't so simple. Washington finished 6-10 in Gibbs's first season back. Nobody could have predicted such a lackluster outcome. He was Joe Friggin' Gibbs—too good, too smart, and too successful. E.B. often pointed out that Gibbs was also a national racquetball champion, as if that guaranteed wins on the gridiron.

Nevertheless, we couldn't help but wonder: Had Gibbs lost his fastball during his years running a NASCAR team? Had he stepped away from football for too long?

For an entire offseason, we pondered whether Gibbs was tarnishing his legacy. On the positive side, he drafted two players who would be building blocks for the future. University of Miami safety Sean Taylor, selected No. 5 overall in the 2004 NFL Draft, was a hard-hitting player who buzzed around the field hunting for quarterbacks and anybody who carried the ball. Meanwhile, Utah State tight end Chris Cooley was picked in the third round and proved to be a steal as he finished with six touchdown catches as a rookie.

But if Gibbs was going to lead the Redskins back to prominence, he needed to find a quarterback. Trading for veteran Mark Brunell hadn't worked. The three-time Pro Bowler suffered a hamstring injury during the 2004 season, couldn't hit the broad side of a barn with his throws, and was ultimately benched in favor of Patrick Ramsey.

Ramsey? He had flopped during his first two seasons with Washington. As the old saying goes, if you have two quarterbacks, you have none.

That's why the stakes were so high during the 2005 draft. Unfortunately, the Redskins held the 25th pick. Amazingly, after Utah quarterback Alex Smith was drafted No. 1 overall by the San Francisco 49ers, no other quarterbacks were selected until the 24th pick. Then, just one selection before Washington, the Green Bay Packers selected future Hall of Famer Aaron Rodgers from Cal. Imagine the Redskins with Rodgers for the last decade and a half. Gibbs might still be coaching today.

Instead, they settled for quarterback Jason Campbell from Auburn. Afterward, we wondered if the SEC Player of the Year who led the Tigers to an undefeated season might turn into the quarterback of the future. Kicking it around on the air, we were aware Gibbs won three Super Bowls with three different quarterbacks. From Joe Theismann to Doug Williams to Mark Rypien, we were not oblivious to Gibbs's quarterback track record, or the Babe Laufenberg, Jay Schroeder, Stan Humphries, and Jeff Rutledge controversies.

Though we had thrived for almost a decade on the radio while the Redskins struggled, we had never been fortunate to conduct the show when they were good. With Gibbs at the helm, was it destiny? Or were we overlooking some ominous signs?

★ ★ ★ ★

The 2005 season got off to an inauspicious start. Sitting at 5-6 after an overtime loss to the San Diego Chargers at FedExField on November

27, the Redskins' playoff chances were dwindling. More of our callers were saying the coach had indeed been out of the NFL for too long. Though it felt like blasphemy, especially to E.B., who worshipped Gibbs and had been known to play "Hail to the Redskins" on his saxophone during the Super Bowl years, we couldn't help but agree. Remarkably, Joe Gibbs wasn't getting a free pass any longer.

Then, the Redskins ripped off five straight wins to close the season as running back Clinton Portis topped 100 yards in each game. Reputation restored! A surprise gift had been delivered to "The Sports Junkies." We had a playoff team to talk about the next morning. And what great timing, too. It was our first show in the morning slot on WJFK.

The winning streak had been improbable, but the fanbase flooded our phone lines as we previewed Washington's wild-card matchup against Tampa Bay. Gibbs had the Redskins peaking, which carried into their 17-10 victory against the Bucs. It was the team's first playoff win in six years, and our phone lines continued to be jammed. One thing holds true: The Capitals, Nationals, Wizards, Maryland, or Georgetown can win championships, but this will always be a Washington football market at heart.

Regardless of what might happen in the divisional round against Seattle the following weekend, we had an attentive audience of fervent fans that wanted to talk Redskins. For years, callers claimed that we loved to criticize the moribund franchise. That wasn't true, but it was easy. We couldn't sugarcoat our opinions either. The realities were in front for everyone to see. The Redskins had become one of the worst-operated franchises in the NFL with a maligned owner who mowed through coaches. While that gave us constant material, winning was more fun and meant more listeners would tune in to the show, so we were always ready to jump on the bandwagon.

Thank you, coach Gibbs. Giddy up.

Unfortunately, the magic ride would come to an end in Seattle. Still, the Redskins going two games deep into the postseason as we kicked off the morning drive show had been a blessing. Having grown up together in the DMV, talking passionately about the Redskins was in our DNA. Now we needed Gibbs 2.0 to take the team even deeper in the playoffs the following season.

When Joe Gibbs coached Washington from 1981-'92, the Redskins finished with a losing record just once. The 7-9 season in 1988 was a dud, but it also came on the heels of the team claiming its second Super Bowl. Nobody questioned Gibbs after just one subpar season. He had already delivered two Lombardi Trophies in just six years.

That wasn't the case during the 2006 season when Gibbs had a losing team for the second time in three years. Instead of building on their unexpected playoff success, the Redskins tanked to the tune of a 5-11 record—inconceivable for a Gibbs team. During the year, quarterback Mark Brunell, who had a career resurgence in 2005, was benched in favor of second-year quarterback Jason Campbell. Starting seven games, the Redskins won only two with Campbell under center.

If Gibbs were going to bounce back during the fourth of his five-year contract in 2007, he would need his first-round draft choice to improve dramatically. If Campbell wasn't up to the task, Joe Gibbs 2.0 could be a bust. During his three seasons back, the Redskins were 21-27 in the regular season with just one playoff win. That wasn't Gibbs. That was ordinary Joe.

Sadly, the 2007 season got off to another rough start as Campbell struggled. For almost every touchdown he threw, Campbell also threw an interception. At 5-6, talking about the playoffs was laughable, especially with their best player, safety Sean Taylor, sidelined with a knee injury.

Taylor had quickly established himself as one of the most feared defensive players in the game and was a Pro Bowler in 2006. Now in his fourth season, Taylor led the Redskins with five interceptions despite missing two games. Adored by Gibbs, Taylor had become the franchise's face (outside Gibbs) and was loved by fans and teammates.

After a disappointing loss at Tampa Bay in Week 12, we were breaking down the team's fleeting playoff chances on the show when the news broke that Taylor had been shot at his Miami home in the middle of the night. Details were sketchy, but Taylor had been recuperating from his knee injury when intruders broke in, surprised he was there. Taylor was airlifted to a nearby hospital, where he underwent surgery for a severed femoral artery in the upper leg and remained in critical condition.

Processing the gut-punch with our listeners, we wondered how it could have happened. Why was Taylor back in Miami and not with the team? Would he recover? Was Michael Wilbon right, or had he jumped to an unfair conclusion when he wrote, "Taylor grew up in a violent world, embraced it, claimed it, loved to run in it and refused to divorce himself from it."

Fair or not, speculation abounded. A year earlier, Taylor pleaded no contest to assault and battery charges for brandishing a gun in a dispute over all-terrain vehicles. Later, his SUV was peppered by 15 bullets. Though he appeared to have turned his life around after he had become a father, we didn't know if Taylor truly had changed.

By Tuesday morning, the conversation had shifted. Details of the botched robbery attempt began to emerge. It seemed Taylor wasn't at fault. While that was a relief, we still didn't know about the severity of the shooting. And, could the Redskins make the playoffs without him?

Driving home after another heavy show, C.K. summoned us from the bullpen. Sean Taylor had passed away. Since E.B. and Lurch were still nearby, they quickly jumped on the air to discuss the tragedy. Everything we had talked about for the last two shows didn't matter anymore.

Not since Maryland basketball star Len Bias died from a drug overdose in 1986 had the local fanbase felt such a loss. Another great one had left us far too soon. Sean Taylor was only 24 years old.

★ ★ ★ ★

The shocking death of the Redskins superstar had consumed the radio show and the DMV for almost a week, but by Sunday, the team faced an important game against Buffalo. Emotions were extremely high. Clinton Portis ran onto the field waving a No. 21 flag. Cornerback Fred Smoot was visibly weeping, and for the first defensive play of the game, the Redskins placed only 10 players on the field, leaving the free safety spot open in honor of Taylor. Fans were given No. 21 tribute towels.

The Redskins held a 16-14 lead as the game wound down, and Buffalo kicker Rian Lindell lined up for a potential game-winning field goal. When his 51-yard boot sailed through the uprights, Redskins fans were heartbroken again. But the kick didn't count. Joe Gibbs had called a timeout just as the ball was snapped to freeze the kicker. What a reprieve.

That's when Gibbs did the unthinkable. With Lindell lining up for the field goal again, Gibbs called another timeout. The problem was that's not allowed. The terrible gaffe resulted in a 15-yard penalty for unsportsmanlike conduct. Lindell easily hit the game-winner and Washington fell to 5-7.

Breaking down the game from every angle the next morning, we were front and center on a common question throughout Gibbs's return: Had the game passed him by? He struggled with challenges of calls, managing time-outs, and seemed a tick slower in decision-making during the game. But how could he not know the rule that you couldn't freeze a kicker on back-to-back plays? We were apoplectic.

Four days later, on a Thursday night against the Bears and just two days after Taylor's funeral, backup quarterback Todd Collins started a rip of four straight wins in December to finish the 2007 season with a 9-7 record. Squeaking into the playoffs, the Redskins were thumped in Seattle, 35-14, in the wild-card round.

Still, Gibbs had managed to lead the Redskins into the postseason for the second time during his four seasons back in charge. No other coach during

Snyder's ownership before 2020 has taken them to the playoffs more than once. Perhaps the best coaching by Joe during the Gibbs 2.0 era came in the weeks after Taylor's murder.

Deeply religious, he pulled the team together in a way the players will never forget. That December was the best stretch of Redskins football in years, and if they could have defeated Seattle, Gibbs believed they were a Super Bowl team.

But one thing everyone overlooked—indeed, we missed it on our show, and the callers did as well—was Gibbs dropping hints he wanted to return home to North Carolina. His young grandson was battling leukemia, and the coach often talked about family, priorities, faith, and how each game in heaven was a journey 1,000 years long. Sean Taylor's death punctuated Gibbs's point.

So when the Redskins were eliminated, the media covering the team pushed long-time Redskins beat writer Jim Ducibella of the *Virginia Pilot* to the front. Ducibella was retiring that day, so he was appointed with asking the big question everyone wanted to be answered:

"Hey Joe, today's my last day. What about you?"

Gibbs gave a little laugh, smiled, and essentially said, "We'll talk about it later."

Then, on cue, red flags were flapping in the breeze to everyone in Washington except for two people—Dan Snyder, and his lackey general manager, Vinny Cerrato. The next day, Gibbs decided to walk away from coaching again. Caught off-guard, Snyder and Cerrato watched Gibbs's announcement at Redskins Park unfold on a TV in the owner's office.

You couldn't ask for better sports talk radio. We discussed the incompetence of the Redskins for not being prepared for Gibbs's departure and the botched process for finding his replacement. Jim Fassel? Jim Zorn? Not exactly awe-inspiring choices.

Gibbs had given us a gift. Sports talk radio couldn't have been easier during his return. Even though he had a 30-34 record, two playoff appearances were near-miraculous, given the quarterback play the Redskins received and the playoff droughts before and after Gibbs 2.0.

Fans still loved him—that will never change—and they were hesitant to label him as another failed coach during the Dan Snyder era. But there was a lingering question that still can't be answered today:

If Gibbs couldn't lead Washington back to the Super Bowl promised land, who could? We had no idea.

19

THE ACCIDENTAL SHOCK JOCKS

"If you are afraid of failure you don't deserve to be successful!"
— Charles Barkley

It was an honor to take over Howard Stern's morning drive slot on WJFK, but it also carried immense pressure. "The Sports Junkies" had to deliver. It was so consequential that the *Washington Post* assigned contributing writer Tyler Currie to follow us for weeks. Extremely thorough, Currie interviewed our parents about our childhood, education, and friendship. While getting media attention was always welcomed, we grew nervous about how the show might be portrayed.

But no matter what Currie was writing, we weren't changing what we were doing from 6-10 a.m. Our radio DNA had long been established. Besides, we knew it would be an uphill struggle to retain Stern's listeners. Many would remain loyal and follow him to satellite radio. That couldn't bother us.

Our goal was to capture the open-minded listeners who might sample the show and see why we were getting so much attention. If we could keep them entertained, they'd come back. And if they started talking to their friends about the show, they might begin tuning in, as well. We always urged our listeners to spread the word. Now it was more important than ever.

★ ★ ★ ★

Nobody ever accused us of being four Albert Einsteins. After basking in the midday slot on WJFK for a year, we returned to morning drive on Monday, January 2, 2006. Regrettably, we repeated our first mistake at WHFS by premiering at 5 a.m. What the hell were we thinking?

"That's right, donkeys, we are back, fresh and ready to go," I started. Then, without pause, Cakes shouted, "Nobody's fresh. It's 5:01!" E.B. asked, "One question, can we reconsider?" And just like that, we were off and running.

We didn't waste a lot of time on nostalgia. Being back at WJFK was a familiar cat bird's seat. So we plowed into the hottest sports topic in the DMV— the Washington Redskins, who had just beaten the Philadelphia Eagles 31-20 in their season finale on New Year's Day. The Redskins' fifth straight win propelled them into the playoffs for the first time in six years. Clinton Portis led the way with 112 yards rushing and two touchdowns, while safety Sean Taylor sealed the victory by returning a fumble 39 yards for another score.

The fanbase was on fire. Rabid Redskins fans jammed our phone lines as we recapped the win and looked toward their wild-card matchup against Tampa Bay. Having grown up together in the area, we knew talking about the Redskins was the ratings pile-driver. Similarly, we figured our predominately male audience would love the addition of the Junkettes. As promised, our new general manager, Michael Hughes, carved out a promotional budget that would allow us to hire women and boost the show.

By offering "Junkies in the Morning" coffee mugs, keychains, and t-shirts, we were ready to hold our "Junkette Search." This would be the first of many. The sales department had arranged for a string of appearances. Investing in our show paid quick dividends as revenue poured in from sponsors who wanted us to hold events at their establishments.

First up was Champps Americana in nearby Fair Oaks Mall. A year earlier, we had packed the restaurant and sports bar for a Super Bowl party. Now their manager Richie Prisco was setting up a small stage so we could hold our Junkette tryouts.

Before trotting out the seven attractive candidates, we had quietly put them through a trial run. We needed representatives who could mingle with our fans. So we gave the contestants our new promotional tchotchkes to dole out to our predominantly male audience and watched how they interacted.

While some of the women bounced around the bar gladly greeting our listeners, others seemed unapproachable. That wouldn't disqualify them, but it didn't go unnoticed. We needed representatives who were likable and enthusiastic about promoting the show. Later, the four of us jumped on the stage, with Cakes and I serving as emcees. After welcoming the excited crowd, we introduced the ladies.

Joining us in front of an ogling audience, Nancy, a cute, petite young woman with an exotic look, took the stage first. After dancing briefly while the deejay played a hip hop tune, Cakes and I began to ask her questions about her background and how much she knew about the show. Once we covered the basics, Cakes upped the ante.

Lobbing the first juicy question, Cakes asked, "Have you ever kissed a girl?" Without hesitation, Nancy nodded, "Yes, I have." The horde of men surrounding the stage roared with approval. Cakes followed up like a "60 Minutes" correspondent, clumsily asking, "Have you ever done more than kiss a girl?" Nancy surprised us, "No. However, I would do more with my roommate, who's standing right there."

As the mass of men hooted and hollered, Cakes went for the salacious,

"Would you do it on stage?" Soon Nancy and her blonde roommate were exchanging a quick peck and dancing as the deejay boomed hip hop music throughout the bar. E.B. shoved Cakes between the two women, clumsily joining them for a moment. While juvenile, E.B. knew the crowd would cheer.

After traveling a similar road with each contestant, it was time to announce our winners. We picked Nancy as our first official Junkette. She was bubbly, fun, and our listeners liked her before she got on the stage. Then we added another lady who had made an impression. Marlies was a shapely blonde with a big smile. We wanted great representatives for the show, and it didn't hurt if they were hot. Now we just had to use the Junkettes to our advantage.

Gracing the pages of *Sports Illustrated* was a career-high for us, but on Sunday, February 26, 2006, we landed on the cover of *Washington Post Magazine*. This was huge. *The Post* had a circulation of over 1 million at the time. So when readers opened their big newspaper with a thick wad of inserts, the Sunday mag flashed a bright yellow headline over a picture of an empty chair and radio board reading, "Can Anyone Replace Howard Stern?" Below, in white script, the sub-headline declared, "The Junkies, four loudmouths from P.G. County, try to seize the Throne of Raunch."

Maybe that's how writer Tyler Currie or the WaPo editors saw things, but we didn't see it the same way. While we may have dabbled in shock-jockery on occasion, our intent was to produce an entertaining show that blended sports, pop culture, and personal stories. If we were enjoying ourselves, we hoped that was infectious and be enough to thrive as Stern's successor.

Inside, a two-page picture of the four of us battling for a microphone felt slightly embarrassing. Ten years in, we still hadn't learned how to say no to a photographer. I was sitting in a chair in front of the radio board, holding onto a microphone for dear life. As E.B. put me in a headlock reaching for the microphone, I pushed Cakes away with a hand to his face while Lurch gave him a wedgie. This was not high-brow stuff.

Within the article, Currie covered the gamut. From Stern's history of generating a reported $100 million a year in advertising revenue to our childhood habits, readers would learn about us from every angle. Describing our content, Currie waxed poetic, "The Junkies often use the banalities of 35-year-old middle-class family life as fodder for their show." Though I had to look up "banalities," I couldn't quibble with his assessment.

Capturing our spirit, Currie highlighted an on-air conversation between E.B.'s mom and the four of us. After E.B. confessed that his 4-year-old son had dropped the "F" word recently, his mom, who called in occasionally, lectured, "I think you're setting a really bad example." E.B. couldn't argue but added, "There's a part of me that does feel some pride. He used it perfectly, but I know it's socially unacceptable."

No matter how we were depicted, thousands of readers might now give us a listen. That was a huge positive. While we may not have loved being dubbed "The Accidental Shock Jocks," Currie had nailed one key thing: "The Junkies aim isn't sophistication," he wrote, "it's ratings, though they won't learn how they've done until April."

That line rang true as anything within the 12-page article. If we could deliver ratings, it didn't matter how the *Washington Post* pegged us. Accidental shock jocks wasn't half bad anyway.

★ ★ ★ ★

On December 14, 2005, Infinity Broadcasting reverted to CBS Radio. The corporate maneuver didn't mean much to us, or so we thought. CBS had acquired Infinity a decade earlier. So long as our checks kept coming every two weeks, we didn't care who signed them.

We shouldn't have been so oblivious. On April 21, 2006, CBS Radio stunned the radio industry with a swift move to fire David Lee Roth. The former Van Halen lead singer had replaced Howard Stern in New York, Philadelphia, Boston, Cleveland, Dallas, Pittsburgh, and West Palm Beach. Less than four months into his new gig, CBS Radio cut the chord with the rock star. Scary.

Now on notice that the suits weren't exercising patience, we nervously awaited our first ratings book. Fortunately, the numbers were respectable, though there was a definite drop from the previous quarter when Stern finished atop the ratings in men 25-54 with a 6.9 share. We landed in fourth place with a 5.0 share. While nobody was thrilled, the ratings hadn't fallen off a cliff. There was work to do, but at least we'd have a chance, unlike David Lee Roth.

★ ★ ★ ★

Over the next several months, the sales staff at WJFK went into overdrive. While some feared advertisers might abandon the station upon Stern's departure, the sales staff actually landed more accounts and set up numerous appearances.

Conducting more Junkette searches, our listeners packed bars and restaurants as we added more beautiful women to our ensemble. In time, we would add Kat, a curvy Persian with a sexy voice; Kara, a beautiful brunette who had appeared in *Maxim* magazine; Shannon, a petite blonde; and Lauren, a vivacious African-American who was a diehard fan of "The Sports Junkies."

We sent the ladies out during the show for our "Junkies Breakfast Club" concept hosted by Dunkin Donuts. While we directed our listeners each week to new locations, our Junkettes would greet them as they picked up coffee and donuts at a discount on their way to work. Leaving with "Junkies in the Morning" t-shirts, coffee mugs, and keychains, we hoped the Junkettes' presence (and presents) would grow our sleep-deprived audience.

As the weather heated, the sales staff closed a deal with Mr. Wash to hold bikini car washes at his locations throughout Maryland and Virginia. Cars lined up as listeners received discounts while gawking at our beautiful representatives in bikinis. Handing out promotional gear and taking countless pictures with fans, the Junkettes began to build a a rabid following.

Just as our Junkettes were beginning to blossom, our "JunksTV" show was ending. We had filmed shows at various bars, restaurants, and country clubs across the DMV for three seasons. During filming, I had played in an ABA game as the celebrity 11th man for the Maryland Nighthawks, battled in Wiffle ball tournaments, and played one-on-one hoops against a former Terps legend Johnny Rhodes—all for the good of the show.

That all changed when Lurch tried to sneak in a mini-bottle of vodka into a Hooters restaurant. Remarking the following day on the radio that our "JunksTV" sponsor only served beer, Lurch proudly described how he cleverly concealed his hooch. Unfortunately, Hooters heard the diatribe and withheld their payment. Our executive producer Carey Smith had to deal with a new headache.

Months after wrapping JunksTV, Carey received a check from Hooters and paid us for our final six episodes. By then, my cohorts had grown weary of the filming. It was time to move on and focus solely on the morning drive.

★ ★ ★ ★

Throughout our radio careers, "The Sports Junkies" majored in silly, which is why our most unlikely relationship was with Maryland Gov. Robert Ehrlich, who became a frequent contributor to the program. While serving in Congress, Ehrlich tuned to the show while commuting from Timonium, Maryland, to Capitol Hill. Then, a few months after being elected governor, he called in for the first time in January 2004 while we were still on WHFS. Answering Ehrlich's call-in, C.K. thought it was a goof.

Surprisingly, the governor's fandom dated to our days of doling out "Friday Night Fatties." He's a huge football fan, having been the captain of his Princeton team. But now, he wanted to make picks on our show. We didn't mind. Erhlich was personable and fit into the show like one of the guys, quickly appealing to our younger audience.

As the relationship developed, he invited us to spend the night at the governor's mansion in Annapolis and do a remote broadcast the next morning. Pranking Lurch, Ehrlich hatched a plan with his state troopers to plant silverware in Lurch's jacket pocket. After the show, metal detectors went off, and security stopped Lurch as we were leaving. They searched his pockets and pulled out the silverware like a smoking gun, leaving Lurch dumbfounded. The room erupted in laughter. The gov had pulled a fast one on our boy.

Ehrlich brought a unique and charismatic perspective to the show, displaying an ease talking sports. We would occasionally throw him a political football by asking about topics that interested our audience, like sports gambling and slot machines. Still, he preferred sticking to sports, especially the Baltimore Ravens and Orioles.

In 2006, Ehrlich invited us to be his guests at The Preakness Stakes at Pimlico. We rubbed elbows with important figures and behaved ourselves for once, which might have been the storyline otherwise. But Kentucky Derby winner and Preakness favorite Barbaro broke down early in the race with a leg injury, ending his career.

While our relationship with the governor was mutually beneficial, we also developed a sincere friendship. Admitting that he never received more feedback than when he came on the show, Ehrlich explained that our listeners frequently approached him in public, professing, "Love the Gov."

We did, too.

When the Spring ratings book was released in July, we felt confident about the show's direction. Taking advantage of our promotional budget to the fullest, the Junkettes were constantly on the road promoting our brand with car washes, the breakfast club, and personal appearances. Though we had to readjust our bodies to wake up early again, it didn't take long to find a stride.

Fortunately, our ratings reflected the effort. Notching a 6.9 share in men 25-54, we equaled Howard Stern's numbers during his last ratings book at WJFK. That gave us more ammunition to ask management for greater support.

Working with new program director Max Dugan, who had come over from 94.7 FM WARW, a classic rock station, we prepared a new wish list. Recognizing you can't always get what you want (but if you try sometimes, well, you might find you get what you need), we requested an Atlantic City bus trip with listeners to gamble, a charity poker tournament, and a Junkies golf tournament as potential promotions. By then, we had hosted the Craig Walden Classic benefit to honor our old pal Crickety. Hundreds of golfers convened, including Cal Ripken Jr.

Our relationship with Ripken had grown stronger since he and brother Billy joined us at the WHFS studios that first time in 2004. So when his publicist John Maroon asked us to broadcast from the Ripken Baseball compound in Aberdeen and help promote his youth leagues, we didn't hesitate to say yes. Unbelievably, we had no luck reaching out to our Baltimore affiliate to set up the promotion. Instead, we arranged the appearance at a nearby Applebee's the night before our remote broadcast.

Happy to meet the listeners who had packed the restaurant and bar, we had a wonderful time hanging out with our Charm City loyalists. But it wasn't a great sign that not one member of Bob Philips's promotion staff at 105.7 joined us. There was no signage and nothing to give away. Not one thing. Applebee's was brimming with our listeners, but this was another red flag. No matter how well our show performed in Baltimore, it might not matter.

By the fall of 2006, the poker craze had grown to new heights. My radio brothers were obsessed. Playing online every day, E.B. would sit for hours in his new theater room juggling 12 tables at a time. Cakes, Lurch and Bret would frequently get together on the weekends with E.B. and friends for poker nights.

Months earlier, Bret was selected to play in a celebrity poker tournament in Costa Rica sponsored by Bodog, an online sportsbook and casino. Pretending to be one of the hosts of "The Sports Junkies," Bret touted our celebrity interviews, including Magic Johnson and Jay-Z, as we filmed his audition.

Weeks later, Bret found himself on a reality TV show set among a cast that included UFC champion Chuck Liddell and actress Shannon Elizabeth. Winning $50,000 at his first table, Bret advanced to compete for half a million dollars. This time he would have to beat some of the biggest names in poker, including pros David Williams and Daniel Negreanu. Though he came up just short, Bret returned $50,000 richer with a brand new relationship.

Bodog agreed to give our show bonus money for listeners who signed up to gamble on their website. Bret would get monthly reports. Before long, he noticed a trend. J.A. from Olney was losing hundreds of dollars every month playing online blackjack. At lunch one day, Bret asked me and C.K. if J.A. from Olney might be Cakes. It had to be.

Coyly raising the topic of online blackjack on the air, we wondered how Cakes might react. Maintaining his poker face, Cakes mocked those who frequently played despite the overwhelming odds against them winning. He called online blackjack players "stupid" while refusing to cop to his addiction.

As Bret saw J.A.'s losses mounting, Cakes cracked a few months later and admitted he had lost thousands of dollars. While Cakes may have known that playing online blackjack was futile, J.A. from Olney was hooked. Fortunately, Cakes had the bankroll to cover his alter ego.

Even though our colleague had fallen prey to online blackjack, Bret and E.B. stuck to poker as they launched a podcast. Booking the biggest names in the professional ranks weekly, "Mediocre Poker" became their passion project. In addition, they bandied the idea of a Junkies Texas Hold'em tournament. Behind the scenes, C.K. worked feverishly with our sales and promotion teams to strike a relationship with the Borgata Hotel Casino and Spa in Atlantic City. Announcing our first Junkies Poker Open, listeners were excited about playing in a big tournament like the ones they had seen on TV.

Arriving at the Borgata on a Wednesday afternoon, we wondered how many of our listeners would make the four-hour trek in the middle of the workweek. We were surprised so many had joined us during a happy hour at the Gypsy Bar inside the casino. When Lurch and Cakes left for the tables, many followed. The lure of gambling at a casino was too intoxicating, especially since there still weren't any casinos in D.C., Maryland or Virginia.

Opening the show at 6 a.m. from the B Bar in the middle of the casino on Thursday morning, November 30, 2006, we were exhausted after a late night of drinking and gambling. As listeners began to gather, our excitement grew. By 9 o'clock, C.K. and Bret had learned hundreds had already signed up for our $300 buy-in tournament, and more were waiting in line. Luckily, Borgata's marketing rep helped us register quickly. Unfortunately, we still had to pay our buy-ins.

As our show closed, the casino's pit boss jumped on the air to offer the final instructions. Announcing that 10 a.m. was time to "shuffle up and deal," the crowd roared its excitement. The exodus to the poker room was swift. Within minutes, the poker tables were full of listeners competing to win thousands of dollars.

The Borgata was ecstatic with the turnout. Gathering in the food court that we dubbed the "losers lounge" after being bounced out of the tournament, we mingled with listeners who had suffered the same fate. Despite losing their $300 buy-ins, nobody left disappointed.

Well into the wee hours of the night, Derrick Childress emerged as our first champion. Interviewing him on Friday morning, he was thrilled, but so were the players who had taken off from work to gamble and party with us in Atlantic City. The only difference was Childress was driving home with $30,000. As Teddy KGB said famously in the movie "Rounders," pay that man his money.

20

CHASING ROCKY

"What would life be if we had no courage to attempt anything?"
— Vincent Van Gogh

Seated at the Patriot Center on September 17, 2005, I anxiously awaited the main event. Jimmy Lange, a boxer from Great Falls, Virginia, was fresh off NBC's reality boxing series "The Contender," starring Sylvester Stallone and Sugar Ray Leonard. Though Lange lost to Joey Gilbert on the show, he was picked as a fan favorite to fight again during the season finale at Caesar's Palace in Las Vegas. There, he defeated Tarick Salmaci by decision, winning $200,000.

Lange's popularity surged, as did ticket sales. A packed Patriot Center awaited his grudge match with Perry "The Punisher" Ballard, an undefeated welterweight from West Virginia. I couldn't wait to see the result when Lange finally faced the guy who had been smack-talking him for two years.

After Ballard entered the squared circle, the lights dimmed, and Jimmy began his slow procession toward the ring. Metallica's "Enter Sandman" pulsed through the arena, and the crowd stood in anticipation. The energy was unreal.

Lange was marching in with his entourage when a crazy thought popped into my head. "*Could I do it?*" Wondering what it would be like to have my own ring entrance and grudge match, I scrutinized the entire production, from the lighting to the music.

Then, when the bell rang, the boxers exchanged haymakers for four rounds before the referee finally stopped the fight and gave Lange another win. That didn't stop me from dreaming about the possibilities. This could be "The Sports Junkies" biggest promotion yet.

Driving home, I came to my senses. I was a weekend warrior who played pickup basketball a couple of times a week and co-ed soccer with E.B. and friends on the weekends. I wasn't a boxer. I hadn't even been in a bar fight.

★ ★ ★ ★

Oscar Wilde once said, "An idea that is not dangerous is unworthy of being called an idea at all." Though my brain was telling me no, I couldn't let the daydreaming go. Floating the trial balloon to my radio brethren, no one took me seriously. They summarily dismissed the thought of me stepping into a professional boxing ring. Was it too ludicrous? Maybe.

Months later, during a Junkies appearance at Jimmy's Old Town Tavern in Herndon, Virginia, I recognized a grizzled man with a weathered face and slicked-back hair. It was Johnny Lange, Jimmy's dad and manager. After engaging in small talk with the boxing lifer, I asked about my preposterous plan. "Would it be possible," I started, "if I trained, to get a professional fight?"

Gazing at me with a wry smile, Johnny Lange didn't outright dismiss me. Instead, he peppered me with questions about my boxing experience and athleticism.

Johnny interrupted as I was answering. "Son, if you're serious, you'll have to commit to this. You can't do this half-ass, you understand?" Nodding, I couldn't imagine what he meant. Then he added, "This isn't a fucking joke. You could get hurt." While Johnny was delivering a warning, he wasn't saying no either.

He began to rattle off the names of possible trainers, including Jose "Pepe" Correa, who famously trained Sugar Ray Leonard. As he dove deeper into his boxing connections, I wondered if I could even get licensed. "Don't worry about those things," Johnny fired back. "If you really want to do this, you can do it."

Weeks later, as we ate an early lunch at Panera Bread in Fairfax after the morning show, Bret and Chris Kinard wondered how we might be able to boost the show. Revisiting my boxing proposition, Bret wondered, "What if you did that fight you were talking about?" Not missing a beat, C.K. followed by employing his best reverse psychology. "You won't do it."

Not committing, I continued to eat my chicken panini as the boys pressed and needled me. C.K. jabbed again, "You won't do it."

They didn't expect my response, but they exploded when I gave them what they wanted. "Fuck it. Let's make it happen," I said.

Our discussions quickly turned to the planning stage. Since we knew the key players, we could move fast. First, I would contact Johnny Lange about finding a trainer. Next, C.K. would call Brian Bishop, who handled the promotional side for Jimmy's fights. But we would keep it a secret until we made a big announcement on the show. Shock and awe.

Chewing on a chocolate chip cookie as we discussed the possibilities, C.K. joked, "Man, you're going to get your ass kicked." As Bret laughed, I had to laugh, too.

★ ★ ★ ★

Soon after, C.K. arranged a meeting with Johnny Lange and Brian Bishop at the station. We wanted to know if we could make this boxing idea a reality. Could I actually be part of Jimmy Lange's next boxing card? While I didn't sign a contract, both were excited. They knew I would help sell tickets. Still, there was one hurdle. Jimmy would have to win his comeback fight scheduled for October 7, 2006, at the Patriot Center.

Eight months earlier, Jimmy suffered his worst defeat as Joey Gilbert beat him up badly in their rematch. Gilbert's size and power were too much as the referee stopped the fight in the third round. If Jimmy lost again, his future would be in doubt, and his popularity would take an even bigger hit.

Knowing so much was at stake, Johnny helped secure renowned trainer Angelo Dundee, who once trained Muhammad Ali, to work in his son's corner. Unfortunately, that didn't help sell tickets. Walking into the Patriot Center with my friend Rob Bokman, it was apparent there had been a big drop-off in fans. Less than 4,000 were in attendance to see Jimmy Lange fight Tommy Wilt.

But when the punches started flying, the crowd was enthralled. Wilt wasn't a tomato can. Landing body shots that left Jimmy gasping for air, the outcome was in doubt midway through the fight. But Jimmy's trainers, Buddy McGirt and Angelo Dundee, noticed an opening. Heeding their advice, Jimmy began to pepper Wilt with jabs and hooks to the body. By the 10th round, Wilt was ready to fall.

Unleashing a barrage of punches in the final minute, Wilt finally succumbed to Jimmy's attack and fell to the canvas. After struggling to get up, the referee stopped the fight. Jimmy won via technical knockout. As the crowd erupted, an exhausted Jimmy Lange raised his arm in victory. His career was back on track.

Exchanging a high five with Rob, we were thrilled by the action. Then I confided in what I had been keeping to myself all night. "You don't know how big that fight was for me?" Perplexed, Rob asked, "What do you mean?" Giving him the details of my plan, Rob was flabbergasted. Driving home, I let him know about the secret planning meeting we had held just a few weeks earlier.

Johnny Lange had promised to find me a trainer, an opponent, and to get me licensed. With his son back on the winning track, I would be part of his next card in December. Rob couldn't believe it, the exact response I hoped our listeners would have when we announced the fight in a month.

★ ★ ★ ★

Two days later, a victorious Jimmy Lange, excited by the promotional possibilities, joined me in the WJFK parking lot at noon, long after my radio partners had driven home. C.K., Bret, and I had agreed we wouldn't let them know what we were planning. The announcement would be even more shocking if they were clueless.

Stepping out of his black Ford pickup truck, a battered Jimmy greeted me with sunglasses and a smile. After congratulating him, he turned to the subject at hand. Warning that I had to take the fight seriously, Jimmy wanted to put me through a workout before giving his blessing.

Leading me to a nearby gym, I wondered what the beat-up boxer would have me do. How do you have a boxing tryout? First, he wrapped my hands with tape and handed me a pair of blue Everlast gloves. Then, asking me to bounce in the ring, Jimmy stopped me quickly. Showing me a proper boxing stance and how to move in the ring while maintaining balance, it was clear I was starting from scratch.

After I received my first lesson in boxing movement, Jimmy grabbed two boxing mitts and asked me to fire punches. Working out for nearly 45 minutes, I was exhausted, and Jimmy had seen enough. Stressing that I would need to dedicate myself like never before and follow my trainer's lead, Jimmy gave me his approval.

Even though I would have a trainer, Jimmy advised me to do extra cardio. He also said I would need to be much more fit. He handed me a seven-day cardio routine and said I could lean on him for advice, but he wouldn't be training me. He had to focus on his fight.

As for my training, I'd have to run. I'd have to learn to box. I'd have to spar. Jimmy couldn't help me do that. I needed a trainer to show me the ropes, and I didn't have any time to spare.

So a few days later, I met with Johnny Lange again. This time we had lunch at Red, Hot & Blue in Fairfax to discuss the gamut, from ticket giveaways to a purse. Though I wasn't fighting for money, I couldn't get Jimmy's bruised face out of my head. I needed monetary incentive to get me through the impending torture.

Recognizing that Jimmy's last fight had drawn a much smaller crowd than his previous bouts, I had leverage. Our Turkey Bowl football game against the D.C. Divas had attracted twice as many fans. Though I had no frame of reference, I told Johnny that I wanted to be paid fairly.

Asking what I thought that meant, I offered, "I'll do the fight for five or 10 thousand." Quickly responding as I had likely underbid, Johnny agreed to split the difference. I would fight for $7,500.

Negotiating the purse was the least of my concerns. Though Johnny had touted a slew of trainers, he hadn't delivered. Issuing an ultimatum, I warned Johnny that I'd walk away if I didn't have a trainer by Monday. The clock was ticking.

★ ★ ★ ★

One month later, it was all coming in focus. The Monday after our meeting, Johnny Lange dropped me in the Arlington Boxing Club and introduced me to Willie "The Heat" Taylor. A stocky African-American, Willie was a veteran who had 36 professional fights to his name. Now Willie was teaching at-risk kids how to box and stay out of trouble.

Trying to scare me out of my fight, Willie had me sparring on my second day. Spitting blood the next morning as I showered, Willie almost had his wish. I was bruised and battered and full of fear.

Thinking he'd never see me again, Willie was surprised when I returned. Gaining his respect, he gave me a crash course in boxing while I got lean and mean. In less than a month, I shed 15 pounds and grew more comfortable during the brutal sparring sessions.

We also settled on an opponent. Jay "The American Dream" Watts was fresh out of prison after serving 13 months for maiming someone. Known as a great trash talker, he was chosen over another potential foe who was bigger and more accomplished. Jay Watts had just one win in nine fights, though he had been fighting as a pro for a decade.

Fortunately, on Thursday, November 16, 2006, my partners remained clueless. None of them had noticed how much thinner I was or knew about my nightly two-hour training sessions in Arlington.

Teasing a big announcement at the top of the show, they grew curious. Bret and C.K. lied and told them we were announcing a new station giveaway to quell their interest. They didn't suspect the bomb I was about to drop.

With Jimmy, Johnny, and Willie waiting in the parking lot at 7:30 in the morning, I asked Cakes, who handled our replay machine full of sound effects, to play the drumroll. C.K. fired up our produced promo. With eerie music playing underneath, the faint sound of a heartbeat began to pulse in the background while a dramatic baritone voice bellowed, "From the ashes of the earth, he will rise. He is a warrior, a man, a beast. He will battle all that is evil. That man is…"

While the voiceover echoed, the heartbeat began to thunder as the music built to a crescendo. After a dramatic pause, BDK's voice shrieked, "J.P.!"

Stunned, my partners tried to process what they had just heard. As Survivor's "Eye of the Tiger" kicked in, the details emerged. "Only J.P. would do something as crazy as this," Cakes kidded in disbelief. "Unbelievable," Lurch added. "You're gonna get killed."

Maybe they were right, but this was the reaction I wanted. We brought Jimmy, Johnny, and Willie into the studios to tell everyone what had been happening behind the scenes for weeks. The fight was just 23 days away.

The phone lines lit up. My boys were shocked, but so was our audience. Later, when Jay Watts called into the show, the intrigue grew. Thanking me for the opportunity, he fired his first shot.

"When I heard a radio deejay wanted to fight me, I jumped at the chance," he said. "You can't just say you're a boxer and think you're going to have a shot. That's an insult. J.P. is going to be in for a rude awakening, and I'm going to shut him up."

Despite his record, Jay Watts was offended. But E.B. had my back. "I got my money on J.P. I've known him all my life. He's a competitor. He'll never quit."

Easy for him to say.

★ ★ ★ ★

For the next three weeks, the hype grew as I continued to grind daily at the Arlington Boxing Club. First, there was a press conference where I was interviewed by the *Washington Post*. Then a local newspaper sent a photographer and reporter to watch me train.

As the buzz grew, tickets sales boomed. To keep the momentum going, I flew to Florida and trained alongside Jimmy Lange for two days. Being part of a professional boxing camp was a strange experience. Johnny's head trainer Buddy McGirt was a former world champion who retired with a 73-6-1 record. Now he trained champions such as Antonio Tarver, Paulie Malignaggi, and Arturo Gatti.

Introducing me to McGirt, who was puffing a cigar outside his gym, Jimmy explained that I was fighting on his card. When he heard Willie Taylor was training me, McGirt's ears perked.

Putting down his cigar, Buddy reminisced. "Willie was a tough son of a bitch." The two had fought 10 brutal rounds in February 1989. Almost two decades later, McGirt vividly remembered what was supposed to be an easy victory for him. At the weigh-in, his trainer confidently taunted Willie by yelling, "Buddy's going to jail because he's going to kill you." Willie didn't say a word. Instead, he went the distance with McGirt and gained his respect.

Since Jimmy warned me to stay out of the way, I jumped rope and hit a heavy bag by myself. While I worked on my combinations, McGirt strolled over and offered me a piece of advice. "Shorten those punches." Telegraphing my punches was not a recipe for success. Leaving my face wide open by dropping my hands was even worse. He noticed my holes immediately.

I returned home to discover the pre-fight hype reaching new levels. A column in the *Washington Examiner* included some bombs from Jay Watts, who proclaimed, "I'm going to kill him. I'm offended this guy gets on the radio to say he has a chance. The only chance is I may let him survive one round, and I may do that so I can punish him, so he never gets in the ring again."

The trash talk was precisely why Watts was chosen as my opponent. He knew how to bring the heat and added, "Don't put your head down. Don't get a drink. The very second the bell rings, I'm going to put the pressure on. My intention is to put my fist through his face."

Then, during my final week of preparation, I had the opportunity to interview actor Sylvester Stallone. In town to promote the new movie "Rocky Balboa," I drove to the Four Seasons Hotel in downtown D.C. to tape the sit-down. Greeted by a publicist, I would have six minutes to talk about the movie. I didn't care. I just wanted to talk to "Rocky" about my fight.

I knew my interview would be different. Passing local movie critic Arch Campbell when I was summoned to Stallone's room, I was blown away by the 60-year-old Stallone's physique. Wearing a shiny blue button-down shirt tucked into his jeans, he looked jacked.

Before firing any questions, I told Stallone that Jimmy Lange had said hello. "The Contender" connection was real as Stallone asked me about Jimmy. When I told him that I was on the undercard, he answered surprisingly, "Really?" Though Stallone seemed interested, the publicist urged me to start the interview.

Turning on my recorder, I asked the Hollywood icon about the latest installment in the "Rocky" series. Proud of the choreography and fight sequences, Stallone spoke passionately about the movie 16 years in the making. Then, just as the publicist told me to wrap, I asked Stallone to get into character. "As Rocky Balboa, what advice would you give me as I step into the ring?"

Chuckling, Stallone's head perked up as he transformed into one of the most famous characters in movie history. "Be first," he muttered. As I started to thank him, he grabbed the microphone and added, "Be first and be lethal."

Though Buddy McGirt warned me to shorten my punches and Willie Taylor had taught me technique for seven weeks, Rocky Balboa had just given me a game plan.

When the publicist tried to usher me out of the room, I asked Stallone for a picture. Maybe it violated movie critic protocol, but I wasn't a movie critic. Annoyed, the publicist grabbed my camera and snapped a quick photo. Me and my best pal Sly.

Fifteen months after I had my crazy light bulb moment watching Jimmy Lange destroy Perry Ballard, it was my turn to step into the ring. When the music faded down inside the dark arena on December 9, 2006, Henry "Discombobulating" Jones grabbed the microphone and announced what thousands in the crowd were waiting to hear: "And now, ladies and gentlemen, from the flagship station of the area, WJFK, please welcome to the ring, J.P. Flaim!"

Hearing the crowd roar with partisan fans chanting my name, Schwartzy led three of our Junkettes into the stands and began to rap over the booming music...

Well, I supposed he's going to throw some blows
Until J.P. goes and explodes his nose
And gives him whiplash, I hope J.P. kicks ass
Lose for the ninth fucking time you bitch ass!

Schwartzy was throwing low blows, but he wouldn't have to take any punches.

While I waited in the bowels of the Patriot Center, I was thinking about everything that had happened in the previous three days. Hours after interviewing Sylvester Stallone, my father-in-law passed away. Mulling whether I should cancel my bout, I decided to move forward. Too many things were in motion. Tickets had been sold. Our listeners wanted to see what would happen. I didn't want to let anyone down.

Beyond that, I didn't want to train again. I had poured my heart and soul into working out. I had been bruised and battered along the way. It was too much sacrifice. I craved a return to my normal life.

Watching Schwartzy and the Junkettes excite the crowd, I tried to focus on the task at hand, but I had spent so much time meticulously preparing my ring entrance that I wanted to enjoy the show. Standing in my black robe, I felt the love of those waiting to see me emerge.

Weighing in at 156 pounds, I was leaner than I had been since high school. Offering me support over the tragic loss of my father-in-law, I knew Junkies fans were in my corner. Some had attended my weigh-in. Their cheers warmed my heart.

With sirens blaring, a countdown began. Bouncing up and down, E.B. smacked me on the shoulders as the clock continued, "Three... Two... One... Fire!" The confetti gun, which cost me $750, fired, and was followed by a bell ringing three times. Then, Eminem's "Lose Yourself" kicked in as the crowd cheered louder.

"Look. If you had one shot or one opportunity to seize everything you ever wanted in one moment, would you capture it or just let it slip?"

I surfaced from underneath the stands with E.B. and my Arlington Boxing Club teammates behind me for the first time. Passing by some of my co-workers, including our boss Michael Hughes and our program director

Max Dugan, I walked slowly toward the ring. Then, stepping inside the ropes, my heart started racing faster.

I saw Lurch and Cakes ringside to call the fight. I began to bounce like I had seen so many fighters do as a fan. Boxing analyst Gary "Digital" Williams said he had never seen a debut "with such pomp and circumstance."

Then, in what seemed like an instant, the ring announcer started. Boos reigned throughout the arena when Jay Watts was introduced. I almost felt bad, but he relished playing the heel. Then Discombobulating Jones shouted over the raucous audience, "Ladies and gentlemen, from the flagship station of the area, 106.7 FM-WJFK, the voice of The Junkies. He's on a mission to stake his claim to fame. Here's the 'Latin Donkey,' J.P. Flaim!"

With the crowd going berserk, I found myself nose-to-nose with Jay Watts in the center of the ring. Unfortunately, my trainer Willie Taylor wasn't by my side. Ironically, he had committed to deejay a party months earlier. So instead, veteran trainer Scott Farmer, who I had met the night before, was tapping me on the back of my neck as we received the referee's final instructions. Then, in a flash, it was time to fight.

Adrenaline pumping, this was so different than my sparring sessions. My mind raced as though I was on speed and couldn't calm down. But this wasn't a practice session. This was the real deal. There was no headgear. There weren't big 16-ounce gloves. And I wasn't fighting a teammate.

Weeks earlier, Jimmy Lange had told me Watts would feel it if I connected with my straight right hand while wearing the 8-ounce gloves. On the flip side, I would probably feel his punch, too.

When the bell rang, everything I had learned and the strategic advice I had been given was forgotten. All I could think about was what Rocky Balboa had told me: "Be first and be lethal."

Standing toe-to-toe against my shorter opponent, I began to unleash a 1-2 combination. Firing a left jab that grazed the side of Jay Watts's face, I cocked my right arm to throw a straight right. Regrettably, I hadn't heeded Buddy McGirt's advice. My punch wasn't short, and I hadn't protected my face.

Throwing a left hook that went over the top of my right arm, Watts connected flush on the right side of my face. Immediately, I was stunned. Getting hit by the 8-ounce glove with no headgear was no joke. As I charged Watts, I walked right into a haymaker. The straight right connected squarely on my chin. My head snapped back, and my knees buckled.

Just 11 seconds into the fight, Watts had knocked me to the canvas. As I popped back up, my head was spinning. Though I should have been thinking strategically, I was embarrassed and couldn't believe what had happened. Through 30 rounds of sparring, I had been dropped only once, and that was by one of my teammates who had been a runner-up in the national Golden Gloves competition when he was a kid. Years later, he was a highly skilled boxer on the verge of turning pro. Meanwhile, Jay Watts was 1-8.

Terrible record or not, Watts was backing up his bravado. Not holding back, he continued to throw bombs. For the next minute, I survived the repeated attacks and landed a few punches, even forcing Watts to grab and hold me before the referee split us apart. As the crowd began to chant my name, I was settling into the fight.

But Watts's experience allowed him to expose my weaknesses. Connecting repeatedly with left hooks as my hands dropped, Watts inflicted more damage. As I tried to fire another 1-2 combination, Watts landed a heavy left hook that left my legs wobbling. Following up with a right uppercut that shot between my gloves, Watts knocked me down for a second time.

Popping back up, I felt fine, but my equilibrium was compromised. As Scott Farmer barked commands from my corner, there was no time to process instructions. I fell into the same trap once again. Pop! Watts cracked me with a wicked left hook that had me falling backwards into the ropes. As I bounced back, I pushed Watts with all my weight, knocking him down. The crowd roared. But they didn't know what was going on. It was a push, not a knockdown. I was in trouble, not Watts.

He had me figured. Just as I went to launch another right hand, he walloped me with another left hook. My legs were gone. I fell to the canvas again.

Referee Malik Waleed counted to three, and I jumped back up on my feet. Then, looking into my eyes to see if I was okay, I smiled and told him that I was fine. I even described the punch that had knocked me down.

There were just 30 seconds left in the round and my corner was begging me to hold onto Watts. Though I had seen fighters do that on TV, I had never practiced that drill during training. Getting off the canvas and figuring a way to survive was new to me. Sadly, I couldn't take a timeout.

As I bounced to my right to throw a left jab, Watts swiped it away with his right hand. Backing me up to the ropes, Watts slipped another of my punches. Connecting with a jab to his chin, Watts fell back momentarily.

Seconds remained in the round. If I could just get to the second round, I was far more fit. But, noticing my cornerman with a stool in his hand ready for the bell to sound, Watts threw a right-handed haymaker that caught the side of my head just above my ear. Off-balance, my feet were tangled with Watts and I slipped to the canvas for the fourth time.

Though I wasn't hurt, I kept my gloves down to try and gather myself as the referee began to count. Just as I started to rise at the count of five, the referee waved his arms and put a halt to the match. There was just one second left in the first round.

Ashamed, I stood in disbelief. As Watts embraced me, I believed I had disappointed the entire audience. When the play-by-play announcer asked what happened, I couldn't fully explain. I believed I had choked.

Discombobulating Jones made the official results announcement, and the crowd gave Jay Watts his due. He had notched his second win in 10 years. Then the ring announcer added, "Let's also hear it for J.P. Flaim. Most deejays wouldn't have the courage to try something like this."

In a nice touch, the ring announcer asked for a moment of silence to honor my father-in-law. Appreciative, I placed my glove over my chest and made the sign of the cross. I was dejected and embarrassed about my performance. Walking back to the locker room, everybody tried to console me. "Don't worry about it, J.P.," someone yelled from the stands. "You did it!" others screamed. But it still had the feel of a walk of shame.

Taking a hot shower, I wanted to cry. I couldn't believe how poorly I had performed, but maybe I shouldn't have been surprised. C.K. had cynically predicted the outcome at Panera—"Man, you're going to get your ass kicked"—and deep inside, I may have expected that result. At least this moment was a massive victory for the show. That was more important anyway. But damn, what if I could have lasted just one more second?

Nah.

21

ATTENTION DOLLARS

"There's no such thing as bad publicity." — *P.T. Barnum*

In his book "Blink: The Power of Thinking Without Thinking," Malcolm Gladwell writes: "We need to respect the fact that it is possible to know without knowing." From the moment we sat down with Bob Philips, we knew our future in Charm City was precarious. It didn't matter if he said all the right things. Sometimes you know. We weren't his guys.

One year later, it was official. "The Sports Junkies" run in Baltimore was over. Though we were disappointed, we felt terrible for the thousands of listeners who tuned into our show regularly.

Being a one-market show had its benefits. We wouldn't have to worry about multiple bosses and ratings in different cities. Now our entire focus would be on WJFK in Washington, where we had already established ourselves as one of the dominant morning drive shows. Our ratings were strong, and management was happy.

Luckily, our success wasn't tied to the fate of the local sports teams. If it had, we wouldn't have lasted very long. What separated us was our chemistry and the way we had fun on the air. Listeners had become acquainted with many of our show characters, including the Homies, Cowboy Todd, and Sactown Mike.

And while we still enjoyed hearing from our most notorious callers, Bret surmised at lunch one day, "We need some new characters." As we ate our Subway sandwiches, C.K. laughed and added, "Yeah, it's been the same shitters for years now." The thing is, we couldn't force new personalities on our audience. It had to be organic. We couldn't just create characters.

Little did we know that a chain-smoking gambling addict was ready and willing to fill the void. Hearing us reflect on the success of our first Junkies Poker Open, Ram the Card Counter became hooked on our show. Smarting from his divorce, Ram gained weight and fell into a personal abyss. Listening to the show became an escape from his spiraling life. The mix of sports, personal stories, and gambling talk filled some of the emptiness in Ram's heart.

The short, pudgy 33-year-old fan wanted to meet his new radio friends. When a Junkies appearance at Clyde's in downtown Washington was announced, Ram hatched a plan. Not only would he meet the four of us, but Ram was also persistent in cracking the inner circle. Since I couldn't make it to Clyde's that day, he fired his first shot with my partners.

Finding Cakes, Ram introduced himself and quickly asked about the Junkies Poker Open, which we were bringing back in November 2007. Hearing Cakes talk about the bad beat that bounced him out of our spring tournament at the Borgata, Ram established a quick connection. While Ram touted some of his biggest blackjack scores and his upcoming trip to Las Vegas, Cakes wouldn't forget the disheveled gambler eager to make an impression.

Next, Ram fawned over E.B. and Bret's pet project, their new podcast "Mediocre Poker." Flattery gets you everywhere. Having E.B.'s attention, Ram bragged about his card-counting prowess. Claiming that he had won thousands playing blackjack, Ram also admitted to losing much of it recklessly playing other table games. Nevertheless, E.B.'s interest was piqued.

Blackjack was the passport to Lurch's soul. Relating most to our resident degenerate gambler, Ram thought he could entice his radio idol by asking about Lurch's card-playing strategy. The approach may have worked, but the appearance was ending. With car keys in hand, Lurch seemed indifferent as Ram rambled. Minutes later, Ram's heroes were gone, but he had planted a seed.

Listening to us debate the mega-bout between Floyd Mayweather and Oscar De La Hoya set to take place in Las Vegas on May 5, 2007, Ram made his first call-in to the show. Flaunting the comp tickets he received for the fight from Mandalay Bay, Ram hoped The Junkies remembered him. When E.B. asked, "Are you the card-counter guy?" Ram got his wish. Instant gratification.

The high Ram felt grew when Cakes said, "Oh, you're money." When E.B. added, "This guy is silly, Lurch," Ram felt a rush similar to hitting blackjack. Maybe it wasn't the same as winning money, but he loved the attention.

Two months later, we convinced management to send us to Las Vegas and cover the World Series of Poker. Being in the middle of the action would mean countless stories and material for the show. Unfortunately, we weren't staying in the heart of the Vegas strip. Instead, the WJFK sales department had secured a sponsorship deal with Tahiti Village Resort and Spa several miles away. Though the location wasn't ideal, the trip didn't cost WJFK a dime, the tagline from Tahiti Village actress/spokeswoman Tanya Roberts, who had starred on the '70s hit TV series "Charlie's Angels."

Broadcasting from the Rio Hotel and Casino, the show would have an added buzz and energy. Still, there were plenty of complaints. Lurch was never comfortable flying. The seats in coach weren't made for tall guys like him. E.B. and Cakes were fearful flyers who had to drink heavily before takeoff. Listening to them bitch and moan about the free trip humored me.

Upon our arrival, there was a mad rush to gamble. You would think none of us had ever been to a casino. After briefly playing craps, I joined Bret and C.K. for dinner while my partners dabbled in poker and blackjack. We returned to Tahiti Village for sleep after dinner since we had to jump on the air live at 3 a.m. in Las Vegas. Rest would be limited.

While I woke up exhausted, I was in far better shape than my guys. Cakes had pulled an all-nighter at the poker tables while E.B. and Lurch had also barely slept. Fueled by Red Bulls, E.B. seemed to be having a manic episode on the air. His mind raced from topic to topic as he talked faster and faster. Inevitably, we knew he would crash.

After the show, I dove into my bed in the room I was sharing with Bret. Our producers had stayed behind to break down the equipment, and Bret burst in half an hour later with unbridled enthusiasm. He was eager to gamble. Having won $500 for sucking E.B.'s toes during an on-air challenge to fund his trip, Bret woke me up and asked, "Hey, do you want to give that guy money?"

Shaking off the cobwebs as I had just drifted off to sleep, Bret added, "He's going to make us money." Knowing about the legend of Ram the Card Counter, I passed. The whole thing seemed shady.

Besides his alleged blackjack prowess, everything I had heard about Ram seemed negative. After meeting him again, Lurch ripped into his wardrobe during an appearance at The Front Page in downtown D.C., where Ram showed up wearing baggy cargo shorts with black socks and black dress shoes. "He doesn't care," I reasoned. "He just wants the attention." Disagreeing, Lurch fired back, "Oh. He cares. He was walking to the bathroom looking at his shoes."

Lurch couldn't have been more wrong.

Nevertheless, he invited Ram to join us in Las Vegas. On their first night playing together, Ram helped Lurch win $9,000 by following his moves during their first blackjack session together. Jealous of the huge wad of cash Lurch was now carrying, the rest of the gang wanted to invest. Meeting at the Mandalay Bay after the show, Lurch handed Ram $2,500. "Cakes wants a piece of you," Jason offered. Cakes had already left for the poker room.

E.B. and Bret also wanted in on the action. Handing the unkept smoker $1,500 each, they blindly placed their faith in a guy they barely knew. Ram was thrilled. His radio heroes were leaning on him. Since he wanted to keep things equal, Ram set aside $1,000 for Cakes and gambled with $4,500 of Junkies funds.

Though card counting gives blackjack players an advantage, there are no guarantees. Eager to win money for the crew, Ram strayed from his principles. Playing too aggressively, he lost the entire investment. Fortunately, the boys were none the wiser. They were all playing poker.

Panicking, Ram retreated to his room and grabbed $10,000 set aside in a safe. Then, on a mission to win back The Junkies money, Ram got on a roll. Flipping the $10,000 to $19,000, Ram doubled their money. Later, when he handed each of the boys their winnings, they glowed with approval. Though it had been a stressful ride, Ram had earned his membership to show character.

★ ★ ★ ★

Winning money is intoxicating. In the wake of the successful trip to Vegas, Lurch and Bret would hook up with Ram again at the Trump Marina in Atlantic City. Handing Ram a wad of cash from Cakes, who was investing from afar, the trio would hit the tables together. Lurch walked away with $7,000 in profits when all was said and done, while Bret and Cakes collected $3,000 each. Ram had delivered.

Unfortunately, this relationship wasn't all smooth sailing. On a subsequent trip, Lurch and Ram joined forces. With a favorable count, Ram increased his bet to $3,000. When Lurch only bet $500, Ram reached over and moved an additional $500 in chips to Lurch's stack. While Lurch had made a strategic mistake, Ram made a tragic one. The eye in the sky noticed his move and flagged him as a card counter. Ram wouldn't be allowed to play blackjack there again.

But the two found their way to other casinos. Though Ram didn't need his new partner in crime to make money, he couldn't quit Lurch. He was getting more on-air mentions and was intoxicated by the attention.

After a few more gambling trips, their magic carpet ride hit a tree. With Lurch becoming impatient after losing more than $2,000 during one blackjack session, Ram urged his new bestie to return to his room. While Lurch chilled, Ram gambled with his money. Regrettably, Ram was running bad and lost $13,000 of Lurch's cash, as well as another $15,000 of his own.

Returning to his room, Ram felt like he was walking the green mile. Afraid of Lurch's impending reaction, Ram had an idea. He guaranteed Lurch that he'd win back his money in full. Ram even promised to toss in another $300 for the headache. "Ramsurance" was born.

E.B. was set to join the two addicts later that evening, but Lurch couldn't wait. Since he didn't have any more cash, he headed home. Speeding his way back from Atlantic City, anxiety got the better of him. Even though he was less than an hour from home, Lurch's stomach was too queasy. Pulling over on River Road just off the Beltway, Lurch found a long driveway on the side of the road and left a present.

Reflecting on the fiasco on Monday morning, Lurch had us rolling as he described the disgusting scene. While we couldn't stop laughing, our audience was stunned. Lurch was almost 40 years old; how could he not control his bowels? The story was immediately legendary.

Later, Ram called in to offer a kicker. Since he decided to follow Lurch's lead and also drive home, Ram offered his empty room and gambling perks to E.B. so he could eat and drink for free. Ram was perplexed when he received a bill for $80. Confessing on-air, E.B. justified running up the tab. Not only had he ordered one adult movie on pay-per-view, but he ordered two—the price of friendship.

★ ★ ★ ★

Over several months, Ram the Card Counter wiggled his way onto the show more and more. During a Junkette Search, he took to the stage and displayed his breakdancing skills, walking "The Egyptian" like The Bangles. Sweating profusely and gasping for air when he finished, the overweight attention 'ho tried to lean on what he thought was a wall behind a WJFK banner. Instead, he fell off the stage. Some in the crowd were alarmed, but most laughed. Ram played the fool once again.

Calling in to mock Cakes about a recent blackjack session, Ram explained he had given Cakes detailed instructions on how to win the most money. After playing for almost two hours, Ram raised his bet from $50 to $300, which should have sounded alarms for Cakes. The card count had finally become favorable.

When Cakes didn't follow Ram's lead, he kicked Cakes's leg underneath the table. Still, Cakes didn't catch on. Explaining the missed opportunity afterward, it finally dawned on Cakes. Though Ram was irritated, he knew making fun of Cakes would be a great call to the show. That was valuable as anything.

Perhaps most memorably, Ram divulged his biggest financial flop. He had started to day trade. Buying 400,000 shares of a stock he believed would skyrocket, Ram borrowed on margin nearly as much money as he had in his brokerage account. His investment ballooned immediately, and Ram's heart raced with adrenaline as his account began to tickle $1 million. Jumping for joy, Ram left his computer momentarily to go to the bathroom. Returning just a few minutes later, his heart sank as he read the monitor. His account had dipped below $100,000. Bailing as soon as he could, Ram was left with just $17,000 when he sold his stock. The entire ordeal had taken just six minutes.

Hearing the implausible details of Ram's incredible ride, we wondered if he was pulling our chain. Tragically, he wasn't. Ram shared his trade confirmation. We were shocked.

While Ram had lost almost everything in his brokerage account, he had also gotten everything he ever wanted. He was the new Junkies character. It didn't matter if we beat him up all the time. It didn't matter if we made fun of his appearance or his chain-smoking ways. Hearing us mock his foibles and follies gave Ram the attention he craved. While he had lost hundreds of thousands of real dollars, he collected what he called "attention dollars." That filled his broken heart as much as anything.

Years later, Ram would remarry and serenade The Junkies during his 2015 wedding reception. Many of the attendees didn't understand what was happening. Wearing a Nationals jersey over his tuxedo that read Junkies on the back and the number 21, Ram didn't hold back as he crooned…

Did you ever know that you're my hero
And everything I would like to be?
I can fly higher than an eagle
For you are the wind beneath my wings.

Maybe he didn't sound like Bette Midler, but he was making another attention dollars deposit. Ram lived for these moments. And though we don't hear from him as much nowadays—his beautiful Russian bride Marina will not allow him to play the fool often—Ram can't quit The Junkies. He craves attention too much. Only now, he collects in rubles.

22

HAIRCUTS SUCK

"If I can make a teacher's salary doing comedy, I think it's better than being a teacher." — *Dave Chappelle*

During the last months of our run on WHFS, protégés Oscar Santana and Chad Dukes started "The Big O and Dukes Show." They were our extended family so we were pulling hard for them to succeed. But just as they were beginning to gain traction, WHFS changed formats, leaving Oscar and Chad out of work.

Landing in Baltimore on 105.7 FM, our pals took over the midday slot. They weren't given much freedom. Hovering over them, Bob Philips, the station's general manager, began tinkering almost immediately. Within months, he added former Baltimore Police Commissioner Ed Norris to the cast. Then, Norris would get top billing, squeezing Oscar and Chad out of the lineup. Once again, our boys were unemployed.

Making a monumental shift, Oscar and Chad, who grew up in the DMV, moved to the southwest, where they replaced the retiring popular talk personality Phil Hendrie. Building a loyal audience of supporters called their "Horde" on 101.5 KZON in Phoenix, Oscar and Chad loved life as their late-night show gained popularity. Even though they were 2,300 miles from home, they enjoyed their new city, the weather, and ardent listeners.

Just as "The Big O and Dukes Show" was reaching its first anniversary, fate slapped them once again. KZON pulled the plug in June 2007. Talk was out, hip hop was in. *Déjà vu.*

Fortunately for them, Alexander Graham Bell's axiom, "When one door closes, another opens," rang true. A month later, "The Big O and Dukes Show" returned to Washington. Like a dream, Oscar and Chad found their way to their favorite radio station, WJFK. Airing in our old nighttime slot, the boys were excited, and it didn't take long for the rivalry shenanigans to begin.

Challenging us to a game of kickball, we gladly accepted. We couldn't imagine losing to these guys in any athletic endeavor. Hyping the contest for weeks, we added listeners to our roster and placed a wager on the outcome. If we won, we'd get a day off with "The Big O and Dukes Show" filling in for us. If we lost, we would host eight hours of radio, including their nighttime shift.

With dozens in attendance, The Junkies squad faced a motley crew that included a guy wearing a Spartacus costume and another wearing a nun's habit. Nevertheless, our lead was just one run entering the final inning. With Lurch calling the shots as our manager, Bret shifted from third base to first. Frustrated that our producer had misplayed a foul ball earlier in the game, Lurch had seen enough of Bret's defense at the hot corner.

Leading off the bottom of the sixth, Chad's brother, Casey, hit a line drive directly to our new third baseman. A listener who was our supposed ringer misplayed the ball, placing the tying run on first. Next, Oscar reached base safely on a controversial kick resembling a bunt, which was against the rules. With two runners on, a lazy kick drifted into short right field over Bret's head. Lumbering back to make the catch, Bret crashed into Oscar, who was running to second base. Instead of making the easy play, Bret watched the ball drop in for a hit. The bases were loaded with nobody out.

Catching a fly ball to the outfield from the next kicker, I hit my cut-off man E.B., who was pitching. Relaying the ball home as Casey Dukes tagged up, E.B.'s throw was late. Tie game. Compounding the problem, our catcher tried to double up Oscar on third base. Instead, he launched the big red ball into the outfield. Oscar sprinted home, and the game was over. "The Big O and Dukes Show" had pulled off the improbable upset, winning 3-2.

Recapping the embarrassing loss during our next show, Lurch started the Monday morning quarterbacking. "I don't know how we lost." Then, turning his venom toward our beloved movie reviewer BDK, who had left runners on base, and Dee Woods, a loyal listener who misplayed a ball in the outfield, Lurch barked, "When other players can't play, you suffer."

Growing more irritated, Lurch trained his guns on Bret, asking, "When are we going to blame Bret, because Bret dropped a line drive right to him?"

As Bret began to mount his defense, claiming it was a difficult play, Lurch shouted, "You blew the game! Let me tell you why you blew the game. Because there's a pop-up to first base, and you ran into somebody. You push him out of the way and you go get the ball! In kickball, if the ball is kicked in the air, it should never hit the ground! EVER! You run around him. You ever play sports before?"

Jumping to Bret's defense, Cakes claimed it was a nearly impossible catch, yet Lurch piled on. "It wasn't impossible. The guy's a freaking tractor!"

The low blows were just beginning, however. Losing to "The Big O and Dukes Show" was humiliating, but the truth? Lurch was livid he would have to work an extra four hours.

"Let me tell you what happened," he argued. "I replayed the game 75 times. I can't believe we lost."

Agreeing, E.B. added, "We lost to guys wearing dresses!"

Bret, our easy-going producer snapped. "E.B., you whiffed! You're the only man to whiff the entire game. If you're so silly, you wouldn't have whiffed!"

Incensed, E.B. fired back, "You think I'm not sillier than you?"

The pissing contest had begun. Bret jabbed, "At least I got a hit!" Screaming angrily, E.B. shot back, "I got a hit, too, dick!"

The temperature kept rising. When E.B. tried to explain he was trying to kick the ball on the ground, Bret poked the bear. "But you missed."

Now raging, E.B. took it to a personal level. "Here's the difference, fat boy! Here's the difference. Now I'm bitter. You dropped the ball! You dropped the ball! You dropped the ball coming right at you. Then you lost a race to Cakes. You lost your manhood on Saturday! Your manhood is cooked!"

Laughing at E.B.'s volcanic eruption, Bret wouldn't back down. "You whiffed at a big red ball the size of a beach ball! You took your big leg, and you missed!"

E.B. didn't want to hear it. "Who do you think is more athletic?" he asked.

As Cakes continued to chuckle, Bret countered, "What do you think, you're Bo Jackson?" E.B. blew up.

"Hey, fat boy! Meathead! Compared to you, I'll beat you in anything! You move like an elephant!"

So it continued with Bret claiming he would beat E.B. in a fight and a game of one-on-one hoops. That was the last straw for E.B., who stood up, slamming his headphones. "Fuck you," he cursed, "I'll challenge you in anything!" Dumping it immediately, C.K. and Bret urged us to go to break. All the while, Chad Dukes giggled while waiting patiently on the phone line, ready to take a victory lap. When we returned, E.B. explained his outburst.

"The reason why Bret touched a nerve with me is it's the most humiliating loss of my life. I couldn't sleep all weekend knowing we lost to guys in dresses. We lost to guys who play Gears of War."

Rationalizing the loss further, E.B. offered his theory: "That ball is the great equalizer. That's why it's a sport for nerds."

Obviously, we couldn't handle the loss. "It's a dark day in Junkies history," Cakes declared. In the pursuit of fun and games, this was infamy.

★ ★ ★ ★

The following spring, on March 13, 2008, Cakes would get his shot at redemption. This time he would play Chad Dukes on the blacktop in a game of one-on-one basketball. With BDK providing commentary and E.B. coaching, Lurch and I listened from the studio. Losing to nerds in kickball was one thing, but we couldn't lose to them in hoops.

Yelling at the top of his lungs, E.B. was exasperated. The game was knotted at nine points each. The on-court battle was the furthest thing from pretty, yet there was so much on the line. "Get up on him, Cakes," E.B. urged.

After another brick from Dukes, a shirtless Cakes pulled up from 10 feet and rattled home a short jumper to take a 10-9 lead. We were just one point away. After Cakes missed a jump hook, E.B. urged, "Play some defense, Cakes, it's straight eleven!"

Fouling Chad hard as he drove to the basket, it was clear Cakes wasn't going to go down easily. When Dukes missed his next shot, Cakes pulled his shorts high above his flabby waist to give the audience a quick laugh. Then it was down to business.

Backing Dukes down under the basket, Cakes hit a two-foot jump hook to win the game. "Winner! Winner!" E.B. exclaimed as the small crowd cheered. Though it was a personal victory for Cakes, it was a win for The Junkies. Reputation restored!

During our last year at WHFS, we held our first spring break party, mimicking the success of MTV's spring break coverage. Staging the show live from a cavernous bar, a crowd of almost a hundred listeners looked on as our first Junkette, Lindsay, stood in a kiddie pool with one lucky listener pouring water over her t-shirt. As the crowd ogled our voluptuous colleague, we knew this was the start of something big.

By 2008, our annual spring break event had grown into a monster, full of sponsorships and prizes for all our reindeer games. And now we had scores of Junkettes.

As the line wrapped around the State Theater in Falls Church, Virginia, on April 5, 2008, Kara, Mina, Lauren, Teresa, and Shannon greeted our listeners in their new Junkette uniforms, which consisted of short mini-skirts and halter tops. Once inside, the drinks flowed as the deejay warmed up the crowd. Then, with a packed house, we jumped on stage and invited some of our wacky characters to join us. We forced them to participate in various contests where we pushed the outside of a few envelopes.

A year earlier and inspired by the movie "Borat," we forced BDK to wear a mankini on stage. Now he would participate in our "Crush It" contest with couples competing to see who could burst a water balloon first without using their hands. The more sexually suggestive, the better.

Later, Ram the Card Counter took the stage for our "Kiss a Loser" contest. Initially declining because he had a new girlfriend, Ram conceded after C.K. berated him. The allure of attention dollars was too great. In the end, he kissed a woman almost twice his age. The crowd roared its approval.

As the night progressed, we gave the audience more of what they wanted. A sponsor had provided our Junkettes with lingerie. Holding a Junkette fashion show, the throng of fans roared louder with each successive introduction of the curvaceous models.

Then we held our biggest bikini contest yet. With thousands of dollars in prizes, word had spread. The field was strong as our boy Schwartzy recruited contestants online. Bringing Cowboy Todd and Sactown Mike to the stage as judges, we sat back and enjoyed the show. Attendees snapped pictures furiously as the ladies danced even more, bringing the crowd to explosive cheers.

After announcing the winner, a cover band took over, and we joined the fans in attendance. Slugging beers with them was a helluva toast to this party.

A few months later, in June 2008, our old pal Justin Gimelstob stopped by for an in-studio visit to promote his upcoming stint with the Washington Kastles tennis team. Little did we know how noteworthy this interview would be.

Revealing his animosity toward tennis bombshell Anna Kournikova, who was playing for the St. Louis Aces, Gimelstob ranted, "If she's not crying by the time she walks off that court, then I did not do my job."

Having played alongside the beautiful internet sensation on tour and during their days in a youth tennis academy, Gimelstob made it clear he thought Kournikova was a terrible person. "Hate is a very strong word," he quantified. "I just despise her to the maximum level just below hate."

Gimelstob gave us more when he discussed the attractive females on tour. Calling French players Tatiana Golovin and Alize Cornet "sexpots," we wondered if he was crossing a line. Then Justin described Czech player Nicole Vaidisova as a "well-developed young lady." While the conversation was undoubtedly misogynistic, we didn't think twice. Gimelstob was an excellent radio guest—engaging, insightful and controversial.

Unfortunately for him, the tennis world was listening, and his comments would come back to haunt him. Ilana Kloss, CEO and commissioner of World TeamTennis said, "Justin's remarks were completely out of line with what World TeamTennis stands for. World TeamTennis was founded on respect and equality for both genders. These remarks were clearly inappropriate and inconsistent with the values of World TeamTennis. We will not tolerate this language or derogatory remarks of this nature."

Gimelstob was suspended without pay.

He apologized, saying, "Anna Kournikova, World TeamTennis, and many others deserve my deepest apologies. My hurtful remarks do not reflect the genuine and deep respect I have for women. I recognize that my access to communicate to the public should be used in a positive way, and this was clearly not the case last week. In addition, I have a responsibility to the numerous outlets that trust me to inform, entertain, and educate their viewers and listeners. I failed them. I am truly sorry."

While we had thoroughly enjoyed our interview with Gimelstob, we also felt guilty. Though we didn't put the words in his mouth, his comments on "The Sports Junkies" had cost him thousands of dollars. That was a first for us.

★ ★ ★ ★

Weeks earlier, we interviewed UFC President Dana White, who was promoting UFC 86. Ribbing him on the air, we asked for tickets to the bout. Of course, we knew it was a "grasper," as we would say on the show, but sometimes you have to throw a Hail Mary.

Amazingly, on Saturday, July 5, 2008, we found ourselves seated in the lower bowl of the Mandalay Bay Events Center in Las Vegas for the main event. White had delivered. As Forrest Griffin upset Rampage Jackson to win the UFC light heavyweight championship, we were thrilled to witness the spectacle.

When the crowd began to pour out of the arena, some of us decided to hit the bars while others went to gamble. Meeting up with Ram the Card Counter, who had tagged along for the trip, E.B. and Bret had a celebrity sighting when they spotted A.J. McClean of the Backstreet Boys.

Messing with Ram, the two persuaded the attention seeker to give McClean a shoutout, but they wanted to punk him. Ram didn't know the singer. Telling Ram that McClean was a member of NSYNC, they dared him to perform the puppet dance from their video "Bye Bye Bye."

With McClean's entourage surrounding him, Ram shouted out to the pop star, "A.J., huge fan! Love Bye Bye Bye!" Embarrassed, E.B. and Bret jumped behind a pillar as they watched Ram perform his version of the puppet dance. While McClean remained stone-faced, his entourage burst into laughter. Ram played the fool once again. He didn't mind. It was just another attention dollars deposit.

★ ★ ★ ★

By the fall of 2008, we had proven to be a consistent force in the ratings, so it wasn't a surprise when WJFK picked up our fourth-year option, extending us through 2009. Since we were due a substantial raise, we were happy that we wouldn't have to endure contract negotiations for at least another year.

Camaraderie at the station was at an all-time high. Over the course of several months, WJFK had gone through a facelift. "The Big O and Dukes" show moved to the midday slot, followed by "The Mike O'Meara Show" in afternoon drive. After Don Geronimo's unexpected retirement in April, Mike took over the top billing with the rest of the "Don and Mike Show" cast joining him.

Having Oscar and Chad follow us was akin to working with our little brothers. We were proud of their journey and how far they had come, but that didn't stop us from cracking their coconuts. The boys had taken to shooting each other with paintball guns as punishment for committing flubs on the air. We were intrigued and asked them to let us fire away in morning drive.

As their producer Drab T-Shirt braced for pain in our cramped studio, Lurch was holding a loaded paintball gun that resembled a military assault weapon aimed at his back. E.B. inquired, "This is like crazy to shoot somebody from this close?" Agreeing, the rep from Pev's Paintball in nearby Aldie, Virginia, warned, "You'll just get a bleeding welt. It's not going to go through his skin or anything," as if that would comfort Drab.

Before Lurch pulled the trigger, Bret wondered, "You won't shoot him in the ass?" Proud of his derriere, Drab objected, opting for the back. Seconds later, E.B. began a countdown, and then it was ready, aim, fire.

"*Ohhh!*" everybody screamed as Drab doubled over in pain, falling to his knees. With Oscar cackling like a hyena in the background, Lurch began to feel guilty while deflecting blame. "What do you want me to do? Oscar told me to do it!"

Lifting his shirt, we all were amazed at the wound already forming. Worried, Drab asked, "they're open wounds?" Uneasiness began to fill the studio. Had we gone too far?

While Lurch pondered how to treat Drab's injury, Cakes lightened the mood. Referencing a Hot Hot Heat song, Cakes had the solution. "Lurch, you need some bandages, of course."

Quickly forgetting about Drab's pain, Lurch began to sing, "Bandages, bandages, bandages." The studio erupted in laughter. We were having such a good time.

The fun continued through Halloween when we were invited to be part of Mike O'Meara's "Boo Bash." Mike had started to involve us more on his show. Inviting us to drink in the studio during his Friday afternoon happy hours wasn't a tough sell. It was a blast, and his promotional ladies, the Buzz Babes, joined the chaos. The audience loved the station synergy with the entire lineup interacting with each other.

On the night of the "Boo Bash," we looked forward to hanging out with hundreds of loyal WJFK listeners attending the costume party. After drinking with fans for hours, there was a hiccup. Our limo had left with some of us still inside the bar.

Scrambling to find sober drivers to take us home, E.B. turned to Ram the Card Counter. Though he had promised to drive Bret home already, there was no room in his car after agreeing to take E.B. and Cakes, as well as our newest intern Matt. Bret would have to fend for himself. He was just a "secondary hero" for Ram.

When Ram pulled into E.B.'s driveway an hour later, he shook his radio hero to wake him up. E.B., dressed like Washington Redskins coach Jim Zorn with gray hair and a headset, arose from his slumber and stammered, "I just realized… it's kinda of freaky… you know where I live."

There was no thank you and no appreciation. But Ram was still happy. He knew he'd get plenty of mentions during our next show. More attention dollars.

★ ★ ★ ★

In 2006, we were part of a massive Free FM campaign when we replaced Howard Stern, who left for satellite radio. By 2007, CBS Radio was phasing out the Free FM brand. David Lee Roth, who had taken over for Stern in New York and many of Stern's east coast affiliates, was fired. Rover, who had replaced Stern in the Midwest, was ousted, too. So when Adam Corolla's morning show on KLSX in Los Angeles was canceled in February 2009, we became the last of the Stern replacements still standing.

Despite our success, we began to hear rumblings of a possible format switch at WJFK. Could this be the WHFS scenario all over again?

Lucky for us, Chris Kinard was still our executive producer and had ascended to program director two years earlier. He was privy to corporate discussions. CBS Radio was moving away from hot talk, but "The Sports Junkies" weren't going anywhere.

Our agent was in discussions with the corporate brass. WJFK was switching to an all-sports format and wanted us to remain their morning show. That was a relief. But C.K. was put in the unenviable position of firing Mike O'Meara, who was thriving in afternoon drive. Ratings didn't matter. He wasn't a sports guy.

Similarly, Oscar from "The Big O and Dukes Show" was let go. Since Chad Dukes was a huge Redskins fan, he survived and was paired with former linebacker LaVar Arrington in afternoon drive. *Washington Post* sports columnist Mike Wise would debut in the midday slot.

The all-sports format would begin July 20, 2009. Fortunately, we wouldn't be asked to change our show. We were relieved to still be working, but we felt terrible for our friends who had lost their jobs. The radio business can be ruthless.

CBS Radio CEO Dan Mason explained, "There's no better way to reach large numbers of male listeners than through exclusive sports programming. We're seeing impressive ratings growth at a number of our stations and clients continue to make big investments in sports marketing."

It always came down to money.

And that included our future, too. If we wanted to continue hosting the morning show on the newly branded 106.7 The Fan, we would have to agree to a new contract. Unfortunately, that meant what our agent described as a haircut. Just four days before the format flip, we signed a new two-year deal. Regrettably, we also accepted a six-figure pay cut each.

That wasn't a haircut, that was a buzz cut, and it sucked!

23

BROTHERS FIGHT

"Everyone knows that if you've got a brother, you're going to fight."
— Liam Gallagher

I wrote several raps for the show during our early years, including two about Washington Wizards star Chris Webber, who was eventually traded to Sacramento. Sometimes E.B. would urge me to pen the parodies as a goofy way to have fun on the air.

Years later, as we supposedly matured, E.B. was mortified. He didn't want our listeners to hear the raps again. Maybe his feelings had changed as he grew older and became a father. Instead of laughing at the self-deprecation, he was indignant.

Coming to a head on the air, our producer Bret said, "The dynamic is so funny. You guys are so embarrassed, but J.P. is so proud." Then E.B. started to take digs. "I'm going to have to write a booklet for J.P. on what works in radio and what doesn't. He clearly doesn't understand 15 years in. Want me to give you a seminar? Come over to my house today and I'll explain how radio works."

With Cakes laughing in the background, Bret added, "It's awkward." Perhaps, but this episode was the floodgate of a simmering feud. Searching for the Webber song on the instant replay machine that housed all of our sound effects, I was unsuccessful at first. "It's probably better that way," Cakes said. "It's better for all parties involved."

Then E.B. claimed, "You definitely won't find it when I delete it. You'll never find it again! Keep looking." I wasn't going to back down.

Seconds later, the beat from "Money, Power and Respect" by The Lox dropped. Cakes started to laugh uncontrollably. "Oh, no!" Then the intro kicked in, and the rap began, *"Yo! This one goes out to the number one pick..."* Moments later, E.B. reached across the console and ripped the wires from the replay machine. He wasn't caving either.

Stunned, Cakes warned, "You're going to break the machine."

E.B. didn't care. "I will break it. I will kick your ass."

While E.B. was enraged, I laughed. I had seen him lose his cool so many times. "That is hilarious," I said. "Do you realize what you just did? You were willing to break a machine because of a stupid rap." Still fuming, E.B. started firing low blows. "Find headphones that fit your peanut head."

Trying to lower the room temperature, Bret interjected, "What's up, Cakes?"

"This is the most awkward five minutes I've ever been involved with," he said, and it wasn't over.

"It's all because of his stubborn ego," E.B. theorized. That struck me as ironic since E.B. had always claimed to like self-deprecating humor. I asked, "Why can't you just let it go and play it? Listeners want it."

"They want it because they like my blow-ups," E.B. asserted.

"And they got it!" Cakes added.

Before the on-air drama was over, E.B. threatened to hit me. Daring him to do so, I stuck my chin out and tested him. "Go ahead, punch me in the face. Go ahead. Right now. Right here. Punch me in the face."

Though no punches were thrown, what started as an on-air dispute had turned personal. Cakes wasn't laughing anymore. Lurch had missed the entire episode while on vacation but wasn't shocked when he heard the details. We had been fighting on the air for years. Bret admitted the screaming matches attracted him to the show in the first place. Our audience loved the bouts. They were raw and real.

Though most of our fights were silly and didn't linger past the show, this one was different. Sitting alone inside a new apartment after my separation, I wondered why an argument about a silly song had escalated to such epic proportions. Maybe E.B. and I had drifted apart. I was at a distinctly different point in life. Even though I saw my kids most days, I was alone at night. It wasn't easy.

I don't think my friend realized the loneliness. I had gone from bathing my son every night to dropping Kelsie and Dylan off at 7 o'clock at their mom's house. How could he possibly know how that felt?

So it stung when E.B. zinged on the air that me and one of our close friends also going through a divorce were "living la vida loca." I let the jabs slide because I never wanted my pending divorce or what I was suffering to be public. Almost all of my friends were married, so most nights I watched TV alone.

But why hadn't E.B. visited once? We were each other's best man. Though I knew his comments weren't meant to be malicious, they had gotten under my skin and hurt. I soon realized the fight wasn't about the stupid rap. It was the culmination of the feelings I had kept to myself. Maybe that's why I wasn't going to cave to his on-air request.

Writing E.B. an email, I argued that Bret was right. I did have a sense of pride in the rap. I knew it was silly, but it was part of the show's history, and I wanted to share that with the audience. Revisiting the rap song was akin to playing Lurch's embarrassing college deejay tapes.

Then, I dove into the more significant personal issues. I was never one to express my feelings, but after years of therapy in a failed marriage, I had to change my ways. There was more to the fight than the facts, so I wrote:

"As I sit here, I have to tell you I often think about the last days of my dad's life. If I could go back to that hospital room right now, I would. And one of my favorite memories is one of the last times I saw him open his eyes. It was when you were there, and I told him, and he was able to open up his eyes, see you and even smile."

Three years later, the memory was still vivid. Growing up, E.B. was like another son to my dad. He was at my house almost every day, and my dad loved him.

Hitting send, I didn't know if I would get a response or if I wanted one. I had finally gotten what had been bothering me off my chest. Still, when E.B.'s email came back two hours later, it was probably for the better of our long friendship.

Much like I did, he hit the facts first. He felt I had disrespected his wishes and didn't like the way I pushed his buttons. That was fair. Adding that he thought there was a condescending tone when I argued, he wrote, "Maybe it's the way they teach people in law school. I have no idea. It irks me. But I will simply fight back and do the same thing."

But now, it was his turn to bring up something that had been frustrating him. E.B. was bothered that I had arrived at the last minute for the show and was occasionally late. He wrote that he was unnerved by the tardiness and disrespect. He wasn't wrong.

"At the end of the day, you are a brother to me," he continued. "We will fight and we will agree. When one of us buys the farm I'm sure the remaining guy will be organizing the funeral. But that doesn't mean it's going to be a smooth ride and that shit isn't going to happen along the way."

We could agree on that.

While Bret had been put in a difficult position as he watched E.B. and I go at it like raving lunatics on the air, in the end, there was no harm, perhaps a few fouls. But it wasn't long after that our young executive producer would be tested again.

Just as we finished our next-to-last segment, Lurch told us that he wanted to leave early. He had a tee time and didn't want to risk holding up his foursome. While we thought his excuse was weak, we shrugged our shoulders and said it was fine.

Bret wasn't so calm. As Lurch began to pack up his things, Bret became annoyed. He felt Lurch was taking advantage of him, so he decided to take a stand. "You're not going to do your job?" You're just going to leave?" Then, as Lurch began to object, saying our final segment would be less than 10 minutes, Bret fired back, "you're just not going to do your job? That's a show!"

Simmering, Lurch reached a boiling point. Reaching into the brown paper bag he brought to work that morning, Lurch fired an orange at Bret. The orange missed him by inches. Our mouths were agape. We couldn't believe what we had just seen.

Sitting down, Lurch was furious. He decided against leaving and remained mostly silent during the last segment of the show. Bursting out of the studio immediately after we signed off, the rest of us stayed in disbelief. Lurch's temper had gotten the best of him.

But by the following morning, the episode was history. Our fights never carried over exceptionally long.

"Shut up," E.B. shouted. "F-you," I countered as we sat just three feet apart. And so it began, this time about Peyton Manning's move to the Denver Broncos in spring 2012. "It's what you said," I continued. Frustrated, E.B. lobbed a warning, "I'm so close to attacking you."

Not willing to back down—some things never change—I challenged him immediately. "Go for it!" Of course, nobody believed it would actually come to that. As Valdez manned the microphone levels from the adjoining production studio, Cakes and Lurch started firing zingers.

"I've got a front-row seat," Cakes offered while chuckling.

"So do I," Lurch joked. "I'll sell tickets."

Jabbing back at E.B., I dug in. "Sorry that you said something that you are now backing off of." Enraged, E.B. screamed even louder, "I'm not backing off of dick. The only thing I'm backing off of is your neck."

As the shouting continued, E.B. foreshadowed his next move. "I'm this close to leaping across the table and ending it once and for all." I retorted snidely, "Just because you can't handle a conversation? If I don't agree with you, you are going to get upset."

Then the unthinkable happened. E.B. stood up, jumped across the console and began to tackle me. Still seated, I immediately wrapped my arms around E.B. as he put me in a headlock. Lurch and Cakes couldn't believe their eyes.

Valdez was scrambling. After countless arguments over the airwaves, nobody fathomed that it might turn physical, including our producer running the board and responsible for us not getting kicked off the air. Immediately shutting off the four microphones in our studio, Valdez took us to commercial break as fast as he could. The listeners would have no idea what was happening.

Within seconds, Lurch and Cakes tried to separate us. As headphones dangled from my head, Jim Jester, who had been filling in to answer our phones, jumped in the middle of the fray. Soon Valdez was in the studio as well, and we finally let each other go. There were just a few minutes until we returned from commercial break.

Convincing E.B. to go downstairs to cool off, Valdez had thwarted a disaster. Resuming the show just a few minutes later, Lurch offered a quick recap and we quickly moved on as if nothing had happened. Some things are better left unsaid.

Unfortunately, C.K. couldn't sit by idly as program director with two of his hosts having a physical altercation on the air. Though I argued against it, E.B. was suspended for the next morning's show. The fight would be scrubbed from the podcast later that day, and we wouldn't be allowed to discuss it the next show.

Later that evening, my friend of 40 years called to apologize. It wasn't necessary. Though he had lost his temper and taken it to another level, I knew it didn't mean anything. We had been down that road countless times, whether it was in my backyard as kids or over the airwaves. We were brothers. Brothers fight.

24

CHANGE IS INEVITABLE

"Don't cry because it's over. Smile because it happened." — *Dr. Seuss*

Hall of Fame Los Angeles Dodgers manager Tommy Lasorda once said, "You give loyalty, you'll get it back. You give love, you'll get it back." With Chris Kinard leaving as executive producer of our show in 2009 and fully committing to his responsibilities as program director of 106.7 The Fan, we had some decisions to make. C.K. had been with us since 1998 and worked faithfully on our behalf for almost a decade. Whether it was dealing with management, sales, or promotions, C.K. handled it all so we could concentrate on the content. He also booked guests and dealt with four prima-donnas who pushed him to work even harder. The job wasn't easy.

Still, it was a no-brainer for us to name Bret Olivero as our new executive producer. Bret had been a loyal foot soldier since he was a teenager, had great instincts for radio, and knew the show as well as anybody. Having done everything we asked for years, Bret deserved the promotion.

We also had a rising star who started interning for us the previous fall. Matt Myers was a burly, broad-shouldered senior at the University of Maryland. After his roommate died in a drunk driving accident, his parents encouraged him to plan his career. The Chesapeake High School graduate who grew up between Annapolis and Baltimore in Pasadena, Maryland, had been introduced to "The Sports Junkies" by his older brother Michael during our days at WHFS. So, Matt started waking up at six every morning before school to catch some of the show before basketball practice.

Continuing to listen religiously during college, the journalism major didn't miss a minute. When Matt finally interviewed with Bret, it was obvious he understood the show's many dynamics, and he was hired immediately.

We put him through the wringer right away. Because he was nervous on the air, Matt tended to trip over his words and stumble. While that wasn't a big deal, we still laughed at his obvious discomfort. But what tickled us more so was his Baltimore accent, known as the blue-collar "Bawlmerese." Having shed his accent years earlier, Cakes was pouncing on Matt whenever he could, mimicking his thick townie dialect with the fronting back vowels.

Off the air, Matt was a valuable asset. Tasked with primarily answering the phones, he would also print out stories that we might use for the show. He took it too far. Each morning he'd hand out a prodigious stack of papers that mostly ended in the trash bin.

Undeterred, Matt kept printing. Did he think we weren't preparing on our own? Why was he handing us so many stories? Cakes jabbed, "You're a bigger threat to the environment than the Exxon Valdez." Likening him to the catastrophic Alaskan oil spill, a new nickname emerged. He was now Matt Valdez.

★ ★ ★ ★

"This crusher claw right here could snap off your toe," Frank Dalton, the executive chef at The Palm in Tysons, Virginia, warned. Our bright-eyed producer Valdez would be sitting atop a dunk tank filled with live lobsters and crabs in just a few minutes. Fresh out of college, the broke 21-year-old couldn't afford the $300 buy-in to play in our 7th Junkies Poker Open. But, desperate for cash, Valdez was willing to do almost anything.

There was no turning back with Bret securing the dunk tank and listeners waiting in the parking lot on Tuesday, November 10, 2009. When we returned from our next commercial break, we stood outside in the cold with microphones in hand. As Valdez climbed onto the small platform just above the water, E.B. began our play-by-play coverage: "There go your feet in the cold-ass water."

Valdez was still smiling. Wearing shorts and a t-shirt with swim goggles and tennis shoes, we began to throw softballs at the target. On my second toss, I hit the bullseye, and the platform was released. Dropping immediately into the frigid, shellfish-infested water, Valdez desperately tried to climb out to avoid any potential bites. The crowd howled while E.B. began to paint the picture for our radio audience.

"He's panic-stricken. He's trying to get out of there." As the crowd cackled, Cakes mocked Valdez's attempt to escape. "You should have seen him flounder after he got dropped."

Still chuckling, Lurch wondered, "Did any of them get you at all?" Hearing the trepidation in his voice, Valdez confirmed, "I could feel them poking at my ankles." Breaking into his best Valdez-like Baltimore accent, Cakes described the challenge for our distressed producer. "He's struggling and flailing to get away from the crabs and the lobsters." It was just beginning.

Next, our movie reviewer BDK grabbed a softball. Having put BDK through a sports challenge months earlier, nobody expected him to hit the target, especially Valdez. Then the unexpected happened. BDK hit the mark, and Valdez was back in the freezing water.

As Bret pointed to the window in the 4-foot-high dunk tank, we could see a crab inches away from Valdez. "There's one right on your ass," E.B. cautioned our panicky friend. So it continued for several minutes. Drenched and shivering, Valdez explained, "As soon as you get down there and your feet get down there, they nip at your ankles."

By the time we were through, Valdez's legs were worse for the wear, having been pinched and cut a few times. Cakes declared, "This is quite a wacky radio stunt." Valdez had earned his money and proved he would do anything for The Junkies.

★ ★ ★ ★

On June 7, 2010, the Washington Nationals selected 17-year-old slugger Bryce Harper with their top pick in the Major League Baseball draft. One day later, their top pick from their previous draft, San Diego State fireballer Stephen Strasburg, took the mound for the first time in a Nationals uniform. The fanbase was buzzing. Even E.B., a long-time Baltimore Orioles fan, felt compelled to attend the historic debut.

By then, Washington had been playing in Nationals Park for three seasons, but there weren't many highlights beyond Ryan Zimmerman's walk-off home run to win their first game in the new stadium on March 30, 2008.

Strasburg's arrival changed the narrative instantly. Because of the hype, the Nationals were forced to distribute over 200 media credentials for what had been dubbed "Strasmus." Everybody wanted to see the phenom.

With 40,415 fans in attendance, Strasburg showed everybody why he had been a No. 1 overall draft pick. Hitting 97 miles per hour on the radar with his first pitch, the crowd burst with excitement. Then over the course of seven innings, as E.B. watched from the concourse with his brother Matt, Strasburg unleashed a strikeout parade. The crowd erupted louder and louder as the Bickel brothers pounded beers, giving each other high fives after each ensuing strikeout. Nationals Park was electric.

When the rookie sensation was pulled after seven exhilarating innings, he had struck out 14 batters, including the last seven he faced. The Nationals would beat the Pittsburgh Pirates 5-2, and Washington baseball was alive once again. They also had a new cheerleader in E.B. and a radio show following their every move.

The astonishing debut of Stephen Strasburg wasn't just a D.C. story. It was a national story. Soon media outlets from across the country were reaching out to "The Sports Junkies" for our take on the Nationals' new star. Since Bret and Valdez knew we didn't enjoy guest stints on other shows, they cooked up something different.

Guesting on the Jorge Sedano show based in Miami, Valdez assumed an alter ego, Rick Valdez. Listening to the interview the next morning, we couldn't be more entertained. Valdez had prepped furiously and was giving a serious breakdown of Strasburg's performance. Hearing Valdez's thick townie accent shine, we couldn't believe the host had no idea this was just a bit.

Then as Sedano wrapped the interview, Valdez unintentionally gave us a gift. Awkwardly signing off, Valdez tried to thank the host, "thanks for being on George." Thanks for being on? Valdez was a guest on Jorge's show, not the other way around. Then again, it was the Rick Valdez show. We loved it.

★ ★ ★ ★

In the fall of 2010, there was a renewed interest in the Washington Redskins. They had a new coach in Mike Shanahan who had two Super Bowl titles on his resume. They had a new quarterback in Donovan McNabb, a six-time Pro Bowler who had led the Philadelphia Eagles to five NFC Championship games and one Super Bowl. There were plenty of reasons to be optimistic.

Nevertheless, they were the same old Redskins as they finished just 6-10. For the ninth time in Dan Snyder's ownership, Washington missed the playoffs. We were used to the lethargy.

Similarly, the narrative on the Wizards and Capitals didn't change much either. Though the Wizards drafted Kentucky guard John Wall with the top pick in June's NBA Draft, his presence didn't impact their record. As a result, the Wizards closed their season with an abysmal 23-59 record.

Meanwhile, the Capitals were winning the Southeast Division for the fourth season in a row. Earning the top seed in the Eastern Conference playoffs, fans were ready for a long playoff run. However, after beating the New York Rangers in five games during the first round, Washington was unceremoniously swept by the lower-seeded Tampa Bay Lightning.

Listeners began referencing the D.C. curse. None of the professional teams in town had won a championship since the Redskins won the Super Bowl in 1992. At least there was next year.

★ ★ ★ ★

Our annual Spring Break Party at the State Theater in Falls Church, Virginia, was a tried and true formula. But each year, we tried to spice things up even more. Maybe it was because we had grown bored with some of our silly contests, but in 2011 we became more homoerotic than before.

First, there was the addition of the "Get Huge Club." Matt Valdez and two fellow employees at 106.7 The Fan, Chris "Blue Shorts" Lingebach and Othello Bouchareb, began to work out furiously in anticipation of the contest. As the hundreds in the crowd awaited our popular bikini contest and Junkette lingerie fashion show, the threesome jumped on stage in their Speedos. Oiled up to accentuate their new muscles, the three began to pose as if they were competing in the Mr. Olympia contest. While many in the crowd groaned, we laughed at their unbridled enthusiasm.

Leaning on the females in the crowd afterward, we held a booty-shaking contest followed by a Junkette kissing contest. The raucous crowd was delighted. Then we debuted one of Bret's wacky ideas. Bringing more guys to the stage, we judged who had the biggest bulge in their underwear during our "Horse" contest. The concept had made us laugh weeks earlier during Bret's pitch, but executing the humiliating competition on stage was absurd.

Though the night was an unmitigated success, we had an epiphany. We were all over 40 years old and had daughters who were growing up fast. Could we keep hosting the debauchery? What 40-year-olds went to spring break anyway?

Months after the Redskins finished their miserable season, we were still dissecting what had gone wrong. When the Redskins traded for Eagles quarterback Donovan McNabb, we assumed he would thrive in Mike Shanahan's West Coast Offense.

Unfortunately, McNabb's first season in Washington was rocky. By Halloween, Shanahan was pulling him out of the game so backup Sexy Rexy Grossman could run the two-minute drill. Citing McNabb's fitness, Shanahan explained, "The cardiovascular endurance that it takes to run a two-minute, going all the way down with no timeouts, calling plays, it's just not easy. If I thought it was the best situation to do, then Donovan would have run the two-minute offense."

That was a new one for us. Plenty of ammunition for good sports talk radio. But then, we were breaking news.

"During the season, at some point, not sure when, Shanahan asked McNabb to wear a wristband with the plays on it," Lurch said. "Tons of quarterbacks do it. So when Shanahan asked McNabb to do it initially, he said 'Look. I can't do this.'"

McNabb felt the wristband would make him look stupid and was bad for his image. Adding more to the story, E.B. said, "And the coach is like, 'What are you talking about?' Tom Brady wears a wristband. Drew Brees wears a wristband. And Kyle [Shanahan] is saying, 'Look, it's better for you. It helps you. It doesn't mean you're stupid. It doesn't mean you don't know the plays. Hall of Famers wear wristbands."

Later Lurch would describe a lunch at the Super Bowl with McNabb's agent, Mike Shanahan, Bruce Allen and the owner Dan Snyder. When the owner caught wind of the wristband dispute, Lurch claimed he grew irate.

"At that point, when Snyder heard that, Snyder apparently went ballistic and said, 'Are you effing kidding me?' Why did I hire you as the head coach? I'm paying you $7 million a year to be the head coach, and you can't get your guy to wear a wristband? Are you serious?"

The story was spreading like wildfire across the country, but some doubted our sources. The day after we broke the story, May 13, 2011, the *Washington Post* noted that many in the media disputed the rumors. Chris Russell, a former colleague of ours, claimed he spoke to five people who said they had no knowledge of the wristband dispute. Meanwhile, Kelli Johnson from Comcast SportsNet called the story "a lot of junk," citing an unnamed team source.

On the other hand, Rich Tandler, one of the most respected reporters in the market, wrote, "I'm about 99% confident that the wristband story is true." Of course, it was. We weren't in the business of breaking stories, so why would we make up something like this?

That's when C.K., our program director, summed it up best on Twitter:

"Multiple sources have corroborated. And McNabb's own spokesman has declined comment. So I would question their story… We have a source with the organization, and one close to the player's agent, saying he refused to wear a wristband with the plays. His publicist didn't respond all day. The team didn't respond all day. You be the judge."

Right or wrong, it didn't really matter. We had made waves. That was never a bad thing.

★ ★ ★ ★

Over the years, we have faced our share of adversity. Our dear friend Craig Walden died in a terrible car accident. E.B. lost his father, Lurch's mother died from cancer, and I lost both parents and went through a divorce. But what do you tell a friend and colleague when their brother, who was so full of life, passes away suddenly?

Derek Oliverio, Bret's younger brother, was an undeniable success story. At just 18 years old, he conceived a fun college restaurant and bar featuring specialty hot dogs, burgers, and drinks. By 2008, when he was just 23, he had fulfilled his dream with Sup Dogs restaurant in Greenville, North Carolina. By 2010, Sup Dogs had become a favorite haunt for East Carolina University students with an annual concert called Doggie Jams. With ECU being one the best party schools in America, hundreds lined the streets to celebrate.

Returning home from the restaurant past midnight into Thursday morning, September 29, 2011, Derek saw smoke emanating from his place. Trying to save his two dogs, Derek never made it out alive. We couldn't believe this tragedy. He was only 27 years old. Having met Derek over the years, it was apparent why he was so accomplished. He was a dreamer with a magnetic personality who worked tirelessly. Now he was gone, and Bret was devastated.

By spring 2012, Bret had been our executive producer for three years and working on the show since he was a teenager, covering 13 years. He decided to leave us and take over Sup Dogs. He had no restaurant or retail experience. The move was a huge risk. Though we didn't want to hear the news, we understood. Bret wanted to keep his brother's legacy alive and make Derek proud.

At Bret's going-away party, local celebrities and newscasters joined us to wish him well. The entire Junkies audience had listened to him grow up as he climbed from volunteer to executive producer and assistant program director. It wasn't easy for him to leave. Bret loved radio, and he was beloved by our audience. But in his 30s, he had gotten married and was ready to embark on a new journey.

Over the years, so many of our loyalists had moved on and were thriving. We were certain Bret would be the next in a long line. Jim McClure, who discovered us in 1996, was climbing the ladder at Sirius XM satellite radio. Amy Szutowicz, who answered phones for us during our weekend stint, became a successful television news reporter and anchor. Our former intern David Bernad, aka Clank David, had moved to Hollywood and was producing movies. That's why we weren't stunned when Bret decided to leave us. In our industry, 13 years together is a helluva run.

Truthfully, while we continued to march forward, so many things had changed. Free FM was long gone. WJFK had been rebranded and was now 106.7 The Fan. Chris Kinard, who started as our intern, was now our boss. We had decided to retire our Junkettes and Spring Break party, too. Maybe, just maybe, we had matured. Probably not, but the pathways of life teach us that change is inevitable.

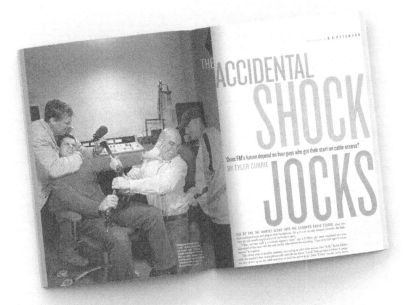

We don't know how to say "no" to photographers.
Our Washington Post Magazine spread, 2006.

The Italian Stallion and the Latin Donkey, 2006.

J.P. vs. Jay Watts at the Patriot Center, December 9, 2006.

Junkette Lauren promoting our Bikini Car Wash, summer 2007.

Junkette Kara as the referee for our kickball game vs. the "Big O and Dukes" show, 2007.

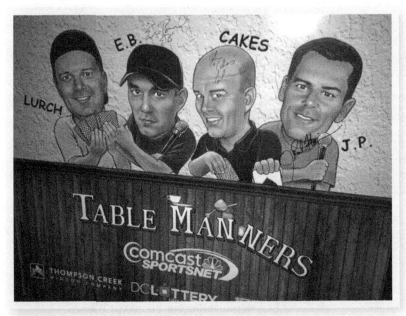

The intro for our "Table Manners" TV show, 2013.

With actor James Woods at the Junkies Poker Open at the Borgata in Atlantic City, 2014.

Backstage with O.A.R. and Ryan Zimmerman before our 20th anniversary concert, 2016.

Four Junkies: Celebrating 20 years at the 9:30 Club in D.C., 2016.

Cakes taking a breathalyzer during our annual Christmas drinking show, 2018.

E.B. and J.P. enjoying the Washington Capitals Stanley Cup parade, 2018.

Stanley Cup in the studio, 2018.

Ram grabbing more attention dollars at the 2019 Junkies Poker Open.

World Series trophy in the studio, November 2019.

Celebrating No. 1 ratings at The Palm, from left: Drab, JP, Lurch, A-Wadd, E.B., Cakes and Valdez, 2019.

The Junkies vs. Producers in a bowling grudge match celebrating No. 1 rating, 2019.

25

DRAB IS THE NEW BLACK

"Flying by the seat of your pants precedes crashing by the seat of your pants." — Bill Walsh

Sitting in front of the four guys who would decide his fate, Matt "Drab T-Shirt" Cahill boldly suggested, "It sounds like you guys don't prepare." It was a harsh assessment, but maybe he was right. After 16 years, the show had become second nature to us. We didn't spend hours brainstorming topics or have meetings to discuss new ideas. We didn't have producers who challenged us, either. "The Sports Junkies" was a well-oiled machine, or so we thought.

Still, when it was time to interview candidates for the vacant executive producer position, Chris Kinard advised us to keep an open mind. He had narrowed the field to three: Matt Valdez, who wanted more responsibility and a raise, Chris "Blue Shorts" Lingebach, and Drab T-Shirt.

Meeting in the station's conference room, Valdez was the first to state his case. He seemed more serious than we had seen. Dressed in a suit and tie, he began by pointing to his experience working alongside Bret Oliverio. Valdez was confident he was ready for more responsibilities, including booking guests and dealing with sales and promotions, but midway through the interview he became distracted.

E.B. was staring at his Blackberry. In the biggest interview of his life, Valdez stopped and directed his ire.

"Eric, come on, man! Can you stop?" Immediately defensive, E.B. fired back, "It shouldn't bother you." Claiming he could multitask, E.B. had Valdez on tilt. Nevertheless, we already knew what an asset Valdez could be.

Next, we interviewed "Blue Shorts," a true wild card. Though we liked him, we didn't know what to expect. Years earlier, the avid Junkies fan had dropped off his resume hoping to be an intern. Instead, he was hired by "The Mike O'Meara Show." He later interned for "The Big O and Dukes Show," with Chad Dukes dubbing him Blue Shorts. After a stint in promotions, Shorts was now writing articles for the station's website.

Answering our questions, Shorts began to blather uncontrollably as he felt like he was in the middle of a firing squad. As he looked at Lurch, who seemed disinterested, Shorts wondered if he deserved to be there. Revealing that he wasn't confident running the board, E.B. said, "That's okay. We'll have you figure it out on the air and we'll just grill you for it." Being a willing target was always part of our producer's job.

Pitching a new direction for the show, Shorts thought we should feature more skits and bits. As appreciative as we were, we couldn't overlook his lack of experience. Shorts had never booked guests or produced a show.

But Matt "Drab T-Shirt" Cahill had been preparing for the job since he was a sixth-grader in Richland, Washington. Grounded by his parents, the door to his bedroom was removed and Drab wasn't allowed to watch TV. He became hooked to his only outlet, sports talk radio, obsessively listening to legends Jim Rome and Scott Ferrall.

By the time he reached high school, Drab knew he wanted to pursue a career in radio. Attending a vocational school at age 16, Drab got his first taste of air time hosting the "MC and Jason Show" on Thursday nights, where he often lifted material from David Letterman's Top 10 lists. Later, one of his teacher's would recommend Arizona State University. Drab heeded the advice and headed south to study at the Walter Cronkite School of Journalism and Mass Communication.

During his time at ASU, Drab's future was nearly derailed. First, he partied and drank too much. Then he fell into a cult. What started as a church trip to impress a young woman became a lure into being baptized by a charismatic pastor who Drab began to follow blindly. Luckily, Drab managed to escape the gravitational pull of following the cult and got his career back on track.

First, he worked in promotions for KYOT, a smooth jazz station in Phoenix. Then, he landed on KZON, working as the midnight board op spinning music and occasionally jumping on the mic. As the weeks passed, Drab began to speak more on more on the air. At 23 years old, he was living the dream.

Just as he began to blossom, KZON switched to the Free FM hot talk format and changed its lineup. Drab's on-air shift was gone. Assigned to answer phones for "The Big O and Dukes Show," Drab resented the new hosts. Calling him out on the air, Chad Dukes lobbed the first bomb. "I'd rather kiss a blowfish than talk to that guy." Hell of a start.

Three days later, the producer working for Oscar and Chad was fired for allowing an inappropriate joke by comedian Greg Fitzsimmons to get aired. Drab would fill in and never look back. After bonding with Chad over the movie "Die Hard," the two became fast friends. Since Drab also worked at the World Market and constantly wore his gray t-shirt, Chad gave him the nickname that stuck for years... Drab T-Shirt.

Following Chad and Oscar to Washington, Drab steered the show admirably from nights on WJFK to the middays. When WJFK flipped to all-sports, Drab began to work with "LaVar and Dukes" while continuing to produce Chad and Oscar's new podcast. Now, just a few years later, Drab was vying to join our show.

Challenging our preparation during the interview caught our attention, but so did Drab's competence. He had worked alongside two distinct personalities and helped build their show into a success. He had experience working with the management at 106.7 The Fan, as well as sales and promotions. He was a hard worker who prepared meticulous notebooks full of material for his hosts and clearly wasn't afraid to confront us.

When the four of us discussed our options with C.K., the choice was pretty clear. As much as we loved Valdez, we asked Drab to join our team. Like a head coach bringing in a new offensive coordinator to call plays, Drab would bring a new voice and perspective to the show, but that didn't mean we couldn't call audibles.

★ ★ ★ ★

Having known Drab for years, it didn't take long for him to fit seamlessly in our group, screening calls and focusing on everything behind the scenes. Valdez was disappointed he didn't get the job, but he quickly gelled with Drab and ran the board. This was a solid team working the show.

CBS Radio was about to start digitally streaming their radio shows across the country. Chosen to be one of their first, we launched WatchTheJunkies.com. Eric Waddon, an avid Junkies listener since he was 12 years old, was hired for the new video producer position, arriving from West Virginia University with ample experience.

Almost immediately, the short, thin 24-year-old was surrounded by the wolves sitting at the console. First, we wondered why he was so quiet. But Eric had heard us ridiculing over-eager interns on the air, so he wasn't inclined to make an impression. Instead, he left us wondering if he cared about the show at all.

Baptizing him on the air, we grilled the noob about his ambivalent personality, receding hairline, and single dating status. He handled it without a flinch. Clearly, he knew the show, and his laid-back personality blended among our brashness. Still, he needed a nickname. Saying his friends called him "E," that wasn't going to fly with E.B., who claimed one of his uncles called him the same nickname. Instead, we dubbed Eric Waddon as E-Wadd. He didn't complain. He was just happy to be part of the family.

★ ★ ★ ★

When Drab took over as producer in July 2012, we knew he wasn't going to be a wallflower. Having listened to the show for five years, Drab noticed a shift in content. Maybe the station flipping to all-sports had changed us without knowing, but Drab was hearing less variety and too many segments about sports that dragged on far too long.

Urging us to mix things up more often with lifestyle stories and tales from our personal lives, Drab wanted a return to our roots. Each day the goal was to have a 50-50 split between sports and non-sports topics—keeping the talking points moving, avoiding monotony, and allowing the fun times to roll.

Drab also felt we needed a jolt of energy by reviving our bikini contest in the studio. These contests were not high-browed, and we knew they were silly. But our audience loved the spectacle and drama. So, instead of frenzied fans ogling the contestants on a stage, our audience could watch the debacle via our new live stream. After Drab secured $2,000 from our sponsors, our producers proposed a new idea. Instead of spreading the prize money among the top five contestants, why not hand out $1,500 to the winner and $500 to the runner-up? Everybody else would go home empty-handed.

Agreeing the new format would create excitement, there wasn't a shortage of contestants. By the time we held the contest, nine ladies were on board.

Not wanting a procession of boring interviews, Drab secured a Shake Weight, hula hoop, and trampoline as props. What better way to boost WatchTheJunkies.com than having attractive ladies hula-hooping in their tiny swimsuits? Not surprisingly, our new video stream reached new heights with hundreds logging on for the first time. First, we did our best play-by-play impersonations, describing the contestants' bikinis and curvy figures. Then, as they began to use the props, we got a glimpse of their personalities. One contestant showed off her kickboxing skills. Using E-Wadd as a prop, we were blown away as the high-heeled harlot came within inches of crushing his skull. We couldn't stop laughing.

Afterward, we invited the contestants back to our crowded studio. Pounding our console to create a drum roll, the ladies waited in anticipation, but we weren't ready to crown the winner. Instead, we announced the top three. Six ladies left the studio dejected. If our producers wanted us to feel uncomfortable, mission accomplished.

Doubling down, we asked the women to give us another drum roll. The three finalists included a statuesque blonde in a blue bikini, a perky Asian with a sexy tattoo in a metallic green bikini, and an African-American woman with ripped abs in an orange bikini. How could we pick a winner? Luckily, we wouldn't have to. Our judges had already given us their scores.

Announcing the top two, we witnessed heartbreak and disappointment again, followed by elation as we crowned the bikini bash champion moments later. The tweaks to the contest had created more intrigue. Drab and Valdez were right. We wanted to add drama and be entertaining. Accomplished.

★ ★ ★ ★

While we had injected more variety back into the show, the 2012 Washington Nationals were becoming a force. After six straight losing seasons, they were atop the National League East with 19-year-old rookie slugger Bryce Harper drawing more fans to the ballpark than any Nats player since they moved from Montreal.

With the playoffs in sight, one topic loomed largest: General manager Mike Rizzo had decided to shut down ace Stephen Strasburg before reaching 180 innings pitched. Strasburg had missed all but five starts during the 2011 season due to Tommy John surgery on his elbow. Rizzo's innings limit meant Strasburg would miss the playoffs.

Arguing about the decision incessantly, my partners agreed with Rizzo's conservative approach. I countered that when you have a chance to win a World Series, you adjust your plans. Like most of our arguments, nobody relented. So Drab booked former reliever and MLB Network analyst Mitch "Wild Thing" Williams on the show.

"I just think it's absolutely absurd," he started. "And I would not want to be Mike Rizzo in September when the Nationals are fighting to win that division and get to the postseason, and have to tell the 24 other guys on that roster 'and oh, by the way, we're gonna take a perfectly healthy Stephen Strasburg and shut him down.'"

Regardless of whether Mitch would be proven right or wrong, he was direct, opinionated, and provocative. Of course, we had expected nothing less.

★ ★ ★ ★

One year shy of 70 years old, Washington Nationals manager Davey Johnson had quickly become one of our favorite guests. Joining us every Wednesday, his charm rested in his storytelling and a keen ability to never take anything too seriously. He also was fascinating.

A rare baseball bird with a degree in mathematics, Davey was one of the first managers to use computer stats analysis. When he played for the Baltimore Orioles in the 1970s, Davey would hand old school manager Earl Weaver a printout to show he could be making a better lineup that would produce 50 extra runs a season.

Weaver would rip up the printouts and cuss Davey's condescension.

But Johnson was equally adept at talking about golf, fishing, or flying planes. He was also sharp at busting our balls and would occasionally weave in some of our lingo. It couldn't get better than hearing Davey Johnson use "monkey tilt" in a sentence.

A few weeks before the playoffs, in an effort to possibly deflect attention from his team's mid-September losing skid, Davey flipped the script and began questioning Cakes about his infamous two-day stint in a pine box. "Was it all right? I'm probably getting close to that time," Davey joked. Nice zing.

But Davey remained focused on winning the division. The Nationals maintained a 5½-game lead in the National League East. "I want to clinch our division. It's the only thing that's important to me," Davey asserted. Before we could sign off, even if we knew the answer, we had to ask him about Strasburg, and whether there was any possibility he would pitch in the postseason.

"That ain't happening," Davey snapped. "Don't even start it!"

How could we not?

After winning the NL East, the Nationals found themselves in Game 5 of the National League Division Series against the St. Louis Cardinals. With 45,966 fans at electric Nationals Park, the home team took an early 3-0 lead. The lead grew to six runs as Bryce Harper and Michael Morse homered in the third inning. The National League Championship Series was within reach.

Alas, baseball can be cruel. With a two-run lead in the top of the ninth inning and just three outs to go, manager Davey Johnson turned to his star 24-year-old closer, Drew Storen, who had notched 43 saves during the season. After Carlos Beltran led off the inning with a double, Storen retired the next two batters. The fireballer came within a strike of closing the game. *Twice.* Instead, he walked two hitters to load the bases.

Then, disaster struck. The Cardinals tied the game on a single and took a two-run lead heading into the bottom of the ninth. When the Nationals went down in order, everyone was shell-shocked.

Still, after waiting 33 years for baseball to return to the nation's capital, the Nationals had proven that baseball could flourish in Washington. As the Cardinals celebrated on the field, the crowd showed appreciation with a "Let's Go Nats!" chant. Baseball was alive and well in D.C.

With young stars like Bryce Harper, we hoped the Nats were primed for another playoff run in 2013. Still, we wondered: What if Stephen Strasburg had pitched in October, and what if the team never made it to a World Series? Would the Nationals regret the shutdown of Strasburg?

★ ★ ★ ★

The end of the football regular season always feels like an early-morning hangover. No matter the offseason drama, some of the show's juice evaporates once the season ends. Anticipating this lull, Drab concocted a bet in advance of the Redskins' playoff game against Seattle. Since E.B. is a huge Redskins homer and Drab is a diehard Seahawks fan, and Seattle is famous for its fish markets, the loser would be slapped on the ass by a fish.

Two days after watching the Redskins lose, E.B. dropped his pants in the studio. Those watching via WatchTheJunkies.com got the pleasure of seeing Drab mercilessly smack a rockfish to E.B.'s bare buns. Writhing in pain, E.B. had taken one for the team as we laughed hysterically. Maybe it was karma. Years earlier, Drab had been peppered with paint balls. Now the fish was on the other foot.

★ ★ ★ ★

Despite being passed over for the producer position a year earlier, Blue Shorts remained devoted to The Junkies as much as anyone. Whenever we needed him, Shorts was ready and willing to help at a moment's notice.

With adult entertainer Asa Akira set to join us the day after Valentine's Day, Drab turned to Shorts for two reasons: 1.) He knew Shorts would say yes, and 2.) Shorts had an affinity for Asian women.

Entering the studio after we interviewed Asa about her appearance at Fantasies Night Club in Baltimore that evening, Shorts was excited but nervous. Since Asa had experience as a dominatrix, Shorts would be her submissive.

Stripping down to blue Speedos, Shorts revealed a smiley face he had shaved onto his chest hair. Meanwhile, Asa began to undress. Wearing only a thong and tank top, the petite porn star prepped her paddle as Shorts bent over the console. "Dominate him. Smack him," E.B. urged. Seconds later, she began to spank away. "Aaah," Shorts screamed after the first few hits. Asa was just getting started.

Cakes implored Asa to hit Shorts harder. "Give it to him, like super hard," Cakes pleaded. Asa followed suit, though she began to feel guilty. "See, you're a terrible dominatrix," Cakes contended. "You should be yelling at him and making him feel like a flea." Vicious.

Before long, Shorts' pale butt had turned beet red. While we continued to laugh uncontrollably as Shorts shrieked louder and louder after each successive whack, Lurch wondered, "Guys actually like this?" We didn't know, but we were enjoying watching Shorts as he squirmed in pain. So were our viewers on WatchTheJunkies.com as our live stream exploded.

Upping the ante, Drab and Valdez brainstormed further humiliation for

Shorts, who soon was on all fours being walked like a dog with a collar around his neck. Asa began to command Shorts to sit and bark, so E.B. grabbed the paddle and battered Shorts. On the floor in the fetal position, Shorts stared at the sexy starlet and shouted, "I still get cised!"

As we began to ask Asa what it felt like to dominate Shorts, Valdez zinged, "Cakes, the breed of doggie, he's a Shorts Tzu." Continuing to have fun at his expense, Shorts proclaimed, "I'm a serious journalist," ironic after Asa had just called him a "good boy" for sitting on her command. "This is committing," Cakes declared. Bit season was in full swing.

★ ★ ★ ★

While Drab and Valdez pushed for a return to our juvenile roots on the radio, we began to embark on our most serious television venture to date.

Pitching a new concept, we reached an agreement with CSN Washington to carry our new show, "Table Manners," on Tuesdays at 11 p.m. The premise was simple. We would sit down with local athletes and celebrities and interview them as we shared a meal.

Under the direction of Lisa Edwards, an established director and producer who had worked for ESPN, CNBC, and ABC, we began to shoot two shows at a time from The Palm restaurant in Tysons Corner, Virginia. The number of cameras and equipment involved was beyond anything we had done since we shot our pilot with ESPN. Beyond that, we secured great guests, ranging from retired hockey star Jeremy Roenick to Michael Jordan's former agent, David Falk.

Holding a premiere party at the Arlington Cinema and Drafthouse, listeners and local celebrities walked the red carpet as Blue Shorts did his best Ryan Seacrest impersonation by asking them what designer they were wearing. After our colleague Danny Rouhier warmed up the crowd with his comedy act full of impressive impersonations, we jumped on stage to introduce our pilot episode.

Fortunately, the show didn't flop when we gave the crowd a sneak peek. Instead, the audience laughed throughout as Roenick weaved classic tales of hockey fights and partying with celebrities.

Over the next two years, we'd sit down with many of our sports heroes, such as Cal Ripken Jr., Maryland basketball coach Gary Williams, and Redskins legend John Riggins. We laughed hysterically as comedian Frank Caliendo took over the show and listened intently as O.A.R.'s lead singer, Marc Roberge, described his writing process.

Though "Table Manners" would never win an Emmy, much to E.B.'s dismay, it was a bona fide hit. And damn, we stuffed our faces during the filming.

★ ★ ★ ★

Faster than at any point during our careers, new forms of media were emerging. Vine's mobile app had become a hit in 2013 by allowing users to post short video clips to social media. Wanting to jump on the bandwagon, we turned to a familiar bit, slapping somebody. Volunteering to take one for the team, E-Wadd would slap me in the face and post the video to Vine.

As I stood up while E-Wadd positioned himself, Cakes said, "Oh, the backhand slap." Lurch wondered, "So you're going to do like Roger Federer and backhand him?"

Building the drama, E-Wadd warned, "If I light you up, do not get rick at me." Hey, I was in on the bit. It was for the greater good.

Turning away because he just wanted to hear the slap, Lurch jabbed, "Every listener is thinking, 'I wish I was E-Wadd.'"

With Drab holding the microphone inches from my face, Valdez barked out, "I'm going to count down one, two, three, then go ahead and do it." Cakes intervened, "How about you go three, two, one… donk? You don't do one, two, three, moron."

Seconds later, as I became increasingly nervous for the impending pain, Valdez began the countdown:

"Three…

"Two…

"One…"

SMACK!

"Oooooh!" E.B. screamed. E-Wadd had delivered what Cakes described as a hatchet job. Lurch, who only heard the force of the wallop, laughed hysterically.

Colleague Frank Hanrahan, who delivered sports updates and served as the play-by-play announcer for the Washington Mystics, said, "I was surprised by the force that E-Wadd laid on that cheek. Jesus." Clearly, E-Wadd didn't want to be labeled as soft.

"That was insane," E.B. added.

It didn't take long for my cheek and ear to turn bright red. There was no denying E-Wadd's strike had stung. Soon after, Valdez posted the video to Vine as we listened to the loud smack over and over. "We are such bottom feeders," Cakes declared.

Maybe, but thousands of other listeners were checking out The Junkies Vine, too.

26

RJESUS

"Hope is everything. Once you've lost that, you don't really have much." – Mya

While we watched Michael Jordan return to the NBA in a Wizards uniform and witnessed Alexander Ovechkin dazzle on the ice, there was nothing quite like the hype surrounding Robert Griffin III in 2012. The Heisman Trophy-winning quarterback from Baylor, known simply as RGIII, was drafted second overall after Washington shipped three first-round picks to the St. Louis Rams for the dual-threat quarterback. The future of the Redskins' franchise was resting almost entirely on his shoulders.

He immediately exceeded the hype. During his first pro game, RGIII led Washington to a 40-32 win against the New Orleans Saints while becoming the first player in NFL history to debut with at least 300 yards passing, two touchdowns, and no interceptions.

Beyond the numbers, his style and flair made him an instant superstar. After connecting with wide receiver Pierre Garcon for an 88-yard touchdown in his debut, RGIII raised his arms in the air to celebrate the score while planted on the ground from a hit. "Griffining" became an instant sensation with memes going viral.

For the season, RGIII had 20 touchdown passes with just five interceptions, earning rookie of the year honors. Orchestrating a read-option offense that was novel to the NFL, he also ran for 815 yards and seven touchdowns, including an electrifying 76-yarder against Minnesota in the fourth quarter of a 38-26 victory. Quarterbacks are not supposed to do the things Robert Griffin III was doing.

He was a true godsend to Redskins fans and our radio show. Apathy had set in when they missed the playoffs four straight seasons before RGIII's arrival, but he led them to the postseason as a rookie. Then, hyperbolic as usual, E.B. compared Griffin to Gandhi and called him "RJesus," suggesting the player could bring everybody together from all races, creeds, and political affiliations during a divisive time on Capitol Hill. Maybe that was a stretch, but our phone lines were constantly flooded by RGIII congregates.

Not everybody was on board. Maybe being a Colts fan blinded me, but I thought fellow rookie Andrew Luck was better. While Luck operated a more diverse passing offense and made more challenging throws into tighter windows, RGIII seemed to benefit from open receivers as defenses were terrified of his legs. The numbers supported my argument. RGIII's air yards were inferior, so I started calling him "RG Screen." E.B. didn't like the moniker. Neither did most of the diehard Redskins fans who deemed me a sinner and hater.

The 2012 season was an undeniable success on and off the field for RGIII until Week 14, when the Redskins hosted the Baltimore Ravens in early December. Behemoth defensive tackle Haloti Ngata hit him during a fourth-quarter scramble, twisting his spindly leg awkwardly. Though he would return to the game, RGIII missed the next week as fellow rookie Kirk Cousins led the Redskins to their fifth straight victory. When RGIII returned to lead Washington to wins against Philadelphia and Dallas, the entire DMV rejoiced as the Redskins won the NFC East and prepared for the playoffs.

There, they seized a 14-point lead over the Seattle Seahawks after RGIII tossed two first-quarter touchdowns. It appeared his magical rookie campaign was going to continue well into January. But that's when everything came crashing down. First, Seattle's Russell Wilson and Marshawn Lynch were too much for the Redskins' defense. Then, trailing 21-14 in the fourth quarter, RGIII appeared to tweak his leg while being sacked. On the very next play, he fumbled the snap as his leg crumbled. The Redskins' season was over, and RGIII had a torn ACL. Devastation ensued.

Questions lingered throughout the offseason. Should the organization have risked RGIII's future by playing him when he was obviously hurt? Should coach Mike Shanahan have protected the franchise player better? And, most importantly, would RGIII be able to come back and have the same impact? You couldn't buy better sports radio fodder.

By the time NFL preseason started in summer 2013, there was no question RGIII was going to attempt to play as soon as possible. Maybe too soon, many believed. His comeback had been documented by adidas, which mounted an "All in for Week 1" campaign. Taking advantage of the buzz, WJFK organized a bus trip full of listeners to attend training camp. Despite not participating in drills, RGIII remained the overwhelming crowd favorite. My daughter Kelsie was thrilled to get a picture and autograph with her favorite player as RGIII happily mingled among his adoring fans.

As much as he smiled off the field, a rift had developed between RGIII and Shanahan. Trying to protect the second-year quarterback, Shanahan sidelined him throughout the preseason. Responding passive-aggressively, RGIII wore an "Operation Patience" t-shirt during their preseason game with Pittsburgh, resulting in an NFL fine and kicking off what would become an extremely disappointing season.

To say RGIII was never the same after his knee injury would be an understatement. After finishing 10-6 and making the playoffs as a rookie, the Redskins crashed and burned with a pathetic 3-13 record. A clearly hobbled RGIII threw just 16 touchdowns in 13 starts. Unfathomably, the former track star didn't rush for a single score while being sacked 38 times with 12 interceptions and 11 fumbles. Fans began to jump off the RGIII bandwagon in droves and Shanahan was fired. That made for easy sports talk radio as we wondered what was next for RGIII and the team.

Heading into the 2014 season, many remained optimistic RGIII would return to his rookie form. Washington hired Cincinnati Bengals offensive coordinator Jay Gruden as its new head coach. With a reputation as an offensive guru and quarterback whisperer, diehard Redskin fans like E.B. held hope RGIII could be fixed.

Ten weeks into the season, he was still broken. With the Redskins off to a 3-7 start, we started "bit season" early by burying RGIII's career. It was almost hard to imagine we had given up on the guy who captured the imagination of every Redskins fan in 2012.

Listeners immediately jumped on the proverbial pile with one fan offering his homemade coffin, which he had built for Halloween. The idea grew quickly with Dan Steinberg from the *Washington Post* noting how E.B. had been RGIII's biggest supporter just two years earlier, calling him "bust-proof."

Our proposed burial was not without objection. Some listeners thought it was in poor taste, while others thought it was premature. We forged ahead anyway. Listeners were invited to throw memorabilia and gear into the coffin before the ceremonial hammering of the nails.

As we symbolically buried the former superstar's career with listeners gleefully joining the fun, the quarterback controversy was well underway with Kirk Cousins, a fourth-round draft pick from Michigan State the same year Griffin was selected. E.B. left room for an RGIII comeback by explaining, "Maybe at the end of the year we say he's resurrected, his career is back, and he's going to be that franchise quarterback we all thought."

The RGIII-Cousins controversy reminded fans, listeners, and media of Gus Frerotte vs. Heath Shuler in the mid-90s, Doug Williams vs. Jay Schroeder in the late '80s, Sonny vs. Billy in the early '70s, and any number of other Redskins quarterback quandaries since Frankie Filchock vs. Sammy Baugh in the early '40s. The Redskins were founders of the quarterback controversy, but Cousins vs. RGIII also fell along racial lines, playing out on Washington talk radio like Williams vs. Schroeder.

The White/Black population around the DMV was almost even at 42-43 percent. So, the "burial" of RGIII's career may have appeared racial and mean-spirited to some. That truly was not our intent. It never crossed our minds, even though it should have. We had been doing stupid bits like this since our BCTV days when we chastised Shuler with a Christmas carol parody. The coffin bit was just another way for us to have fun.

But, truthfully, we didn't know if RGIII's career was over. He still had a chance to change the script. The Redskins would play the 49ers in San Francisco in just two days, and he could prove us wrong. Instead, he threw for an anemic 106 yards and didn't change the narrative one bit. The Redskins were in the middle of a six-game losing streak. It had become evident he wasn't going to develop into the franchise quarterback most everybody envisioned. E.B. had finally seen the light and reached his boiling point.

With countless fans excusing RGIII's poor play on an inept offensive line, E.B. stood up and erupted, "Robert doesn't even throw downfield, and he gets sacked all the time!" Comparing sack rates to Cousins and Colt McCoy, who had also seen action during the season, E.B. continued to rant. "Robert only throws sideways and gets sacked every other play. It doesn't even make intuitive sense!"

As E.B. became more and more animated, Cakes and I began to chuckle. We knew our friend was about to go on a ranting binge. While Cakes reached over to the replay machine for the "It Does Not Make Sense" sound drop, E.B.'s eyes bulged as he began to scream, "It makes no sense! It makes zero sense—other than he *suuuuuuuuuuucks*! He *suuuuuuuucks*, people!"

Finally, sitting down as Cakes and I couldn't stop laughing, E.B. added, "That's the only conclusion that a reasonable person can come up with." Then, with veins popping out from his neck, E.B. shouted deafeningly once again, "He *suuuuuuuuuuucks*!"

We fed him more stats to back his case, and E.B. exploded once again. "He's scared to throw it downfield. He's a tough guy physically. Mentally, he's shot!"

It was harsh, but he wasn't wrong. After a momentary pause, E.B., who once believed RGIII was destined for the Hall of Fame, began shrieking even louder, "He's scared to get hit! Everybody knows that! He's scared to throw a pick. *Everybody knows it! Everybody knows it!*"

Cakes and I were dying from laughter. As E.B. gathered himself for a split second, Cakes chimed in, "This is the meltdown we've all been waiting for." Finally, E.B. had seen the light, wondering how the rapid decline of Robert Griffin III was genuinely possible. What started so promising had become the latest Redskins quarterback tragedy.

Heading into the 2015 season, RGIII famously said, "I feel like I'm the best quarterback in the league." A few weeks later, he was benched. Cousins, drafted 100 picks behind RGIII, was named the regular season starter. Jay Gruden called the Redskins "Kirk's team."

As it turned out, Gruden made the right call. Cousins finished the season with 29 touchdowns and just 11 interceptions while leading Washington back to the playoffs. Even though they lost to the Green Bay Packers in the wild-card round, hope was restored.

That season had been a gift for sports radio. From a quarterback controversy to a surprising playoff run, the Redskins delivered one of the most compelling seasons in recent years. That continued in the offseason when RGIII was released. He wasn't the savior of the franchise. Not even close.

27

SKITS AND BITS

"At the end of the day, if I can say I had fun, it was a good day."
– Simone Biles

While we marched toward two decades on the radio, the media landscape continued to shift. After XM and Sirius merged in 2008, satellite radio grew exponentially. With big names like Howard Stern enticing more people to pay for radio and Sirius XM partnering with automakers to be in nearly every new car, there were over 25 million subscribers.

The popularity of podcasts was booming, too. Personalities such as Adam Corolla were now garnering hundreds of thousands of listeners per episode. Comedian and Ultimate Fighting Championship mouthpiece Joe Rogan had millions of fans, and Barstool Sports was rapidly expanding as a digital sports media outlet.

The lure of hosting a more raw and unfiltered show was appealing, but we weren't willing to gamble with our careers. We were all married with children. Signing contracts with CBS Radio meant guaranteed money and hopefully more ratings bonuses.

In the fall of 2014, agent Bob Eatman began negotiating our new contract. This time we asked Eatman to ensure the right to add an uncensored podcast if we decided to do so. For years, CBS Radio had been podcasting our show successfully. Throughout its more than 200 radio affiliates in the country, we consistently finished atop our company's podcast charts with hundreds of thousands of downloads each month. Unreasonably, we didn't receive a penny.

Moving forward, we knew we weren't going to be paid above what we were contractually obligated to do from 6-10 a.m., but if we wanted to start a separate podcast, we wanted that property monetized.

Lurch dipped into the podcast world with "Big, Fat Winners," which he launched with childhood friend Scott Torregrosa, aka Skippy, and Matt Valdez. Since gambling had been in Lurch's veins for decades, hosting a podcast where he made picks made perfect sense, even if he wasn't getting paid.

Occasionally Lurch's side venture would spill into "The Sports Junkies." Since Skippy made us laugh, he became a regular, mixing in the sordid details of his love life with his picks. Though we didn't know if he had actually worn his wife's underwear to a doctor's appointment when he ran out of clean boxers, it was hilarious hearing him weave such tales.

Nobody took the "Big, Fat Winners" podcast too seriously. Lurch's passion project was just a way for him to have fun with his pals. That said, his frustrations were mounting. While Valdez was crushing the bookie with a sizzling 20-9 start to the 2014 season, Lurch whiffed on four of five picks and dropped to 8-22. Embarrassed that he couldn't pick a winner to save his life, he began to bet against his instincts.

"I don't care about the record. I faded myself this week," he claimed.

Had Lurch pulled a George Constanza and done the opposite of what he would normally do? We found it hard to believe. "Listen. I'm up 1,364 real dollars," Lurch said. "I'm going to collect $900, and I'm going to roll $464, and I'm going to fade myself."

Warning Lurch that his new strategy was unsustainable, E.B. ignited our sidekick. The obsessive gambler began to shout passionately, "I've got no luck. I lost two games by half a point. And the other quarterback doesn't play and I thought he was gonna play!"

We started laughing. Lurch's bad beat stories always made for loud radio.

"LSU's up 13-10, the kicker kicks it out of bounds!" he screamed. "Fifty seconds left! Unbelievable." Now standing and pounding the console, Lurch fumed, "Goddamn! I can't win a game!" Finding a silver lining, E.B. reminded Lurch his bank account had swelled. Lurch didn't care. He roared louder than ever, "I want to win on the podcast!"

Our partner's frustration left us bellowing in laughter. Before E.B. could ask him if he'd trade his financial gain for wins on his side project, Lurch ranted again. "UTEP's winning the entire game against Western Kentucky. *The entire game!* Two backdoor scores. Unbelievable.

"I can't control the incompetence of these kids," he preached, "College kickers SUCK! ALL OF 'EM! Every single college kicker, including your dumbass kid over at Maryland. He sucks, too! They all suck. They should take kickers out of college football. Take 'em out! Make 'em go for two, I don't care! I hate 'em all."

As Lurch began to calm, Cakes reminded, "You knew this was simmering over the last few weeks. You knew that was happening." Then, standing up once again, Lurch bellowed, "I know too much about college football to be 9-23!"

★ ★ ★ ★

Four more years. Bob Eatman had worked his magic as we signed a new deal, effective January 1, 2015, to keep us with CBS Radio through 2018. Though we still hadn't reached the salary heights before our six-figure haircut in summer 2009, we were endorsing more products and cashing more bonuses.

Since CBS Radio wasn't willing to give us a big raise, our shrewd agent negotiated other ways to make money, including a $10,000 bump in our bonus structure. If we were able to finish in first place in morning drive, something we still hadn't achieved, we'd net $25,000 apiece. And if we decided to move forward with a podcast, we would split the profits 50-50 with CBS Radio.

Feeling like it was a long shot with all-news WTOP entrenched at No. 1, Lurch promised to hold a house party for our listeners if we finished atop one of the quarterly books. Teasing him on the air, we wondered how the neat freak might handle the chaos and mess if he had to host our rowdy fans. The reality wasn't a stretch. We had finished second twice in just the past year.

But the Washington sports teams were not helping us and the fanbase seemed more ambivalent and dispassionate. It was not a great recipe for sports talk, even though there was plenty to complain about. Given our cynical nature, we wallowed in the complaining and forged ahead.

No matter how much media evolved, one constant remained in radio: If you worked behind the scenes, you were probably underpaid. We handed out bonuses to our producers during the holidays, but we couldn't keep some from moving to more prosperous positions. As much as video producer E-Wadd loved working with us, his salary was so anemic that he had a second job to survive. Eventually, he left us for the Discovery Channel, where he would make more money and receive benefits. Who could blame him?

Losing E-Wadd wasn't easy. His laid-back personality had grown on us as he was yet another crash test dummy in a long line of loyalists willing to do almost anything for The Junkies. From embarrassing himself with drunken messages to exposing his rap alter ego "Blizz," E-Wadd took it on the chin regularly for the show's good.

His most memorable moment began as an innocent claim during a commercial break. Joking with Drab and Valdez after a second intruder had scaled the White House fence, garnering national headlines in the fall of 2014, E-Wadd maintained that he'd follow suit by wearing a WatchTheJunkies.com t-shirt. Overhearing the conversation, Cakes immediately brought it to the air. Not backing down, E-Wadd asserted that it would be great for ratings. None of us took him seriously.

The Secret Service did, however. At 11:30 that night, during "Monday Night Football," E-Wadd received a surprising call from his father. The Secret Service was at his house. An hour later, two men in tactical vests were in Arlington, where E-Wadd shared an apartment with two roommates, to ask questions. Explaining it was an on-air bit, the Secret Service officers understood, but they still had to do their diligence.

The next morning we couldn't believe it. We knew E-Wadd wasn't going to jump the White House fence. We knew he wasn't that stupid. Maybe.

★ ★ ★ ★

The video producer position to run WatchTheJunkies.com was a part-time job that paid just $13 per hour with no benefits. Still, there wasn't a shortage of applicants. In the end, C.K. hired Adam Epstein, a recent graduate from Virginia Commonwealth University who had interned at 106.7 The Fan a few years earlier.

The 22-year-old baby-faced strawberry blonde who studied communications in college was a D.C. sports fanatic. Adam listened to "LaVar and Dukes" religiously during his rides home from South County Secondary School to his house in Burke, Virginia. Now he was working on his favorite radio station about to get baptized by The Junkies.

The line of questioning was familiar. Adam was fresh meat. E.B. wanted to know about his luck with the ladies. No matter what he claimed, we had our doubts. He dressed like a slob and sported a Washington Wizards velcro wallet. There was no chance he was a player.

Regardless, Adam asserted himself on the air. Loud, bold, and brash, he touted everything from his video editing skills to his prowess on the basketball court. Letting us know his "broskis" called him "A-Eps," we had to put him in his place. We weren't his broskis. We'd dub him A-Wadd, son of E-Wadd.

★ ★ ★ ★

Basketball challenges weren't new to The Junkies. I had battled with Bret in the parking lot in Fairfax years earlier during the nighttime show. Cakes had played Chad Dukes in a grudge match, too. But this live on-the-air hoops challenge in June 2016 loomed large as any.

Now 45-years-old, Cakes would square off against the upstart, A-Wadd, who had been caught lying about his basketball resume. Making it seem like he had played for his high school team, we uncovered the truth. A-Wadd had only played summer league.

With Pete Medhurst, who offered sports updates on 106.7 The Fan, in uniform as our referee, a smattering of fans surrounded our make-shift court on the concrete in front of our parking garage entrance.

When the action began, it was apparent this would be ugly. The two combatants missed the first five shots of the game. While A-Wadd showed a quickness advantage— after all, he was 20 years younger than Cakes—he appeared winded almost immediately. Cakes's limited offensive arsenal consisted of repeated attempts to back down A-Wadd before unleashing his (*cough*) deadly (*cough*) jump hook.

After Cakes scored the first point of the game, E.B., who had bet $20 on A-Wadd, declared, "Cakes is going to win this. I can't believe I bet on that loser." Right away, Cakes drove to the basket and shot the ball *over the backboard*. Airball! "That almost ended on South Capitol Street," E.B. joked. It was going to be a long game.

But A-Wadd was making a run, seizing a 5-1 lead. "He can't stop A-Wadd. He's got too much size. He's dominating him on the boards," E.B. announced. Lurch was distraught. He had bet on Cakes. "I'm so bitter. It's going to be 11-1," Lurch predicted.

The forecast was premature. Thanks to his jump hooks, Cakes tied the game at 5 while A-Wadd gasped for air. "Don't give up any more points," E.B. shouted at A-Wadd. After a few more misfires, the score was knotted at 6-6 as we broke for commercials.

The break served A-Wadd well as he stormed to a 10-6 lead. Needing just one more point to claim victory, he pleaded for the crowd to cheer him. They booed instead.

Then A-Wadd left us dumbfounded. Hunched over while dribbling, he began to spit up on the court. "He's throwing up!" E.B. yelled. The crowd howled. Some even yelled "forfeit." That wasn't happening.

Allowing A-Wadd a cup of water, Cakes couldn't stop the inevitable. Moments later, he'd succumb to the younger man: A-Wadd 11, Cakes 7. Though he was victorious, A-Wadd had lost his dignity as he lost his lunch. Unbelievable.

★ ★ ★ ★

Two weeks later, on July 8, 2016, it was my turn in the spotlight as my boys were betting on whether I would puke during a beer mile run. Operating as the show bookie, Lurch declared, "The latest line on J.P. puking is minus 120." In just a few minutes, I would attempt to run alongside beer mile world record-holder Lewis Kent, who had run a mile while drinking four beers in an astounding 4 minutes 47 seconds.

Years earlier, in spring 2009, Chris Farley, owner of several Pacers running stories in D.C. and Virginia, was listening to "The Sports Junkies" when he heard me say running a marathon was on my bucket list. Soon afterward, he sent free shoes and set me on a path to run my first marathon. The store's website chronicled my training with a YouTube web series called "The Marathon Junkie." After I completed the Marine Corps Marathon that fall, Farley brainwashed Cakes to follow suit the following year.

Now we were all fast friends. So when I heard Pacers was holding its first beer mile to promote a new store location at the Navy Yard, just blocks from our D.C. studios, I had a crazy idea: What if I raced Lewis Kent on the show? Chris was all-in. So was his celebrity runner.

Arriving at the radio station at 7 a.m. with a case of Budweiser and his official measuring wheel, Farley prepared a course just outside our studio. An oversized digital clock was positioned underneath our windows while three cameras would chronicle every step of the way for WatchTheJunkies.com.

With Valdez playing "I Ran" by A Flock of Seagulls coming out of the commercial break, I stood near the starting line next to Kent, ready to give the beer mile a go. Looking down from his perch in our studio, Lurch jabbed, "J.P., I just noticed something about body types. Lewis Kent probably has about 1.8 percent body fat. You don't."

Chuckling, Cakes offered his two cents. "You can look down and see Lewis is wearing all the latest, greatest Brooks gear. He's got the running tank top. And J.P. looks like he is going to play pickup with A-Wadd." Cakes wasn't lying.

Before we began, the boys placed their wagers. "I'm going to say he will not puke before 10 a.m.," Lurch offered. Cakes disagreed. Farley guessed that it was a 50/50 proposition. After Farley explained the rules—we had to drink a beer before each quarter-mile—he made the official announcement to start the race: "Runners set. Chug!"

In just six seconds, Lewis Kent finished his first beer and was off running like a gazelle. Amazed, I grabbed the microphone, saying, "That's unbelievable." Then, after downing my first beer in 20 seconds, I started my run. "Oh, he looks hurting," Valdez ragged. "Cakes, your money might be so safe right now."

Two minutes in, Kent was pounding his second beer while I continued to jog slowly. "If you're driving down South Capitol, make sure to honk at him. He's the one that looks like a North Carolina walk-on," Valdez zinged.

Completing my first quarter-mile, I attacked my second beer at the three-minute mark. "He is struggling," Lurch keenly observed. I was. But I finished, nonetheless.

"Second beer is doneski for J.P. He's off. 3:33," Lurch described, offering his play-by-play. Chris Farley added, "I'm impressed. J.P. is hanging in there."

Lurch agreed. "Well, he's competitive." Two beers down, I still had a long way to go.

Just after the four-minute mark, Kent crushed his third beer. He wasn't even trying. When he set the world record, Lewis ran the mile in 4:18 while finishing his four beers in just 29 seconds.

"He is a freaking machine," Cakes stated.

"So Lewis Kent is like the LeBron James of this event," Lurch posited.

"And who's J.P.? What's the comp there?" Cakes asked mockingly.

"He's like a D-League player," Lurch joked.

At the 6:14 mark, I started to drink my third beer while Kent chugged his last. "Props to J.P. for doing this because he's going to feel like butt all day," Lurch offered. True, but the question was, would I finish?

"Oh, I just saw J.P. pat his stomach," Cakes said excitedly, "And he had a look of disgust on his face. Puking could be imminent."

Nevertheless, I finished my third beer and began to run the second half of the beer mile. Seconds later, Lewis Kent crossed the finish line in what Farley described as a "pedestrian time for him of 7 minutes 31 seconds."

As I finished another lap, Kent cheered me on, "Let's go, J.P." Then he casually grabbed the phone and filled in the boys on the air about his run. "I'm feeling pretty good. That was a nice little loop there." He couldn't have sounded more casual.

My stomach was full and I was laboring. I couldn't imagine putting away another 12 ounces. "This is the telling beer," Cakes opined. "Beer number four." As I began to guzzle, Cakes continued, "He grabbed that Budweiser like it was a can of rat poison."

Nine minutes 45 seconds had passed, and all I had to do was finish one more beer and one more lap. "Puke," Cakes shouted, "I need him to puke to win the bet." Patting my stomach and burping, I hunched over momentarily. Jumping out of his seat, Cakes thought I was on the verge of vomiting. Gathering myself, I lifted the can and poured the rest of the beer down my gullet. With the finish line in sight, I began to sprint.

While Cakes pleaded for me to puke, I continued to run faster than I had the entire race. Lurch called me a drunk Forrest Gump as I crossed the finish line in just under 12 minutes. "That is awesome," Lurch said, recognizing the accomplishment. "He beat 12 minutes. I didn't think he had a prayer doing it."

Though I finished the beer mile, I didn't jump for joy. Lurch was right. I felt like butt. Still, it was a good bit and proved a Junkies axiom once again. Always bet against Cakes.

★ ★ ★ ★

In September 2016, the show would be simulcast on Comcast SportsNet, home of the Redskins, Ravens, Wizards, and Capitals. Our content would remain unchanged, but our reach would grow with CSN in more than 4.5 million homes across the District, Maryland, and Virginia. Though they were hardly paying us, it wasn't like we were doing extra work.

For the next year, we saw our ratings increase steadily. Still, we hadn't crossed the mornings threshold and finished in first place yet. We wondered if we might finally hit No. 1 when the 2017 Summer ratings book would be released.

Sadly, before we would find out, our agent Bob Eatman passed away at the age of 65 after battling cancer. We were heartbroken. Bob had done so much for us.

Fifteen years earlier, he took us under his wings while we were on the verge of losing our national syndication deal. Miraculously, he negotiated a raise for us even though we lost 50 radio affiliates across the country.

A few months later, Bob helped us move from the nighttime slot on WJFK to morning drive on WHFS. Our salaries climbed even higher. Though many wondered if we could succeed in the highly competitive morning drive slot, Bob never had a doubt. He always believed in us.

Thanks to Bob, we were given the opportunity to replace Howard Stern in the mornings on 106.7 FM and prove that we had staying power. Though we had never climbed to the top of the ratings, we were knock-knock-knocking on the door.

Just a few days after Bob died, C.K. sent his monthly ratings email. He started, "The headline goes to the Sports Junkies, who finished #1 Men 25-54 for the month of September and the entire Summer book. This is a milestone achievement for The Junkies, and J.P., Eric, John, and Jason should be congratulated, along with their dedicated team of producers, Matt Cahill, Matt Myers, and Adam Epstein."

Notching a 10.4 in our target demographic, we had finally dethroned WTOP, which finished with a 9.8. This was a huge accomplishment. The question was, would Lurch host a ratings party at his house with our loyal listeners? We didn't have to ask. We knew the answer. There was no chance.

Though the feat was rewarding, so was our first-place bonus. Bob Eatman had negotiated a $25,000 windfall for each of us if we ever hit No. 1. Bob had helped guide us through the ups and downs of our radio career, giving us credibility and stability in a tumultuous industry. We would miss him dearly and remain forever grateful for his guidance and belief in our talents. We knew he was proud of what we had finally accomplished.

28

EVERYBODY LOVES A PARADE

"The critics are always right. The only way you shut them up is by winning." — *Chuck Noll*

For years, we marveled at the fantasy of hosting a sports talk radio show in Boston. The Red Sox had broken the curse of the Bambino in 2004 to win their first World Series since 1918. They won again in 2007 and 2013. The Celtics took the NBA title in 2008 while the Bruins lifted Lord Stanley's Cup in 2011.

Then, there were the greedy Patriots. With coach Bill Belichick and Tom Brady forming a perfect union, New England reached the Super Bowl eight times and captured five Lombardi Trophies in 17 years.

Around the Beltway, we couldn't relate.

In 2016, *USA Today* did a comprehensive look at sports cities and listed Washington as the sixth-worst behind Buffalo, San Diego, Atlanta, Cincinnati, and Minneapolis-St. Paul. The criteria were based on winning seasons, playoff appearances, championship berths, and championships for pro football, baseball, hockey, and basketball since 2000.

The Redskins' three Super Bowl championships from 1983-'92 were a distant memory. And before the Expos moved from Montreal to Washington in 2005, the Capitals and Wizards kept us humbled. One was constantly choking in the postseason, and the other was never really a championship contender. When their seasons predictably ended, we turned our attention to dissecting the Redskins' offseason, when fans still had hope.

And then, something magical happened. Within 16 months between 2018-'19, there were two Washington championships and two victory parades through the streets of the nation's capital.

The Caps and Nationals brought us seasons and playoffs we'll never forget. Given the history of our sports teams, no one is taking them for granted. In Washington, we were stuck covering a perennially disappointing football team. Finishing 7-9 during the 2017 regular season, the Redskins missed the playoffs for the 14th time in Dan Snyder's 19 seasons as owner.

But the Capitals were a different animal. Led by three-time most valuable player Alex Ovechkin, they had a legitimate chance to win the Stanley Cup most every season. During coach Barry Trotz's first three years as coach, starting in 2014, they twice received the Presidents' Trophy for best record in the NHL and won their division three times. Sadly, they never made it past the second round of the playoffs. Ovechkin's Hall of Fame career was withering away—until spring 2018.

Simultaneously, the Nats were breaking hearts every October. Hosting the Cubs in the deciding game of the 2017 National League Division Series, manager Dusty Baker turned to Cy Young Award winner Max Scherzer in the bottom of the fifth inning with the Nationals leading by a run. With their ace coming out of the bullpen, what could possibly go wrong? How about an intentional walk, passed-ball strikeout, catcher's interference, and hit-by-pitch in one interminable inning. Losing 9-8, the Nationals were eliminated from the playoffs far too early for the fourth time in six seasons.

That would change in 2019, but in the meantime, Washington sports fans were reminded again that Prilosec doesn't alleviate heartbreak.

★ ★ ★ ★

During Game 2 of their 2018 opening-round playoff series against Columbus, the Washington Capitals fired 58 shots at Russian goaltender Sergie Bobrovsky. Incredibly, the two-time Vezina Trophy winner saved 54 of them as the Blue Jackets beat the Capitals 5-4 in overtime at Capital One Arena. Trailing the series 2-0 with the next two games on the road, the Capitals seemed primed for another playoff failure.

Starting our show the next morning, Monday, April 16, 2018, with a question, I asked my partners and our listeners, "Do you hold out any hope for the Washington Capitals to get back in the series?" Logically speaking, it wasn't over. The first two games were decided in overtime with Philipp Grubauer starting between the pipes. In Game 2, Coach Barry Trotz inserted veteran Braden Holtby during the third period. Maybe he could be the difference?

"It's not over yet," Lurch said sarcastically. "It's an 87 percent chance over."

Piling on, E.B. pointed out Lurch's statistic didn't consider Washington had lost its first two games at home: "It's gotta be worse [losing] at home."

Frustrated, we began to talk about the future. If the Caps lost in the first round again, should they fire the coach? Even though we loved Barry Trotz—he joined us regularly throughout the season—it was a fair question. E.B. conceded, "I would try and roll the dice with another coach. That would be the one concession I would make."

Exasperated, Cakes, the most ardent Caps fan among us, having attended countless games with his dad as a kid, blurted, "I'm on record. I'm fine with changing anything and everything. The players. The coaches. The front office."

Years of demoralizing playoff losses had taken a toll on Cakes. "It's exhausting being a Caps fan," he added. "I had to throw a third beer in for overtime. Crushed that. And then they crushed my soul.

"You know what the Caps are?" he asked. "They're a floater in the Potomac. That's what the Caps are right now. A bloated floater."

Down two games with their next two on the road, how could anyone disagree? Deep down, we hoped Cakes was wrong. Remember, always bet against Cakes.

★ ★ ★ ★

Steve Jobs, the co-founder of Apple, once said, "I don't really care about being right. I care about success." Though that was true to a degree on "The Sports Junkies," we always wanted to be right.

Cakes couldn't have been happier to be wrong this time. The Capitals weren't dead. With Game 3 tied at two, Blue Jackets winger Artemi Panarin fired a slap shot that would have given Columbus a 3-2 lead with 1:15 left in the game, all but burying the Caps. Instead, the puck went off the goal post, sending the teams to their third straight overtime.

Nine minutes into the nerve-wracking second extra period, Blue Jackets defenseman Zach Werenski tried to clear a puck in front of the goal. Instead, it caromed off Caps center Lars Eller and then back off Werenski before crossing the goal line. Washington had its first win in the series. After the game, Trotz said, "We're fortunate the puck went in for us. We got a bounce."

For once, puck luck was on the Caps' side.

The next morning, our phone lines exploded. Caps fans pounced on us for giving up on the home team prematurely. That was okay. They were engaged. Now that hope was restored, we knew they would be listening.

After winning Game 3 dramatically, the Caps won the next three games and advanced to the second round. Goalie Braden Holtby proved to be the difference-maker, but Caps fans remained nervous. A familiar foe, the two-time defending Stanley Cup champion Pittsburgh Penguins, awaited them.

Dating to 1995, the Penguins had eliminated the Capitals from the playoffs in seven straight matchups, including the previous two seasons. Two-time most valuable player Sydney Crosby and running mate Evgeni Malkin owned the Caps in the postseason. When Capitals winger Tom Wilson was suspended for three games for an illegal check to the head that broke the jaw of Penguins forward Zach Aston-Reese, we wondered if they could overcome the loss of their chief enforcer. They did. Dramatically.

In Game 6, yet another overtime, Caps center Evgeny Kuznetsov beat Penguins goalie Matt Murray to give Washington the 2-1 win, eliminating

Pittsburgh. The Capitals advanced to the conference finals for the first time since 1998, when they reached the Stanley Cup finals, being swept by the Detroit Red Wings in four games.

Finally getting over the hump by defeating their dreaded rival, Caps fans were brimming with confidence. The Eastern Conference finals were no pushover. Once again, Washington found itself in a Game 7. Delivering a masterpiece, Holtby and the Capitals shut out the Tampa Bay Lightning, 4-0. For the first time in 20 years, one of Washington's four major sports teams competed for a championship.

With the Capitals in the Stanley Cup final, casual fans jumped on the bandwagon more than ever. We reveled in taking phone calls from the uninitiated who couldn't pronounce Alex Ovechkin's name. That didn't stop them from pulling for the home team. Everybody loves a winner, including "The Sports Junkies."

Though Cakes was the only diehard fan among us who watched the Capitals religiously, there was nothing like playoff hockey. For six weeks, all of us were glued to these games. The edge-of-your-seat tension was like nothing else in sports and left us emotionally drained. Beyond that, we were more sleep-deprived than ever.

For Game 1 in Las Vegas, more than 11,000 fans rocked the red inside Washington's Capital One Arena for a watch party. Unfortunately, they'd witness a 6-4 loss. Far from discouraged, even more fans showed up for Game 2. When Alex Ovechkin ripped a shot past Golden Knights goaltender Marc-Andre Fleury to give Washington the lead, the arena erupted. So did every Caps fan watching from home.

Holding on to a 3-2 lead with two minutes to play, Vegas forward Alex Tuch fired a shot toward a half-empty net. Capitals goalie Braden Holtby threw his stick across the crease and miraculously stopped the puck. The play would become known as "The Save." The series was tied 1-1, and the Capitals were just three wins away from being crowned Stanley Cup champions.

Somehow, this Caps season felt different. Fervor for the home team reached new levels as Game 3 approached. While Capital One Arena was sold out, the streets outside the arena were lined with fans watching on a big screen. They wouldn't go home disappointed as the Capitals won again. The crowd grew even larger for Game 4, when Las Vegas was overwhelmed, 6-2. One more win and Washington's championship drought would be over.

The scene outside Capital One Arena on Thursday, June 7, 2018, was unlike anything we had witnessed. With Game 5 back in Las Vegas, Capitals owner Ted Leonsis had pulled out all the stops. The watch party inside the arena was sold out, but now there were thousands of fans packing 8th and G streets to watch the giant board above the McDonalds. There was music, chants, and fans desperate to see the Capitals deliver a championship to the nation's capital for the first time since 1992.

In a back-and-forth contest, Washington trailed 3-2 entering the third period. Then Devante Smith-Pelly, who scored just seven goals during the regular season, found the back of the net midway through the third period to tie the game. The unlikely star had scored seven goals during this playoff run.

Three minutes later, Lars Eller gave the Capitals the 4-3 lead. Washington was minutes from the Stanley Cup. When the clock expired, the celebration began. Fans danced on the streets, jumping for joy. Many cried as they watched MVP Alex Ovechkin hoist the Stanley Cup. This team proved that they weren't the "same old Caps."

Incredibly, five days later, on Tuesday, June 12, 2018, The Junkies found ourselves lined up behind a bus full of players. Though we felt sheepish about being invited to be part of the championship parade, we weren't going to say no. Instead, we were reveling in history.

Sitting atop red convertibles, we didn't know how we would be received. Thousands had lined the streets of D.C. to celebrate. As we made our way through the parade route, we were pleasantly surprised that thousands of fans cheered for us, too. I couldn't believe that so many rabid Caps fans were chanting our names.

"E.B.!" they would scream.

"Lurch, I love you," I would hear.

"Cakes!" they shouted.

"J.P.!" It didn't stop for the better part of an hour.

During a live radio hit on the "Grant and Danny" show, Lurch described the incredible scene on the parade route. He mentioned that his latest man-crush, forward Jacob Vrana, was on the double-decker bus directly in front of us. Grant Paulsen and Danny Rouhier urged Lurch to get Vrana on the air.

Jumping out of the convertible, Lurch yelled at the young star and tossed his cell phone to the top deck of the bus. Little did Vrana know that he'd be joining our colleagues for a live chat. Luckily, Vrana didn't fumble the phone—or interview.

The entire experience was unforgettable. The four of us hadn't done anything to deserve being there. We hadn't scored one goal or made a single save. Still, there we were, right in the middle of the action on the historic day the Capitals and their go-crazy fans celebrated winning a championship. Amazing.

★ ★ ★ ★

In 2018, the Washington Nationals missed the playoffs for the first time in three seasons. Davey Martinez's first season as manager—having replaced Dusty Baker—proved to be a bust. Things got worse in the offseason when superstar slugger Bryce Harper left via free agency for a division rival, the Philadelphia Phillies. We questioned whether the organization had made the right moves.

Fifty games into the 2019 season, the Nats were off to a disheartening 19-31 start and trailed the Phillies by 10 games in the NL East. We couldn't help but be pessimistic. Callers questioned Martinez's leadership constantly. Though Baker was criticized for poor lineup construction and decision-making, at least the Nationals made the playoffs during his two seasons in charge.

Joining "The Sports Junkies" weekly during the season, the Nationals president of baseball operations and general manager Mike Rizzo reminded us the season was far from over. Maintaining complete confidence in his manager, Rizzo wasn't buying into the criticism. Then again, what else was he going to say?

As it turned out, Rizzo was right. It was a long season, and after the anemic start, the Nationals started playing better baseball. Maybe it began with what seemed to be an inconsequential addition to the roster. Venezuelan outfielder Gerardo Parra wasn't a starter, but his clubhouse presence spiced things up.

On June 19, Parra changed his walk-up song to "Baby Shark," hoping to break out of a slump. But, when he homered, he decided to keep the song. By October, Pinkfong's popular children's tune had become the team's anthem, with fans snapping their arms like shark fins during games and players snapping their fingers after big hits.

Remarkably, the Nationals managed to make the playoffs again. On Tuesday, October 1, 2019, before their wild-card game against the Milwaukee Brewers, "The Sports Junkies" were asked to shout out the ceremonial "Play Ball" in front of a packed Nationals Park with 43,000 fans in attendance.

Sadly, Lurch wasn't able to join us. His spice-of-life mother Peggy Suntum, who had worked in the White House for decades and raised him as a single mom, had lost her battle to cancer on August 19. An only child, he was left in charge of planning a service in Peggy's honor and had business to attend. We understood. Regardless of how much we might fight and bust each other's chops on the air, we always have the other's backs.

Standing in the concourse directly behind home plate with E.B. and Cakes when the game began, we watched the Nationals fall behind 3-0 with ace Max Scherzer on the mound. After shortstop Trea Turner homered in the third inning to curt the deficit to 3-1, Nats fans were energized.

By the eighth inning with Washington still trailing, hope was waning. The Brewers turned to their star relief pitcher Josh Hader, who sported a monstrous mullet and a 100 mph fastball. The All-Star closer had struck out 138 batters in less than 73 innings during the regular season. The Nationals' chances of coming back to win the game were slim.

Striking out Victor Robles to start the inning, the lanky southpaw looked unhittable. But when a Hader pitch hit outfielder Michael Taylor on the hands, the Nationals had the tying run at the plate. After Turner struck out, Ryan Zimmerman, the face of the franchise, stepped to the plate as a pinch-hitter and delivered a bloop single that kept the inning alive.

As the Nats free-agent-to-be All-Star third baseman Anthony Rendon stepped to the plate, E.B. turned to me and said, "You realize this is probably the last time we'll see Anthony Rendon in a Nationals uniform."

It wasn't. Rendon walked to load the bases, and now it was time for 20-year-old superstar slugger Juan Soto to face Hader. Ripping a single to right field, two runners scored, but when Milwaukee's rookie outfielder Josh Grisham misplayed the ball, Rendon rounded third to score the go-ahead run.

E.B., Cakes, and I jumped for joy like we did when we were kids. Nationals Park was on fire. The Nats had seized the lead.

Nevertheless, there was still doubt. Years earlier, we had seen closer Drew Storen come within one strike of leading Washington to the National League Championship Series. But this time, closer Daniel Hudson, a savvy midseason pickup by Mike Rizzo, locked down the clincher. The crowd roared at the unlikely victory as the Nationals advanced to face the Los Angeles Dodgers in the next round of the playoffs.

Driving home, I wondered if this could be the start of a Caps-like run.

★ ★ ★ ★

In the National League Division Series, drama was at an all-time high with the deciding Game 5 against the Dodgers going to extra innings. In the 10th inning, the Nationals mounted a rally. With the bases loaded, second baseman Howie Kendrick hit a grand slam that propelled Washington to its first National League Championship series.

Their fortunes would continue as the Nats mowed through the St. Louis Cardinals, sweeping them in four games and advancing to the World Series, facing the heavily favored Houston Astros. With Ryan Zimmerman and Juan Soto launching homers in Game 1, the Nationals beat starting pitcher Gerrit Cole, who hadn't lost since May. Then, in Game 2, Stephen Strasburg outdueled Justin Verlander as the hometowners took a 2-0 series lead. With two more wins, they'd be crowned world champions.

On the air, fans who had suffered so much heartbreak from the Nationals during their disappointing playoff exits were suddenly bursting with confidence. And so were we. With the next three World Series games at Nationals Park, "The Sports Junkies" began dreaming of another parade. While Cakes didn't want to "jinx" things, I started imagining a Bostonian-like run for the D.C. sports teams. Lurch and E.B. warned I might be getting ahead of myself. The history of sports calamity in Washington is real, if not organic.

Just a few days later, my partners were proven right. The Astros won three straight and were now on the brink of eliminating the Nats. Fans were restless, and we could feel the nervous energy on the phones. *Hell, we were nervous.* But back in Houston, where the closed stadium roof amplifies the crowd noise, Strasburg coolly delivered his fifth win during the postseason, knotting the series at three games apiece.

In the deciding Game 7, Nationals ace Max Scherzer scuffled early. With Washington trailing 2-0 through five innings, Martinez turned to starting pitcher Patrick Corbin to pitch in relief. As Corbin stifled the Astros, the Nats' batters weren't having any luck against Astros starter Zach Greinke, who allowed just one hit through six innings.

But the Nationals wouldn't go down quietly. Like they had done all season, they mounted a comeback. In the seventh inning, Anthony Rendon got Washington on the board with a solo home run. Then, after Dodgers manager Dave Roberts surprisingly pulled Greinke after he walked Soto, Howie Kendrick sliced a drive that clanged off the foul pole for a two-run homer. Sweet music for Nationals fans. Kendrick had done it again, providing a 3-2 lead.

After tacking on insurance runs in the eighth and ninth innings, the Nats turned to Daniel Hudson, who slammed the door on the pesky Astros. The Nationals were world champions, the first baseball title in Washington since 1924. The city was ecstatic.

After the game, Zimmerman said, "What a story. The way this game went is the way our whole season went." One hell of a ride.

We were honored when the Nationals asked us to be part of their historic day on Saturday, November 2, 2019. After jumping on the radio briefly, we lined up behind our station's red SUV. This time we would walk the parade route and bask in the celebration.

Prepared for the festivities, E.B. brought three champagne bottles. As we walked along the packed parade route with rabid fans screaming incessantly, E.B. sprayed them with bubbly. Nobody complained. Everybody was drunk on the world championship.

Hundreds of fans cheered us, yelling, "Junkies!" Wanting to collect their attention dollars, too, Valdez and Drab alternated between driving and walking by our side.

We took photos and exchanged high fives with countless listeners who were celebrating their favorite radio show being included in the spectacle. Once again, "The Sports Junkies" were in the middle of one of the most significant events in Washington sports history. It was a mind-blowing experience. Of course, everybody loves a victory parade. Not only had we been a part of two championship parades, but they happened in less than a year and a half. Who could have predicted that?

29

NO SPORTS, NO PROBLEM?

"Every negative—pressure, challenges—is all an opportunity for me to rise." — *Kobe Bryant*

In early 2020, we were starting to learn about the coronavirus known as covid-19. Though we always aimed for the show to be a diversion from the news, we couldn't escape the impending danger. We wondered what it might mean to the world of sports, but none of us could imagine the severity and widespread consequences of the imminent pandemic.

During our early years, road trips were some of our best times together. Whether we were interviewing quarterback Peyton Manning at the NFL Draft or bumping into random celebrities like actor Tom Arnold and hockey legend Wayne Gretzky at a Super Bowl party, hitting the road was a constant source of show material. Watching a fight with the great Muhammad Ali still lives in Junkies folklore. But so did stories of missed flights, drunken stupors, and awkward photos.

As much fun as we had, gallivanting across the country grew more infrequent. Maybe we lost some of our zeal to travel as our families grew or maybe the budgetary hurdles became too difficult to clear. Regardless, we didn't mind. As the pandemic drew closer, we were down to one trip a year, our annual junket to West Palm Beach to cover the Washington Nationals in spring training. Though our complaints about travel and fleabag hotels never ceased, we were excited about this trip. The Nats were defending World Series champions, and March in South Florida is pretty close to paradise after cold, gray Washington winters.

Days earlier, we had flippantly done a segment about a decline in Corona beer sales. After mocking those who thought the beer had something to do with the virus, E.B. vowed to drink Corona at the airport bar. On the one hand, the worrywart had been the most prescient about covid-19, predicting doom and gloom from the virus that we were just learning. Consequently, he was armed with hand sanitizer when we arrived at the terminal. He was also a ball of anxiety and fear, unable to stop talking about the virus.

That wasn't going to stop E.B. from doing his bit. Like a poker player who can't fold their hand, E.B. moseyed up to the airport bar and ordered a

Corona. But, before grabbing his glass, he doused his hands with sanitizer. Then, instead of enjoying his beer and being excited about the trip, E.B. began droning about the virus once again.

As I grabbed a burger at a Five Guys near the airport bar, Drab texted me: "Where are you eating? I can't sit with E.B. anymore. He's already driving me crazy." The coronavirus talk was too much. We all just wanted to have a good time.

★ ★ ★ ★

Despite the apocalyptic news, sports were still in full swing. As we broadcast just outside the Nationals' training facility the following morning, we focused on the conference basketball tournaments and the Nats' upcoming season. We interviewed manager Davey Martinez and hulking slugger Eric Thames, who won us over with his charm and muscles.

Afterward, Cakes bolted to the nearest casino, and the rest of us headed to The Woods, golfer Tiger Woods's restaurant in Jupiter, much to E.B.'s delight. He's a Tiger sycophant and coaxed us into going for the third time in three years at spring training. Two years earlier, E.B. missed his flight home after becoming violently ill following a visit to The Woods, but that didn't scare him from pushing us to return. Though there would be no Tiger sighting, we enjoyed the ambiance and food as we sat at the bar while E.B. continued to pound Coronas.

Later that night, we looked for a nearby beachside bar before landing at The Breakers, a five-star historic luxury hotel opened in 1896. In a rare moment of group reflection, we talked about how much longer we'd want to do the show and where to retire. Then, surveying the exorbitant prices on the menu, we wondered if Entercom would flip the bill.

Meanwhile, a listener had tracked us down by following us on Twitter to say hello. This wasn't the first time, but that didn't make these encounters less awkward. We were in the middle of dinner. Still, guys like Bo made our careers possible. We were genuinely appreciative.

Enjoying the evening to its fullest, Lurch ordered one last cocktail before we left. Twenty minutes later, that drink proved to be too much. He needed to take a whiz, but we were walking back to our car. Instead of marching back inside The Breakers for a restroom, Lurch fouled the parking lot. Show fodder.

The next morning, we weaved tales of our trips to The Woods and The Breakers while Cakes lamented losing money and bad beats at the casino. Later, we interviewed one of our favorites, veteran Nats first baseman Ryan Zimmerman. After talking about the World Series and the upcoming season, we went to break and shook hands with the all-time face of the franchise.

Before he returned to the clubhouse, however, Zimmerman asked us an ominous question: "What do you guys think about this virus?" We honestly had no idea.

Little did we know how much our lives would change. Less than two weeks after returning from Florida, the coronavirus had grown from a curiosity to a full-fledged pandemic. As a result, all sports came to a jarring halt as the NBA, NHL, NCAA, and PGA tour suspended play. There would be no March Madness college basketball or Masters golf tournament in April. The NBA and NHL seasons were on hold, and baseball spring training was canceled.

The news surrounding covid-19 was unnerving. The virus was spreading rapidly. As more information poured in, our company prepared for quarantine. We were given equipment to broadcast from home. As I dropped off a Comrex recorder at Cakes's house in Olney, I stayed in my car, keeping a distance. A new term had become part of our national dialogue—social distancing. I wondered when I would be able to shake my friend's hand again.

Soon all four of us were linked to conduct the show from our homes. Not having to commute into D.C. and being able to sleep longer was not unappreciated. Nevertheless, we faced new challenges. Since our radio show was simulcast on television daily on NBC Sports Washington, we aimed to find spots in our homes that would look presentable.

E.B.'s theater room featuring Len Bias and Gilbert Arenas jerseys became his new radio home. Lurch settled into his office even though the two televisions behind him didn't work. Cakes started in his living room with a Washington Capitals jersey hanging behind a black leather couch.

I didn't have a great spot in my townhouse to broadcast from daily. Ultimately, I opted for the basement, which served as my wife's office and gym, featuring a large mirror with a ballet bar. Since it was less than ideal, I switched to a green screen a few days later with our station's call letters in the background. Even if it didn't look great, at least I was pimping the product.

Playing around with our green screens became a bit on the show. Soon Lurch was having fun broadcasting from Fenway Park, and I had a tropical background with palm trees. Laughing about the ridiculousness of our backgrounds brought levity to the show. It also helped fill the four hours.

Still, there were frustrations and complications. Equipment failures were frequent and highly aggravating. Sometimes our Zoom connections would go out, while other times, our microphones sounded like crap. While Drab and Valdez remained in the studio, they were somewhat helpless. All they could do was guide us in an attempt to address our issues. Though our technical problems usually didn't last long, they certainly didn't help our broadcast—or moods.

Equipment failures were compounded by doing a daily show within normal, everyday life around the house. My toddler was heard crying on occasion. Then, throwing out what he hoped would be a funny zinger, Lurch asked jokingly, "Can't your wife control your little one?"

Uh, boy.

Jess did not take kindly to that question. She was doing her best to corral energetic Isabella each morning without us hearing a peep. This wasn't an easy task and, like almost every home in America, being in quarantine required patience much longer than your middle finger.

So when Lurch's dog Luka started barking during the show a few days later, I shot back at him. My wife was still salty about his snark. Plus, a little drama never hurt the radio show. But when his housekeeper started vacuuming during the show, E.B. and Cakes jumped on the pile, too. Couldn't his housekeeper do her work later in the day?

Busting each other's chops had always been part of the show. We had been doing it since we were joaning on each other in high school. We knew that it was all in good fun and served as content material, and we badly needed content. Though we never relied solely on sports, we now faced the challenge of filling four hours without them. Speculating about their return could fill some time, but it wasn't enough.

As we were groping through this hazy darkness, we weren't always on the same page (which is nothing new). While Cakes and I were less frustrated by the precautions being taken in the sports world, E.B. and Lurch became increasingly more vocal. They wondered why some collegiate athletic conferences were already canceling sports in the fall and why outdoor sports were deemed problematic.

Beyond talking about the virus and the mundane nature of our new daily routines, we threw some darts at the wall for the sake of entertainment. One week we held a listeners talent show. The following week we tried a doggie happy hour on Facebook Live with pet owners showcasing their canines. Anything to pass the time and avoid the reality of what was happening all across the country.

Entercom was about to put us in an impossible pickle. With people out of work and businesses shutting their doors, advertising dollars were drying up, as well. Entercom's radio stations were struggling across the country. By the time April 2020 rolled around, we were asked to take a "voluntary" 20 percent pay cut.

Though we preferred to stick with our contract—we had just entered the second of a four-year deal—we knew we didn't have much choice. Entercom would likely fire our producers to save money if we didn't agree to forgo our bonuses and take a reduction in pay. We were not taking that risk with our friends and co-workers' careers. We also didn't want to piss off our new company. What would Entercom think of us if we said no? Would they get rid of us the first chance possible? The reality was, so many people were unemployed. At least we were working.

But was anybody listening? Nobody was commuting to work anymore. Much of our audience was working from home. Besides, we are "The Sports Junkies" suddenly without sports. Radio was our lifeblood, and our ratings were tanking, big time. It didn't matter that *Talkers* magazine had just ranked us as the country's eighth-most important sports talk radio show.

Months earlier, we had received our January ratings. Riding the wave of the Redskins firing team president Bruce Allen and hiring Ron Rivera as their new head coach, we hit No. 1 again with an 11.1 combined rating (including our stream). Six months later and approaching three months into the pandemic, our numbers had plummeted to a 3.5.

We wondered how much patience Entercom would exercise. Even though we had already agreed to a pay cut, could they fire us next? Having no sports to talk about would be an easy, convenient excuse. We were in a ratings crisis that threatened our show and livelihoods during a highly contagious disease. There was no precedent or playbook for us to follow. We were nervous, man, nervous.

30

SOCIAL DISTANCE

"Do what you can, with what you have, where you are."
— *Theodore Roosevelt*

In July 2020, four months into working from home, Jake Burns, the executive vice president of business operations for the Washington Nationals, joined us via Zoom. "You guys should all have a box in front of you. Everybody have a box?" he asked. We were armed and ready. The box was the size of a small cigar humidor.

Then Jake said the magic words: "On behalf of the Washington Nationals, we just wanted to thank you guys, thank Entercom, Grant and Danny, Chad Dukes, for the tremendous support that you guys provided to us, always, but particularly during the 2019 championship season. So as a token of our gratitude, we wanted to give you guys your own World Series rings."

Unbelievable. Our ratings had slumped during the pandemic, but now we were being blessed with another championship ring. "The curly W at the top has 30 custom-cut rubies," Jake explained, "There are 32 custom-cut sapphires surrounding the curly W and 108 diamonds." The rings were stunning. Our names graced one side with the team's motto, "Fight Finished," on the other. The rings are genuinely spectacular.

As Valdez played Queen's "We Are the Champions" in the background as he had a year earlier when we received our Washington Capitals Stanley Cup rings, Cakes said what we all were thinking. "First of all, thank you. Thank you very much. Second of all, we are not worthy. We are not deserving. But we will take the gift!"

It was almost unimaginable. In 1995, when we started on cable access, we were ecstatic when the Los Angeles Lakers sent us one warm-up jacket to dress up our set. Now each of us had two championship rings. How lucky were we?

★ ★ ★ ★

The shiny new rings couldn't blind us from our ratings reality. Though this wasn't the first time our ratings had dipped, it felt different. The pandemic had changed everything. Many of our listeners had lost their jobs or worked from home, leaving fewer people in their cars from 6-10 a.m.

Instead, they were sleeping in and missing big chunks of the show.

Podcasting was now working against us, too. Far too many listeners were grabbing our podcasts instead of listening live. Being the most downloaded show for our company, which owned over 230 radio stations across the country, stroked our ego but meant nothing to our bottom line.

The simulcast of our show wasn't doing us any favors, either. Our ratings had grown since NBCSports Washington began televising our radio show in September 2016, but now, faced with no live games to broadcast, they were running our replay every night. That was eight hours of "The Sports Junkies" on television every day. We were overexposed.

Additionally, broadcasting on the weekends wasn't helping our cause. Months earlier, program director Chris Kinard had asked us to be team players. Due to budgetary constraints, the radio station couldn't afford to pay their weekend hosts, so they asked us to fill the time—for free.

Soon we were being paired in various time slots. Lurch and I led things off on Saturday mornings. Typically we'd book three to four guests to help us get through our three-hour shift. Cakes was often paired with either Grant Paulsen or Danny Rouhier from "The Grant and Danny Show," where he was just as likely to take a Star Wars quiz as talk sports. Similarly, E.B. teamed with Chad Dukes, where the two bantered about fire pits while hawking t-shirts. It was admittedly fun at times—listeners enjoyed the different pairings and how each show was editorially unique— but we wanted our weekends back and a return to normalcy.

The world wasn't returning to normal anytime soon, and the coronavirus wasn't washing through like the regular flu. But sports were returning, though they wouldn't look the same. To protect its players from covid-19, the NBA was returning in a "bubble" in Orlando. Players wouldn't be allowed to leave until their teams were eliminated from the playoffs. Testing would be prevalent, and fans would not be allowed to attend.

Similarly, the NHL would return to action, but only in two hub cities. Major League Baseball would hold a second spring training with games being played in empty stadiums. PGA Tour golfers would play without galleries.

As strange as it was, at least we could talk about the competition. Sports would provide a welcome escape from the reality of what was happening around us.

While we hoped the return of sports would boost our ratings, the interest just wasn't there. Ratings for all sports plunged dramatically. Even with LeBron James and the Los Angeles Lakers in the NBA Finals, television ratings declined by 37 percent from the previous year. The NHL and MLB numbers were even worse. When the PGA Tour held the U.S. Open in September, ratings were down more than 50 percent.

With thousands of Americans losing their lives each week, sports just weren't as important anymore. They also felt different. The NBA season concluded in October instead of June. The Masters was rescheduled for November. Would the famous azaleas at Augusta National be blooming at that time of year? Answer: No.

Though I argued it didn't bother me that fans weren't in the stands, I was in the minority. My co-hosts, and many in the larger public, especially the athletes and team owners, didn't feel that way. The leagues countered by piping recorded crowd noise through the public address systems while teams placed cardboard likenesses of fans in the seats. It was the phoniest thing this side of alcohol-free booze.

The political atmosphere in the country was reaching a fever pitch with the presidential election in November. For months, the news was filled with reports about the primaries, the impeachment of President Donald Trump, and the government's handling of the virus. Sadly, the response to the pandemic had become yet another political football in a highly polarized electorate. To our detriment, we carried that rock far too often.

Aiming always to be a diversion from life's daily forces, we often found ourselves derailed. Diving into topics like the Ivy League postponing all sports in the fall of 2020 became a delicate tightrope. Though we never wanted to silence our opinions, it may not have been wise to voice them when half of our audience disagreed, especially while our ratings were near all-time lows.

In particular, E.B., the loving father of a collegiate lacrosse player and a rising high school volleyball star, was perturbed sports were being canceled. He often criticized the measures taken to combat covid-19, from masking to social distancing. At the beginning of the pandemic, E.B. had lauded Dr. Anthony Fauci, director of the National Institute of Allergy and Infectious Diseases. Now he was mocking him.

Our producers and program director asked us to stop when tweets began pouring in from long-time listeners threatening to quit tuning in to the show. They couldn't take the political rants. Unfortunately, as much as we tried to stay clear of any topics that might stir the political pot, it was unavoidable at times.

Eventually, we held a heated conference call to address the issue. Though our ratings had increased by more than a point since our low point in June 2020, they weren't where we wanted them to be. In August 2019, we had finished with a 9.6 share in our target demographic. One year later, our ratings stood at 4.7. The last thing we wanted to do was tick off half our remaining audience. Instead, we had to focus on having fun and being a diversion to the new everyday life of inconveniences.

Feeling attacked, E.B. dug in, refusing to be silenced. Frustrated, I leaned on a phrase I had learned years earlier during marital counseling: "Does it serve us?" I asked. Whether E.B. had data or charts to back his arguments didn't matter to me. But did voicing his opinion on the show help or hurt us?

With Drab and Valdez engaging but Jason and Cakes mostly silent, I challenged my friend. "It doesn't matter if you are right," I said. "And by the way, nobody knows. It's hurting us. You're part of a team. Be a team player. Be a good teammate. Everybody wants you to stop."

Nobody balked.

E.B. correctly noted I had brought up my stance on guns and we had veered into politics on occasion throughout the show's history. I argued this time was different. Our ratings were historically low, and, most importantly, countless listeners were telling us to stop. So I asked him once again, "Does it serve us?" I almost fell out of my chair when I heard his response.

"It serves our country," he shot back.

Was he serious? Did he think he was the surgeon general?

The pandemic had taken so many lives, and thousands upon thousands of Americans were dealing with loss and depression. In some ways, his reaction may have been understandable. All of our lives, and our children's lives, had changed so dramatically. Still, his co-workers were asking him to stop with his political comments on our show.

After butting heads for another 15 minutes, E.B. finally relented. "I'll stay quiet on the air," he started, "but I'm not going to stop tweeting." While it wasn't exactly what we wanted to hear, it was progress.

A few weeks later, in the middle of my family getaway to Rehoboth Beach, Delaware, I received an ominous text. "Call me," Drab asked. I wondered why he was reaching out during my vacation. Had the station flipped? Were we fired?

Sounding like a beaten dog, a disheartened Drab asked, "Did you hear?" I had no clue. "Out of nowhere, E.B. just called Joe Biden senile." Continuing, Drab suggested, "He can't stop. He's out of control."

Broadcasting over two blue states and the District of Columbia that skewed overwhelmingly Democrat, that couldn't be a good thing, especially just weeks before the election. As I tried to understand the context surrounding E.B.'s comment about Biden, an exasperated Drab said he couldn't remember. "We weren't even talking about politics," he said, "It was the last segment of the show. I don't know what to do."

The reality was there wasn't much any of us could do. We had collectively urged E.B. to stop. There weren't any new angles to express our frustration. All we could do was remind him again and ask him to be a team player.

Sensing Drab was not just calling me to vent, but that he wanted me to confront my friend, I cut him off before he could ask. I wasn't going to start an argument while on vacation. Instead, I offered my two cents.

"It sucks, dude. I don't know what to tell you. We told him to stop. He's not stupid. He sees the tweets. He has to know it's hurting us," I reasoned. "But here's the deal, and I know it's not easy. You're our producer. You're going to have to take the bullet. It's your job. You have to say something. Otherwise, we all might be looking for jobs."

That's the last thing any of us wanted to do. What the hell were we qualified to do anyway?

★ ★ ★ ★

Fortunately, our renewed efforts to stay clear of politics were largely successful. Why should we dive into the same murky pool since political discourse was everywhere around us on radio, TV, and social media? One of our strengths has always been that we never took ourselves too seriously. We didn't want to become a political hot button. So we focused on getting back to what had made us successful.

Football season consistently garners our highest ratings. And like most seasons, the newly dubbed Washington Football Team was giving us plenty of fodder during the fall of 2020. After hiring former Carolina Panthers coach Ron Rivera in the offseason and changing the team name, focus turned to second-year quarterback Dwayne Haskins, who struggled to live up to his potential.

Debating how many starts the disappointing former first-round draft pick should get before making a switch felt so much better than discussing the efficacy of covid-19 testing. The roller coaster season provided us with plenty of material. Rivera was battling cancer while remaining on the sidelines. Haskins was benched after just four games, and former starter Alex Smith came to the rescue amid a miraculous comeback from a broken leg in 2018.

Though the team had a losing record, they were in playoff contention. As a result, more fans were tuning in, or so we thought. When the October ratings were released, our numbers didn't skyrocket. Inching up, we finished in sixth place.

But talking about football reinvigorated the four of us who still hadn't seen each other in person for months. Working from home, we focused on the ups and downs of Washington's season, a welcome escape from the world around us that was hyper-focused on covid-19 and presidential politics.

Finishing with a 7-9 regular-season record, Washington managed to win the NFC East with the unlikeliest of heroes. An undrafted free agent quarterback from Old Dominion University, Taylor Heinicke halted his pursuit of an advanced mathematics degree to join WFT as the team's quarantine quarterback. After Rivera released Haskins for breaking covid protocols at a birthday party full of strippers, Heinicke was elevated to backup status.

Incredibly, on January 9, 2021, Heinicke, who was never supposed to see the field, started in Washington's playoff game against Tom Brady and the Tampa Bay Buccaneers. Playing the game of his life, Heinicke threw for over 300 yards with one touchdown pass and an electrifying touchdown run where he dove from the 4-yard line to hit the end zone pylon. Despite the 31-23 loss to the Buccaneers, the entire fanbase had fallen in love with their spunky new quarterback.

Joining us for an interview, we dove into Heinicke's unexpected journey back to the NFL before beginning to pry. Lurch asked, "What were you doing for income?" Heinicke didn't hesitate, "Nothing." Following up, I wondered what he planned to do with his degree. Heinicke answered bluntly, "That's a great question. I have no idea."

I asked, "Does Taylor Heinicke have a wife or girlfriend? What's the status?"

"Nope. I'm a single man. Trying to stay away from it all. Focused on ball."

Before closing, we'd touched on his golf game. Figuring he excelled on the links, we were surprised to learn he wasn't a low-handicap player.

"Damn, you guys are giving me way too much credit," Heinicke replied.

"Are you a chop?" E.B. asked. "Not a chop," Taylor responded, "but I'll say I shoot like an 86. I have my moments, but I'm definitely going to lose some balls."

We could relate. Taylor Heinicke was our guy.

★ ★ ★ ★

Almost one year into the pandemic, a small group of Reddit users decided to take on corporate America in early 2021 by undercutting hedge fund managers who were making millions by shorting companies on the verge of collapse. As more people banded together online in the GameStop short squeeze frenzy, the company's share price skyrocketed, hedge fund managers lost millions, and the little guys investing made huge profits.

The story of GameStop's climb from just under $20 per share to almost $350 grabbed the country's attention, including our producer Drab.

Buying shares of AMC Entertainment Holdings first, Drab saw an opportunity. While the Reddit community pumped the stumbling company, its stock price jumped from $2 per share to almost $20 in less than a month. Drab was riding the new wave. You no longer need to watch CNBC for insight on the market or have a financial advisor at a traditional brokerage. Instead, regular Joes like Drab were making a fortune online.

So, our man Valdez became curious (or nosey). Who was Drab leaning on for financial advice? And that's when Valdez stumbled onto a radio gold mine. Drab wasn't getting his stock tips from a Wall Street wizard, but a guy in South Carolina with a mobile barbecue business and fewer than 25 Twitter followers. Valdez dropped the hammer on Boonjug's Hillbilly BBQ & Hash.

"You're not going to believe the person Drab is putting his savings into," Valdez said. "This is Drab's Jim Cramer." But as Cakes chuckled, Drab vowed, "I trust him with my financial life."

Then Valdez countered, "You gotta listen to Boonjugs. I want you to tell me how much money you would invest in Boonjugs's picks." Our inquisitive producer had uncovered Boonjugs audio, and soon we were listening to the proud cook introduce his food truck with a deep southern twang.

"Good morning, everybody. Boonjugs Hillbilly Barbeque and Hash," he started. Just hearing his voice cracked us up. What could the barbeque man know about investing? Becoming defensive, Drab claimed that he was no different than the rest of us.

"You guys are always talking about Bitcoin and your 401ks. I'm out here with the common man. Me and Boonjugs. We're grinding." Valdez zinged. "Yeah, investing in Ribcoin!"

When Drab began to explain more about Boonjugs's recommendations, Valdez kidded that his portfolio was diversified. One-upping him, Cakes clowned, "His porkfolio!"

We finally connected with Boonjugs, who explained he had just joined Twitter six weeks earlier to learn more about the stock market. "I love to gamble, and stock is a legal form of gambling," he correctly explained.

Boonjugs said when the Dow Jones had dipped below 20,000, he took out every penny he owned and invested in the market. "I put $40,000 in the stock market in March," the pitmaster started, "by the middle of June, I tripled it."

Impressed by the remarkable return on investment, we clapped and started to praise his instinct. Stopping us, Boonjugs continued, "Wait a second, it gets better. So the only thing I put in was 40 grand. I tripled it by mid-June. By Christmas, I doubled that. And then yesterday, I probably needed to change my drawers."

The studio erupted in laughter. Boonjugs could weave a tale.

"I'm becoming a believer," E.B. declared as Boonjugs's Twitter account shot up like his stocks. Whether or not he was the next Warren Buffet, Boonjugs made us laugh.

Fortunately for us, more people were returning to the show, and our ratings were ticking up with "The Sports Junkies" back in the top five in our target demographic, men 25-54. Maybe it was our renewed effort to avoid political hot buttons, or perhaps more of our listeners were driving to work and commuting back to their offices. Either way, we were laughing more and having a blast, albeit still from home.

Our parent company, Entercom, was rebranding itself as Audacy, effective March 29, 2021. It wasn't the first time we dealt with corporate name changes. We had worked for Infinity Broadcasting, CBS Radio, Westwood One, Entercom, and now Audacy. It never really mattered so long as our show was left alone.

Nevertheless, corporate was implementing guidelines regarding the imminent return to our studios in downtown Washington. Audacy employees wouldn't be allowed back until they were vaccinated. With the four of us scheduling our covid-19 shots, it was just a matter of time.

We would miss sleeping in and not commuting, but we also knew the show didn't have the same vibe and rhythm without broadcasting from the same studio. Dating to our days hosting "The Sports Junkies" on Bowie Cable Television, there was something spontaneous, outrageous, electric, passionate, and wildly unpredictable when we sat together and started barking back and forth.

Twenty-five years later, as the world changed so quickly and dramatically around us, I hoped for the same old magic when we finally got back together.

31

"I LOVE YOU, ITA"

"Lots of people want to ride with you in the limo, but what you want is someone who will take the bus with you when the limo breaks down."
— Oprah Winfrey

In March 2021, we bought a new house and moved in with my mom at my childhood home in Bowie. The stay was expected to be only a week while the new house underwent some renovations. Double vaccinated, my mom, a widow who lived by herself, was excited to host us. Each night she would ask what we wanted for dinner, and I loved her cooking and spending time with her, but things went south quickly.

After testing negative for covid-19 days earlier, I became extremely ill following a round of golf just a few days into our stay. Managing to get through 18 holes with E.B.'s brother Matt, I felt and looked like a zombie. I was exhausted. Arriving in Bowie later that evening, I skipped dinner and went straight to bed.

Hours later, my wife Jess was taking my temperature, which hovered around 102 degrees. I was sweating profusely, struggling to breathe, and I could barely get up. There was no way I could do the show in a few hours, so Jess texted the guys that I was out of commission and needed another coronavirus test.

Lying in bed for almost 12 hours, I mustered enough energy to drive to a nearby clinic. This time I tested positive. As the doctor gave me instructions, all I heard was quarantine. Now I would have to find a place in mom's house to stay for two weeks without contact.

I settled in my brother Eric's childhood bedroom, which mom had transformed into a playroom for her six grandchildren. Uncle Carlos, a cardiologist in Puerto Rico, called to reassure me. While his input was appreciated, I didn't believe I was going to die. I'm relatively young and healthy, even though I felt like a Mack truck had run over me. I would follow his advice, take some meds and vitamins, and figured I would get better.

Two days later, I began to worry. My condition hadn't improved much, my temperature remained high, and I was barely sleeping as I sweated through my clothes each night. I couldn't take a deep breath. Still, my condition paled in comparison to what was happening outside my door.

First, I learned Valdez had been hospitalized. We had crossed paths for just a few minutes three days before, when I conducted the show from our D.C. studios because I was worried about my mom's internet connection. Valdez was having difficulty breathing and his parents had taken him to the hospital when he tested positive for covid-19. I felt responsible. Now all I could do was pray that he would get better.

Meanwhile, Jess was concerned about my mom, who asked to cancel her dialysis appointment for the second time that week. Though mom needed the treatment—she had suffered kidney damage six years earlier due to Wegener's disease—she was still in charge and claimed she didn't have the energy to go. What could I do about it anyway? I was quarantining behind a closed door.

To further complicate things, Jess began to feel sick. Responsible for taking care of our 4-year-old Isabella and my mom, Jess was battling fatigue and a high temperature. Soon she'd have to lie down, leaving me with no choice but to break quarantine. Someone had to take care of our daughter. Someone had to take care of my wife. And someone had to take care of my mom. So I was the next man up because I was in the best condition.

Juggling my new responsibilities as caretaker kept me busy, but I was now racked with the guilt that I was to blame for everything. A coronavirus test confirmed Jess also had covid-19.

Later, when everybody had fallen asleep, I called my brother Eric. I was overwhelmed, not feeling well, and needed help. Given my diagnosis, I wouldn't be allowed to take our mom inside for her dialysis appointment the next day. Without hesitation, he offered to drive from his home in Summit, New Jersey, to help.

Mom's condition worsened overnight. While I tried to ready her for treatment, she wasn't moving. Eventually, after several hours passed, she made it to the bathroom, demanding a shower before leaving.

My brother had already arrived from his four-hour drive by the time she was ready. Since he had received just one vaccination shot, the last thing he was going to risk was entering a house ravaged with covid-19. I understood.

While I begged my mom to move faster and helped her get dressed, she demanded her space. Lourdes was still in charge, and despite my pleading, she wasn't going to leave without combing her hair. Anxieties were elevated.

Finally, I managed to help her walk slowly to my brother's SUV. We all wore masks and Eric kept his distance. Jess brought Isabella outside to wish her grandmother good luck. "I love you, Ita," our little one shouted.

Retreating inside, I prayed that dialysis would revive mom. Years earlier, my brother warned she could die if dialysis was skipped for a week. It had been five days. I was scared. Would dialysis work? Would the vaccine ward off the coronavirus? I prayed to see her in a few hours.

Mom never came home. After her treatment, a chest X-ray showed some cloudiness in her lungs. The doctor recommended my brother take her to the hospital. There, her condition quickly worsened as tests showed she had covid-19.

Responsive at first, her oxygen levels began to drop. When doctors gave her an oxygen mask, she soon became disoriented. A few hours later, she was unable to answer the doctor's questions.

Trying not to alarm me, my brother kept me in the dark. He knew I had my hands full with Isabella and a bed-ridden Jess. Luckily, my 14-year-old son Dylan Carlos had tested negative and was able to stay at his mom's house while my daughter Kelsie was away at New York University.

My brother delivered the shocking news the next morning: Our mom had coronavirus and was on a ventilator. I was rocked. I didn't understand how this could be happening. I had taken her for the second vaccination shot weeks earlier. That had given us comfort, but now she was stricken with the deadly virus, and my deep burden of guilt became unbearable.

Uncle Carlos arrived from Puerto Rico to be by his sister's side and offer his medical perspective on her health. Mom had multiple issues beyond the virus, from her heart to kidneys, and her condition wasn't changing.

While my uncle remained optimistic and analytical about her chances, I wondered if he was merely trying to keep us positive and hopeful.

A few days later, I returned to work remotely from my mom's home office. The guys understood the situation, but at least I was physically able to sit in front of my laptop and do the show. Still, under covid protocol, I wasn't allowed to visit mom in the hospital.

The next morning, the bomb dropped.

My phone rang at 7:30 during a show segment, and I had to take the call. Walking off camera, I listened to the doctor intently as she uttered the most devastating words I've heard in my life: "I just wanted to tell you that your mom is dying. I don't know how long she has, but it won't be long. And just so you know, we've lifted the restrictions. You can come and be with her."

My heart sank. Immediately I slammed my laptop. There was no time to explain that I was leaving in the middle of the show. I woke up Jess and shared the awful news. We embraced and cried together before I hopped in the car and sped to the hospital.

Emotions poured out of me like never before. *How could this be?* When my dad died in 2007, we were not caught off-guard. His health had been declining for years, and after several scares, he had become wheelchair-bound and dependent on my mom. When he died at age 78, I was thankful he had lived that long. But mom was expected to live longer. Much longer. Her mother, my grandmother, had died six years earlier at age 96. How could my mom be dying at 75?

Arriving at the hospital just as my brother and uncle pulled into the parking garage, we embraced, understanding the gravity of the moment. Though mom was technically alive when we finally reached her room, she was already gone. My cousin Paolo, a missionary priest, joined us on the phone to deliver her last rites and offer prayers that we recited to her. Eric, Uncle Carlos, and I watched mom take her last breath, fortunate to have spent those final hours by her side. As I sobbed while holding her hand, I took comfort that Lourdes Josefina Nieves Flaim would not suffer any longer. She was reuniting with my dad.

★ ★ ★ ★

One week later, I was standing in front of over a hundred friends and family at St. Edward's Catholic Church in Bowie. My brother had done a masterful job capturing our mother's life, and now it was my turn to deliver the eulogy.

On the evening mom died, E.B. called to offer his sympathy and implored me to not rush back to work. He was also hurting. Having grown up across the street, he considered her his second mother.

After thanking him, I suggested E.B. address on-air what happened when I left in the middle of that day's show. And, when he asked if I wanted him to say anything about my mom, I was confident he would handle it perfectly. She was his family, too.

The next night, after a full day of funeral preparations, I finally checked my phone. Hundreds of listeners had tweeted their sympathies. Dozens mentioned how E.B.'s words moved them. Some said they were in tears after he broke down while describing my mom. Cakes spoke affectionately about her parties and signature brownies, while Lurch glowed over mom's cheerfulness and warm-heartedness. He had lost his mother 20 months prior, so this couldn't have been easy for him.

Even though I could have listened to what E.B. said on the air, I didn't feel the need. I knew my boys would do mom justice. Listening was only going to make me more emotional. I needed a break from the sorrow, but I tried to answer all the tweets that had poured in throughout the day. The next thing I knew, it was 4 a.m. I was barely sleeping. Nothing new.

But now, at the funeral, it was my turn to talk about mom. It had occurred to me the night before that she *wouldn't* want me to heap praise on

My youngest daughter Isabella, my mother Lourdes, and my wife Jessica, 18 months before mom passed away in April 2021. Jessica called Isabella "Little Ita" because of her striking resemblance to her grandmother.

her. She *would* like for me to thank everyone who had been part of her life and brought her joy. That's what I set out to do.

After dealing with the unbearable sadness immediately after she had died, I emerged with a sense of gratitude. Mom had lived a great life, full of celebration and happiness. The Marc Anthony song "Vivir Mi Vida" spoke to me, and captured her spirit.

As I stood in front of everyone preparing to belt out the lyrics, I noticed my close friend Jason Bishop sitting in the back pew, wearing the gray suit I had seen him wear so many times at weddings. Next, I spotted my close friend Eric Bickel, who I had asked to be a pallbearer. I was thankful he rushed back from Poughkeepsie, New York, after serving as the color commentator for his son's lacrosse game. At the beginning of the eulogy, I had read from a card I received from my close friend John Auville's mother Paulette. She wrote, "Lourdes was such a good friend to each of us who knew her. She treated us like family. I thought of her as a sister."

Then, as friends and family looked on, I did my best Marc Anthony impersonation:

Voy a reír, voy a bailar
Vivir mi vida, la la la la
Voy a reír, voy a gozar
Vivir mi vida, la la la la

Voy a reír, voy a bailar
Vivir mi vida, la la la la
Voy a reír, voy a gozar
Vivir mi vida, la la la la

Loosely translated, it means, "I'm gonna laugh, I'm gonna dance, I'm gonna live my life. I'm going to laugh, I'm going to enjoy, I'm going to live my life." My mom did that to the fullest, and her family is forever grateful.

I was also grateful to have Eric, Jason, and John there with me. Since the funeral, I've held onto that seminal moment when I was about to deliver mom's eulogy, scanned the audience, and saw them out there. We're always by each other's side, we're always brothers. We have been rowing life's boat in the same direction for 25 years. In some ways, it feels like only yesterday that we were at Jason's childhood home in Lanham, Maryland, deciding if we were going to give radio a full-time shot. But, in other ways, life is so much different.

Back then, we were in our mid-20s, living a carefree life with little responsibility. Now we're all married with a combined 11 children between the four of us. Many of our kids aren't kids anymore. This year, my oldest daughter Kelsie is a senior at NYU. Eric has a son at Marist and daughter at Cornell. Jason's two daughters attend Virginia Tech, while John has a daughter at the University of Maryland and a son at the University of Maryland School of Medicine. We couldn't have imagined that when we were downing beers on Jason's deck and deciding our future.

Instead of late-night bar appearances after the show, we now find ourselves talking about the benefits of early dinners at home. Instead of staying up until 2 a.m. playing video games or pulling drunken all-nighters at a casino poker tournament, we lament the late starts of "Monday Night Football" and the NBA Finals. Instead of discussing what we are going to buy, we talk about funding our kids' 529 plans so we can pay their outrageous tuition bills.

Regardless of life's stresses and realities, "The Sports Junkies" has always been a way for us to have fun together. Sure, there have been arguments along the way—we'll always bust each other's balls on the air—but that's just part of being family. Even though we are a little heavier... a little grayer... a little balder, we're still making each other laugh and living the dream, just as we did when we started on cable access in 1995.

Of course, one day it will be over and the show will come to an end. Who knows, we might even get fired. But that's okay. Our friendship and brotherhood will always remain.

For now, we aren't done. Not even close. After 25 years, we're still barking.

JUNKIES GREATEST MOMENTS!
★ ★ ★ ★

Mayor Rob Ford

Thursday, December 5, 2013

When we returned to the Borgata Hotel, Casino and Spa in Atlantic City for our 12th Junkies Poker Open, producers Matt (Drab) Cahill and Matt (Valdez) Myers were working together like Stockton and Malone. Always brainstorming ideas, they threw a Hail Mary a couple of weeks prior as they attempted to book an interview with one of the most embattled people on the planet, the mayor of Toronto, Rob Ford.

At the time, Ford was all over the tabloids and international news because he was entangled in a scandal surrounding his drug use, causing the Toronto City Council to reduce his mayoral powers. So Drab and Valdez appealed to Ford's love of football. They pitched the idea of the mayor making NFL picks on our show, but didn't expect a reply.

Through the years, we have been rejected by President Obama, Katy Perry, Arnold Schwarzenegger, and Wayne Rooney, among others, to be guests. We are great at aiming high and failing fearlessly. But, surprisingly, the mayor's chief of staff responded immediately and agreed to the interview. We were flabbergasted.

Mayor Ford knew football—and handicapping a game. He admitted to making college and pro football bets. As a teenager, he attended a Redskins youth camp three times. The mayor had played and coached and was a massive fan with team jerseys and game balls in his office.

But then, the day before his scheduled appearance on our show, Ford was accused of trying to purchase a video allegedly showing him using crack cocaine. He was stiff-arming the Canadian media. We had doubts he would actually call in the next morning.

Two hours before the show and with a superstorm blowing around Atlantic City, we were chugging shots with our listeners at the Borgata. Lurch pulled an all-nighter at the blackjack tables. So when the phone rang with the mayor on the line, we were shocked, and Lurch was still

wearing the same clothes from the previous day.

After promoting his appearance all morning, we knew the political world would be listening. We're not journalists, and we didn't need to know politics. We just wanted to get the mayor talking football.

Easing into the interview with the goal of keeping him on the line as long as possible, Mayor Ford quickly won us over with his charm. Though he may have been a villainous figure in Toronto, he was full of charisma and easily laughed at himself. We couldn't help but like him.

Asking the mayor why he should be re-elected the following fall, he claimed, "We have property taxes lower than any Northern American city." Of course, we had no clue, but we weren't going to fact-check him either. We bantered for four minutes before addressing the elephant in the room. Lurch dove in and asked about the video—a question the mayor had been dodging.

Lurch: "Obviously, everyone in the world has heard about this story where you allegedly offered money for the video of you doing crack. What do you say to that? These are wire-tapped from gang members who say you offered $5,000, if not more—$150,000 and a car—to confiscate the video of you doing crack on the tape.

Ford: "Number one, that's an outright lie. And number two, you can talk to my lawyers about it. But I'm here to talk football guys, so if you want to talk football, talk football."

Lurch: "I at least had to ask ya."

The news media listening to our show thought we should have pressed Mayor Ford harder, but we're not "60 Minutes." And since we didn't want the mayor to hang up, we turned back to the NFL. Surprising us with his passion and knowledge, Ford touched on various football topics, including a possible Redskins name change.

"Like, where do we go with this?" he began. "[The name has been] been around for years and years and years, and if they were offended, they should have come out when the name was first initiated." We knew Washington owner Dan Snyder agreed. He vowed never to change the team's name.

Later, Mayor Ford sounded like a grizzled handicapper as he picked winners against the spread. We loved it and invited him to come back. Though his staff members expected a two- to three-minute interview, he chatted with us for 24 glorious, historical minutes.

Soon after the segment ended, we were being mentioned on the national morning news shows. NBC's Al Roker and Willie Geist poked fun at our name on the "Today" show. CNN's legal correspondent tossed to the audio of Lurch's back-and-forth with the mayor. Toronto's all-news station CP24 carried Ford's appearance live, and their reporters tweeted the segment in real time.

What started as a long-shot guest request by our ambitious producers had become a reality. "The Sports Junkies" were international newsmakers. Go figure.

JUNKIES GREATEST MOMENTS!

BORGATA BOXER BRIEFS

Friday, December 9, 2011

The road trips to Atlantic City for the Junkies Poker Open at The Borgata Hotel were a big highlight for us each year. Our shows from the B-Bar in the middle of the casino were always fun, chock-full of bad beat stories and tales of drunken stupors. Whether it was E.B. showing up to work still buzzed the following morning or Lurch raging over his blackjack luck, or lack thereof, memories from the Borgata often became instant Junkies classics.

So, we strapped in when Cakes told us at the 10th Junkies Poker Open that he had a story to share. "For some reason, I guess because God hates me, he wakes me up at 3:30 in the morning," Cakes started. "We did the wine pairing at dinner. I had too much to drink. So I get up at 3:30..."

Interrupting, E.B. asked, "What are you wearing?" Standing up, Cakes dropped his sweat pants and lifted his shirt in front of the small crowd gathered at the B-Bar, including a police officer, revealing his gray boxer briefs.

"This is what I'm wearing. I'm sorry, officer. It's for the good of the story," Cakes explained as the crowd began to laugh. Posing for a quick picture that E.B. snapped for social media, Cakes continued, "I'm wearing these sillies. Yeah."

"You don't even have a good package in there," E.B. jabbed, while Cakes stood up and flaunted his dad-bod physique. Lurch piled on about Cakes' droopy drawers, and E.B. fixated on his meager presentation.

"It's covered territory," Cakes responded flippantly. Sitting back down, he continued with his saga.

"So that's all I'm wearing. Boxers, that's it. That's it, baby! So I open the door, which I thought was to the bathroom—it was the door to my room. Then I'm standing in the hallway at 3:30 in the morning. It's like something out of a movie. Locked out of the room. Middle of the night. No phone. Me, in my boxers, stranded. Don't know what to do."

Howling hysterically, none of us could get the picture of Cakes out of our heads where he's stuck outside his hotel room in his underwear. This was every man's nightmare coming true—being somewhere in public without pants.

Wondering how he didn't recognize that he was in the bright hallway versus his room's bathroom, Cakes explained, "It's all a blur. I don't remember getting out of bed. The only thing I remember is being in the hallway and realizing I didn't have my room key. I wasn't in the bathroom. Hammered and disoriented. I just opened up the wrong door.

"I heard the click of the door," he continued. "I said, 'Finished! Finished. This is trouble. This is real trouble.'"

"What floor are you on?" I asked. "I'm on the 29th floor," Cakes replied, "so in my infinite wisdom, instead of processing what's happening, I didn't gather myself and go to the elevator and take it down to the bottom floor cause that would take me right to the lobby. It would take me right to the security guard—minimal exposure. I didn't do that. Why would I do that?

"Why would I do the right thing or the smart thing?" Cakes offered sarcastically. "If I go the elevator route, there is very minimal exposure. It's 3:30 in the morning."

But that made too much sense. Cakes was panicking. Leaving us dumbfounded, he described his dreadful decision-making process.

"It's better than that. Instead of going to the elevator, I said, 'Well, I'm going to take the steps from the 29th f'ing floor!' Walk down steps. Walk down the steps. All the way to the bottom floor. Okay? And I come out in this hallway, this corridor, like the bowels of the Borgata. And all I see are these doors. I'm in a maze. I'm in a labyrinth. I'm still drunk, and I'm wearing my boxers! Love handles everywhere. Combo."

When E.B. asked, "Don't they have phones on every floor? Cakes responded, "My brain was in a fog, foggier than usual. I was drunk and disoriented.

"So I go all the way to the bottom floor. I haven't seen a soul yet. So then I open the door into the casino. I look out and say, 'Well, I have to walk to the lobby now.'"

We slapped our knees in disbelief.

"I come out by the Long Bar," Cakes continued, "It's not far, but when you're wearing zippy, it's a long friggin' walk!" Luckily for him, the casino was mainly desolate at that time of the morning.

"So I walk out. Into the lobby. No clothes. Just my boxers. And at the Borgata, they have a security guard that stands in front of the elevator banks to make sure you have your room pass. I've got nothing. I don't have pants. I don't have a shirt. I've got boxers. I don't have a room key. I have nothing!

"So I'm walking down, and luckily only three or four people saw me, and they're just giving me the hairy eyeball. I have tunnel vision at this point. I was walking pretty fast. So I walk up to the security guard, and he looks at me like, 'I'm going to have to arrest you. You're clearly crazy.' I'm in my underwear. And I said, 'Officer, I locked myself out of the room. I don't know what to tell you.' And he goes, 'All right. Hold on. What's your room number? What's your name?' Making sure I'm not some psycho that wandered in off the streets of Atlantic City."

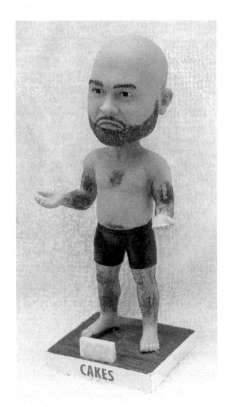

A bobblehead commemorates Cakes's drunken hotel foray.

Then Cakes waited for two other officers to escort him to his room.

"While I'm waiting, by the way, I'm hiding behind one of those little signs that advertise the Borgata, hiding behind it so nobody can see me, and this group of guys that is partying all night walk in, and one guy looks at me and goes, 'Yeaaah! Yeaaaah buddy! Woooooh!' Drawing all the attention that was already on me, squarely right back at me."

Cakes couldn't have been more embarrassed.

"So the two officers escort me up to the room, and before they even let me in, they're suspicious, even though they've checked my name and everything. They're like, 'Can you describe the room for me, sir?' I'm like, 'It's a hotel room. My suitcase is on the floor. I've got my license on my bathroom vanity.' So they let me in. They buzz me in. I go back to bed. And I woke up at 5:43, and here I am!"

Our listeners clapped. It was yet another classic Junkies yarn, one of the best.

Still amazed, we were desperate for the security footage. Cakes explained, "It's a lock; it's there. I don't know how I didn't get tackled by a hundred security guards!"

Though the story was almost unbelievable, we had photographic evidence. One of our loyal listeners, Matt Chang, was scanning Facebook and saw that one of his poker pals had posted a picture with the caption "Borgata Faithful," not recognizing the half-naked man right away. Sure enough, it was Cakes in all his glory, so Matt had to tweet the evidence for us to enjoy. Some might call him a hero.

A few years later, celebrating our 20th anniversary, the infamous Borgata Boxer Briefs moment was memorialized with a Cakes bobblehead in his boxers. The image lives in Junkies infamy.

JUNKIES GREATEST MOMENTS!

BAR EXAM BLUES

Tuesday, November 11, 1997

During the summer of 1997, the Maryland bar exam loomed over me like a storm cloud on a golf course. "The Sports Junkies" was my passion, but I still wanted to become a licensed attorney. Even if practicing law was my fallback, I needed to pass the test. Not taking it would feel like running 26 miles of a marathon without crossing the finish line.

So, each morning I'd take my tree-hour Barbri review course and study another three to four hours before the show. Not fun.

Soon my boys were busting my balls. Though I don't think they wanted to see me fail, they didn't mind predicting my demise. Neither did some of our listeners who predicted a catastrophe.

Though I knew the ribbing was in good fun, it still got under my skin. Talking to my friend Mike Fraser, I explained, "I can't wait to pass the test so I can say fuck you to each of them and rub it in their face." Then he proposed an irresistible idea. "If you want to do great radio," Mike started, "you'll open your results on the air."

Brilliant! It would add drama to the show, and I was supremely confident that I'd pass anyway. What could be the downside?

Pitching the idea to my cohorts, they were on board immediately. That didn't stop them from grilling me when they learned I had been studying and napping on the bleachers at a nearby youth baseball field before the show. Sitting inside the Fairfax library day after day had become drudgery. I couldn't wait until it was all over.

More than three months after taking the two-day bar exam in late July, I was still rewinding some of the questions in my head. Had I spotted all of the legal issues? Did I cite the correct rule of law? Did I reach the right conclusions? I wasn't sure. I was a nervous wreck.

After months of torturing myself and wondering if I'd have to do it all over again, there it was, staring me in the face. An envelope from the

State Board of Law Examiners had arrived. My personal D-Day was here.

As tempted as I was to open the letter, I couldn't. We had built up the moment on the radio too long. Though I cared deeply about the results, "The Sports Junkies" was more important to me.

Anxiously arriving at the station, I handed E.B. the envelope that would decide my fate. If I passed, I could take my victory lap. If not, I'd be humiliated in public.

Once the show started, we began to sell the drama. Announcing he had my results in hand, E.B. opened the phone lines for predictions. While some wished me luck, others predicted a spectacular embarrassment. As each minute passed, I grew more nervous. The anticipation was killing me. I would endure months of studying again if I failed.

Finally, it was go-time. As our producer played a drumroll sound effect, E.B. ripped open the envelope and began to read verbatim, "We regret to advise you..."

The tone of his voice changed suddenly from excited to empathetic, but I had heard enough. I was devastated. Though they had teased me for months, I felt my boys' compassion. They knew I was crushed. They could see it in my face.

As much as I wanted to cuss and scream, I was too sad. I thought about my parents and how disappointed they would be. Even though they supported me no matter what, I wanted to make them proud.

Regardless of how distraught I was, we were still in the middle of a show. I wasn't about to leave or make an ass of myself. Even though the results hadn't gone my way, Mike was right. It was great radio.

Soon the phone lines exploded with callers commending my bravery and expressing sympathy. Some still needled me, but it wasn't going to faze me anymore. I couldn't feel any lower. I knew what the next several months entailed for me. It was going to be drudgery. And yet, hearing some of our listeners tease me made me chuckle.

Later, in an attempt to make me feel better, a fellow examinee called in to explain that it was Maryland's lowest pass rate in years. Only 63 percent had passed, but that wasn't overly comforting. I was part of the 37 percent that had failed.

After nearly an hour of pity calls, I had heard enough. It felt like a funeral. It sucked. But at least I could take the test again. I would, and pass. Still, everyone would remember I had failed the bar the first time. The agony of defeat.

JUNKIES GREATEST MOMENTS!
STANLEY CUP RINGS

Friday, February 1, 2019

Ten months earlier, we were writing off the Washington Capitals. After they lost the first two home games of their 2018 first-round playoff series against the Columbus Blue Jackets, we suspected they were destined for yet another heartbreaking postseason exit. Cakes, the biggest Caps fan of the bunch, likened them to a "floater in the Potomac." We thought there was no chance they would win the series, let alone the Stanley Cup. So instead of focusing on their series at hand, we started speculating about the team's future and whether coach Barry Trotz should be fired.

Miraculously, the Capitals stunned us and delivered something we hadn't experienced during our careers. Not only did we celebrate the Capitals bringing a Stanley Cup championship to D.C., but we were invited to be part of their victory parade through the city. This was incredible, especially to the hardcore Caps fans perturbed that we had buried the team prematurely in the postseason.

Now they would grow even more bitter. Jim Van Stone, president of business operations for Monumental Sports, was walking into our studio, and we could barely contain our giddiness. We knew why he was here. Months earlier, we had been asked to submit our ring sizes.

Still, we couldn't believe it was happening. As producer Matt Valdez played Queen's "We Are the Champions" in the background, we received a decorative box with a picture of the Stanley Cup trophy. We couldn't wait to see what was inside. Moments later, we were amazed.

Made by Jostens, which makes most of the handcrafted jewelry for the NFL, NBA, NHL, and Major League Baseball, the Caps championship ring features bright red rubies, blue sapphire, and dozens of diamonds, plus inscriptions of our names. The level of detail blows you away. They may not have been the same rings the players received, which allegedly were valued in the neighborhood of $100,000 each,

The Junkies show off their Washington Capitals Stanley Cup rings, which they wear for special occasions.

but our rings weren't lifted from a Cracker Jack box, either.

The rings are enormous, bulky and heavy, and we weren't sure how to wear them. "What finger are you supposed to put it on?" Lurch asked. Correct answer: Right-hand ring finger. Though he wasn't into jewelry, Lurch was ready to show off his new bling.

"We will wear this," he promised. "I will wear this when we are out and about. A hundred percent, so people can see it and enjoy it."

Cakes quipped sarcastically, "Oh, I wonder if I'm going to wear this to the Caps game next weekend." We couldn't contain our excitement. Staring at his flashy new jewelry, E.B. was astonished. "Wow. That is crazy." And it was.

We hadn't done one thing to earn the Stanley Cup rings. Hell, I could barely skate. And although I felt sheepish about wearing my flashy new hardware—it has mostly stayed inside the box for safekeeping—the ring was the first thing my buddies asked about when we got together for a round of golf. They wanted to see the bling. So when we met up for drinks afterward, I picked up the ring from home and allowed them to try it on and take pictures. They were flabbergasted.

"Do you know how lucky you are? What did you do to deserve this?" they wondered. The answer was simple. *Nothing*. But I wasn't giving it back.

JUNKIES GREATEST MOMENTS!
★ ★ ★ ★

MANNING V. LEAF

Monday, September 28, 1998

For months we debated who should go higher in the 1998 NFL Draft. Then, as we broadcast live from Madison Square Garden, we watched the Indianapolis Colts select Tennessee quarterback Peyton Manning first overall ahead of Washington State's Heisman Trophy runner-up, Ryan Leaf, who went to the San Diego Chargers.

Interviewing Manning minutes after he was selected, we were impressed by his demeanor and eloquence. Still, the battle line of debate was drawn before the draft and lingered into the NFL season. Even though I was a Colts fan, I didn't have confidence in Manning. His 0-4 record against Florida tainted my opinion. Meanwhile, Lurch was in Manning's corner, even though he thought both quarterbacks would shine.

Three weeks into the season, both rookies were struggling and the national discourse was, "What if they are busts?" Though we were a D.C.-based show, the topic was as big as anything to us, especially with another hapless start to the Washington Redskins season.

So when Leaf fumbled four times and completed just one pass in a comical loss to Kansas City, Lurch gloated, leaving me multiple messages on my answering machine. After Week 4, I had my ammunition. Manning had thrown three interceptions in an overtime loss to the Saints. The supposed savior of the franchise had tallied 11 interceptions as the Colts were off to an 0-4 start.

What did all this mean?

Bringing up Manning's penchant for interceptions on the show, Lurch pounced. "People who criticize Peyton Manning and Ryan Leaf and call them butt-trifling quarterbacks like J.P. has called Peyton Manning are morons. They are moronic."

Shots were fired, and this segment became one of our most intense on-air arguments.

"First of all, they're rookies in a ridiculous league with fast defenses," Lurch defended. "Much faster and much more difficult to read than in the college ranks. When he's at Tennessee, he can pretty much look at one receiver and hit him any time."

Cakes, who rarely gets in the middle of our arguments, began to laugh as Lurch's irritation grew, and his voice boomed louder and louder. I readied a rebuttal.

"Just to clarify one thing," I started. "I'm not saying [Manning is] never going to be a decent quarterback. I'm just saying he's a dork, and I like needling you, just like you like needling me when Ryan Leaf fumbles the ball four times against the Chiefs, and you leave three messages on my machine."

Then I stupidly offered a bold prediction: "I don't think Peyton Manning is going to be a terrible quarterback. I think he can be competent. Kerry Collins-like." The year before, Kerry Collins had thrown 11 touchdowns while tossing 21 interceptions for the Carolina Panthers. The comparison wasn't a compliment.

Annoyed, Lurch shot back, "I think both of these quarterbacks are going to be good quarterbacks." Then, without letting him continue, I jumped back in. "I just think Ryan Leaf is going to be better."

Although the lawyer in me preferred to rely on logic and statistics to validate my arguments, I had become an emotionally frustrated Colts fan as I began to shout at the top of my lungs, "He blows! Worst interceptions I've ever seen."

Next, I argued that Manning's interceptions were worse than Leaf's, pointing out that Manning had thrown more pick sixes. That didn't score points with Lurch, who erupted, "So that makes him a worse quarterback because there are two more touchdowns scored? You're kidding me! Is that your knowledge of the NFL? That's preposterous! Leaf has 13 turnovers in four weeks!"

Incensed, Lurch, who had just argued against my use of stats, turned to some of his own, pointing out Manning had thrown for over 300 yards against the Saints.

While Cakes continued to offer a constant laugh track, E.B. waited patiently, like a cheetah stalking its prey. Then, finally, E.B. threw his first jab. "I wouldn't put a lot of stock into yards thrown. Trent Green threw for 383 yards, and we got waxed." The week before, the Redskins starter compiled a huge stat line during yet another loss in their 0-7 start.

Then E.B. took it to another level by screaming, "That yardage doesn't mean dick! That means you're down by 20! That means you're throwing every goddamn down! That doesn't mean dick!" Half-joking as he began to lose his voice, E.B. tossed in an "F-U and your family, too."

But that wasn't the end. Lurch countered, stating simply, "992 yards." That was the total yardage Manning had amassed in four NFL games. E.B. wasn't moved. He grew more irritated, roaring back, "That doesn't mean dick! Look at the won-loss record!" The Colts were winless. Lurch fired back again, asking E.B., "His completion percentage mean anything?" Shrieking to new levels, E.B. answered angrily, "No, because he's throwing to Marshall Faulk all the time."

Exasperated that it had turned into a 2-on-1 pissing match, Lurch sarcastically proclaimed, "You're right. You're both right. You know so much about the NFL."

The dig touched a nerve with E.B., who wouldn't back down, "And you know so much? You know so much more!" Lurch responded, "I read the numbers," as if his ability to review box scores was unique.

"Who doesn't read the numbers?" E.B. yelled indignantly. "Are you saying I don't read the numbers? I gave you the numbers! You called *me* to give *you* the numbers!"

For nearly five minutes, Cakes hadn't spoken a word, but his laugh said everything. He was wholly entertained, and we hoped our listeners were as well. As Lurch tried to make another point in vain, E.B.'s headphones broke.

"I don't care about your goddamn headphones!"

E.B. instantly shouted back and threw a haymaker: "I don't care about you!" Touché.

The f-bombs started flying next. We knew the language was going to be dumped by our producer, but it was still funny. "Wait a minute. Am I arguing with you about Manning versus Leaf, or am I arguing with fucking J.P?" Lurch barked. E.B. didn't care. "Whenever I want to needle, I jump in!"

Amused by Lurch's sense of superiority, E.B. challenged him: "Oh, you analyze and break the games down?" Lurch claimed he had watched two games, but E.B. wasn't sold. "You sit there and watch four quarters? Now you're lying."

"No, I'm not!" Lurch emphatically denied. E.B. screeched even louder, "You're lying!"

Just another fun day of mudslinging among old friends.

JUNKIES GREATEST MOMENTS!
★ ★ ★ ★

COFFIN CHALLENGE

Friday, September 12, 2003

We were mesmerized the moment we watched illusionist David Blaine's "Street Magic" special in 1997. Blaine's card tricks were mystifying, and whether he was burying himself alive or standing on a 100-foot-high pillar for 35 hours, we were so obsessed that we debated whether he could actually levitate. E.B. joked that Blaine might have super-human abilities.

As we fixated on Blaine's latest exhibition, "Above the Below," we wondered if this was a genuine trick or merely testing his body's limits. This time he was encased inside a glass box dangling over the Thames River, surviving without food or nutrients for 44 days. He lived off 4½ liters of water a day.

Reflecting on some of Blaine's previous feats of endurance, Cakes was less impressed. In particular, he thought the magician's "Buried Alive" stunt in 1999—where he was interred in a Plexiglas box under three tons of water for seven days—was overrated. A sleep-deprived family man, Cakes boasted he would welcome uninterrupted rest for hours, given the same opportunity as Blaine.

We weren't buying it, though, and neither were our callers. There was no way Cakes could be "buried alive" for two days, so our next radio antic was afoot.

First, a listener offered to build us a coffin. Then, when one of Lurch's friends offered a $2,500 reward to Cakes, the coffin challenge was born.

A few days later, Cakes prepared to dive into the homemade pine box placed inside our studio.

The rudimentary casket, painted black, consisted of nothing more than a few 2x4s and plywood sheets. Good enough for the bit.

But there was some family drama leading up to the interment. Cakes' sister-in-law called into the show and announced his wife was not happy about the gimmick, and his kids were scared. They didn't want their daddy to do the stunt, but that wouldn't stop him. Cakes saw dollar signs and was even more determined.

Armed with blankets, a pillow, beef jerky, and Gatorade bottles, Cakes laid inside his new home during our final segment. We closed the box just before 10 a.m., and the clock started ticking. Could he last 48 hours inside the makeshift coffin?

As E.B., Lurch, and I left the studio a few minutes later, we turned out the lights as an eerie silence enveloped the room. Alone in the darkness, we wondered if sensory deprivation would get the best of our pal. Fortunately, we wouldn't have to serve as hall monitors all night. The deejays at the station would keep him honest. If he left the coffin for one second, he would lose the bet. We figured it was a matter of time.

With Cakes still going strong the next morning, we opened the show with him describing how weird it was inside the box. He had lost track of time. But much to our dismay, he wasn't tested as much as we would have liked. The deejays spinning the music chatted with him throughout the day and put him on the air. Now Cakes was using the same microphone connected through one of the holes inside the coffin to pound his chest. He wasn't shaken after 20 hours inside the coffin. On the contrary, he was confident of success.

Cakes' plan was working. By only eating jerky, he had averted intestinal issues, and his now-empty Gatorade bottles were used so he could relieve himself. It was disgusting but oddly impressive, nonetheless.

Later that day, the sales staff had arranged a public viewing at a local car dealership. Cakes was transported in one of WHFS's promotional vans. After a couple of interns lifted the rickety coffin out of the van, dozens of listeners cheered Cakes on, even though they couldn't see him. Still, they wanted to will him to victory.

After returning to the station, the challenge nearly came to an inglorious end. While I helped the promotions staff carry the coffin on the elevator, Cakes began to fall out as the boards separated. Luckily, the poorly constructed casket was salvaged as we frantically pushed the boards together, managing to get Cakes back inside the studio with the coffin still intact. There were 24 hours to go.

By Friday, it was obvious he was going to collect the cash. He had come too far. Though he may have been disoriented inside the dark box, you could hear the bravado in his voice as we got closer to the end.

Finally, as Cakes reached 48 hours inside the coffin, producer Lee Anne Smith played a drumroll sound effect, and Cakes slowly emerged, raising his hands in victory. As he adjusted his eyes to the light, it was apparent he had been through the wringer. Disheveled and in need of a shower, he was also $2,500 richer. We were impressed—and jealous.

JUNKIES GREATEST MOMENTS!
Celebrity Shootout

Tuesday, May 30, 2000

When we started on the radio in 1996, our task was to be entertaining for three hours every Saturday night. One year later, given the opportunity of a lifetime when we replaced *The Greaseman* at WJFK, our mission was to figure out how to do that night after night.

To get listeners engaged while giving prizes to winners, we tried a segment called "Game Show Wednesday." The new feature worked, though it was a challenge to keep things fresh. Over time we added new game shows, including one of our favorites, "Celebrity Shootout."

The concept was simple. We asked athletes basic questions that covered the gamut from sports to current events. Then we'd play our interviews on the show, stop the tape after playing the questions, and have listeners bet on whether the athletes knew the answers.

Asking members of the Washington Wizards if they knew the goalie on the Washington Capitals was revealing. Most were clueless. Even better was learning NBA ballers such as Elton Brand, who attended Duke University, had no clue Washington, D.C. was the nation's capital.

Regardless of whether pro basketball players knew how many were in a baker's dozen (fyi: it's 13) or whether they could finish a rap lyric, the game was fun. Through the years, we farmed out the "Celebrity Shootout" responsibilities to our interns.

First, that was easier than doing it ourselves.

Second, that meant we didn't know the answers upfront.

Third, we could bet along with our listeners, which made the segment even more fun. Of course, that was the entire point anyway.

In the summer of 2000, our two teenage interns began to form a dynamic duo. Bret Oliverio and "Clank" David Bernad were earning their stripes on the air as we constantly busted their chops. Young, eager and naïve, they would soon hit the road for "Celebrity Shootout."

Armed with questions such as "Who discovered electricity?" Bret and Clank David worked their way into the Baltimore Orioles' locker room. After interviewing center fielder Brady Anderson and pitcher Sidney Ponson, the interns were pleased. Both players were good sports. Brainiac Brady wanted more questions as he flexed his knowledge.

Combing through the audio, Slow Joe unearthed a few gems. Swatting at the first question like a straight fastball down the middle, Brady promptly quoted the Billy Crystal movie "City Slickers," by saying, "Scoop of vanilla, scoop of chocolate. Don't waste my time."

Something about Brady's response tickled us, but we had to give him credit. Aside from his rigorous workouts that helped Cal Ripken Jr. extend his consecutive games played streak by a few years, Brady was also a well-read man. For an athlete, he had an uncommon curiosity and absorbed all forms of information. So maybe it was his slight lisp or intellectual prowess that you could palpably feel, but we had to convert the tape to a sound drop that we could play in perpetuity.

Ponson was funny, too, but for different reasons. A widely known partier hooked on heavy metal bands and allergic to athletic discipline, the 23-year-old pitcher from Aruba was utterly clueless. When Bret asked about Benjamin Franklin, the fireballer responded with his raspy native Papiamento accent, "Have no clue." We all started to laugh. Ponson is naturally funny and always ready for a good time.

Done with their questions, Bret and David wondered if Ponson was okay with how he came across. Was he embarrassed? Nah. "I did enjoy it," Ponson replied, his accent leaving us in stitches once again.

But there was nothing like their encounter with Orioles first baseman Will Clark. As Clark began pounding a postgame Budweiser, Clank David and Bret sheepishly approached the notoriously intense slugger. Clark immediately challenged Bret, who admitted he was nervous. "Nervous, man, nervous," Clank David offered in the background. The segment was about to go off the rails.

When Bret asked "Will the Thrill" the first question about who invented electricity, things escalated quickly. "Oh, you're trying to be smart," Clark shot back. Before Bret could respond, Clark put our 18-year-old intern into a headlock. Maybe he was joking or truly pissed off, but Clark was cutting off Bret's air supply as Clank David stood by dumbfounded.

"Easy! Easy," Bret pleaded. After a few seconds, Clark finally let go. He had made his point. Will Clark wasn't going to play our silly game, but he had given us something so much better. Touch 'em all, grand slam!

JUNKIES GREATEST MOMENTS!
LIE DETECTOR

Friday, February 12, 2016

One week after Peyton Manning and the Denver Broncos won the Super Bowl, our 2016 "bit season" kicked off with a bang. First, we brought a polygraph examiner into the studio to learn if our video producer A-Wadd was a habitual liar.

Over a few months, we had suspicions the young protégé tended to exaggerate, to say the very least. Whether it was A-Wadd's high school basketball resume or supposed perfect score on the math portion of the PSAT, his claims didn't add up. The baby-faced, ginger-haired radio neophyte looked more like a couch potato than a hoopster. A simple Google search revealed he never played for his high school team. Instead, he had only participated in their summer camp.

And there was no way he landed a perfect score on *any* portion of the PSAT. Perhaps A-Wadd knew the entire Washington Wizards roster, but he couldn't name the Vice President of the United States. He wasn't exactly Oxford cloth, and we weren't entirely sure if he had actually graduated from Virginia Commonwealth University.

So when it came to A-Wadd's boasts about hooking up with women, we doubted everything that came out of his mouth. His bravado seemed like overcompensation as if he was trying to impress us. With the lie detector test, we would finally learn the truth.

Weeks earlier, A-Wadd had bragged that he took an attractive young woman home from Don Tito, a popular club in Arlington, Virginia. Hooked up to the polygraph, he stuck to his guns. When examiner Robert Smith read the results as "no deception indicated," A-Wadd jumped out of his chair and shouted his glory.

"Don't get amped. There are three more to go," Lurch warned, but A-Wadd couldn't help himself. He was already drunk on attention for the extended air time, and now he felt vindicated that he had told the truth about his dalliance.

Next, we delved into his relationship with executive producer Matt "Drab" Cahill, who he followed around the radio station like a lap dog. Though it was mostly a joke, we had the examiner ask, "Have you ever had sexual thoughts about Drab?" Once again, no "deception indicated." We figured as much, but just hearing our question read verbatim in the most serious tone made us laugh. Immature, sure, but funny, nonetheless.

Question No. 3 tackled whether A-Wadd showered before a recent show. Surprisingly he had. Three-for-three. A-Wadd celebrated once again. "I was squeaky clean," he boasted.

Regardless of whether he was honest about the first three questions, the most critical query was over the truthfulness of his sexual conquests. At 23 years old, A-Wadd was a self-proclaimed sports nerd who carried a Washington Wizards wallet—not pricesely the moves of a ladies man—and claimed to have slept with more than 10 women. We might be middle-aged, but we had 10 kids between the four of us at the time. We know fibs, fiction, falsehoods, fabrication, subterfuge, hyperbole, fanciful invention, and little white lies. We weren't buying A-Wadd's Fables.

With the four of us sitting on the edge of our seats, "The results are," Robert Smith began, "deception indicated."

The studio exploded. "What? No, no, no, no!" A-Wadd screamed. Then, as Cakes stood up to clap, E.B. offered his best Ric Flair impersonation. "*Wooo!* I told you. The big one. The big one. *Wooo!*"

In the case of The Junkies v. A-Wadd, the defendant was found guilty. Adam Epstein, aka A-Wadd, was a lying liar. Case closed. Hammer delivered.

JUNKIES GREATEST MOMENTS!
★ ★ ★ ★
9/11

Tuesday, September 11, 2001

In the early days of our nighttime show, I would often sleep until noon. But now that I was the father of a beautiful baby girl who was almost a year old, I wasn't afforded the same luxury. So instead, I was up bright and early most days, taking care of my little Kelsie while watching television.

Like everyone else, I couldn't believe my eyes when the Twin Towers of the World Trade Center in New York City were struck by passenger planes. Not knowing what to make of these moments, I connected with Cakes on AOL instant messenger, who instantly thought I was reaching out to talk about the fantasy football implications from the "Monday Night Football" game between the Broncos and Giants. "You gotta turn on the TV!" I implored.

This wasn't fantasy football. *This* was the real world, and we had never seen anything like *this* happening in real-time. Our lives were changing, even though we didn't know that yet.

I quickly began to worry about my brother Eric, who worked near the Ground Zero scene in Manhattan. Fortunately, he was several blocks away, but he would witness panicked people jumping to their deaths to avoid the fires.

As the hours passed while the country remained glued to our televisions, we began to wonder how we would handle the show that night. Like everyone, we still didn't have a firm understanding of what had happened—and why. Of course, sports were irrelevant and came to a halt. Major League Baseball, NFL, NASCAR, pro golf, college football, and more postponed games and events that week.

Later that day, Jim McClure, the operations manager at WJFK, informed us that he and his boss, Jeremy Coleman, our program director, had decided we wouldn't run commercials during the show. They weren't worried about our national syndication deal or our Westwood

One affiliates. If they couldn't handle our show being commercial-free, so be it. Many of our listeners worked at the Pentagon, which had been hit by another passenger plane after the Twin Towers came down. Running commercials would trivialize the gravity of the situation.

In the studio, emotions were raw and real. We had never tackled something so serious as terrorism. Now we had no choice. As we talked with our audience and took countless calls over four consecutive hours, we heard eyewitness accounts from listeners who worked near the Pentagon. Most of us learned on the fly about al-Qaeda and Osama Bin Laden.

For the next several days, our show sounded different than ever before. We booked terrorism experts, talked to grief counselors, and eventually turned to the implications of 9/11 in the sports world. We weren't known for being serious on our show, but we connected with our audience in a completely different and emotional way.

We were truthfully no different from most of our audience. (We also worried we might expose some of our ignorance about world affairs.) So when we talked to experts like Anthony Cordesman from the Center for International Studies, we were genuinely curious:

Why were we attacked?
Who were these scumbags?
Why did they hate America?
Was this just the beginning?

We knew we weren't the only people thinking this way. But through tragedy, we grew closer with our listeners. It wasn't that we had any answers to the madness. We didn't. We were angry. We were sad. We were scared. We were confused. We were just like everybody else.

JUNKIES GREATEST MOMENTS!
★ ★ ★ ★

Car Crash

Thursday, October 27, 2011

KABOOM! It sounded like a bomb went off just outside our studio on Main Street in Fairfax, Virginia. It was 7:40 in the morning and we were in the lull of a rather uneventful commercial break when we heard the deafening eruption. Even though this was 10 years and six weeks after 9/11, many people around Washington were still edgy.

Moments later Adam "Noodles" Gracia, filling in that week to answer our phones, burst through the door and shared the news. A car had just crashed into our building.

We rushed out to survey the damage. Walking into the show's call screening room just down the hallway, the front end of a silver Honda Civic had smashed through the window and wall, sending glass, brick, furniture and equipment flying. The cool air from the chilly, drizzly morning was quickly enveloping the destroyed room.

Stunned by the wreckage, I wondered about the driver. Was he alive? Did he need help? Meanwhile, E.B. and Cakes, standing behind me, began to speculate it might be a terrorist attack. This possibility seemed absurd. Why would a terrorist target 106.7 The Fan? Because John Beck was starting at quarterback for the Redskins?

Don't smirk.

With my boys retreating to fetch their phones—they had to tweet photos of the scene—I stepped over the shattered glass and what was left of the wall to reach the driver's side of the damaged vehicle. As I opened the door, I was relieved to see the man behind the steering wheel alive, although he was dazed and confused.

Asking him whether he was okay, the Latino man didn't respond. I turned to Spanish and said, "*estas bien*?" The man nodded. E.B. and Cakes began taking pictures. Clearly, they were more concerned with social media followers than the man's welfare.

Producer Matt Valdez was reviewing the scene. Luckily for him, he

The show's call screening room following a wandering car intrusion.

was running the board while executive producer Bret Oliverio was off for the week, so Valdez wasn't answering calls from his usual seat next to that smashed window.

While pondering the calamitous coulda-beens, Valdez turned his attention to the show and reminded us that our commercial break was almost over. Four minutes had passed since the crash. As we jumped back on the air, Valdez played "Crash" by the Dave Matthews Band in the background as we described what happened. Fire and rescue arrived on the scene minutes later, but we still had questions.

Maybe they were joking, but E.B. and Cakes still considered terrorism as a possibility. I wasn't sure if they were entirely serious. Lurch offered a more probable scenario. The driver may have fallen asleep at the wheel. The tire tracks seemed to support this theory because the car appeared to drift off Route 123, narrowly missing a tree before plunging into our building.

Regardless, it was radio gold and, *noooo*, it wasn't a ratings stunt. Listeners flooded E.B. and Cakes' Twitter accounts to peek at the pictures. Then they filled our phone lines with their own theories. Luckily, nobody was seriously injured. The driver walked away from the accident, telling authorities he had swerved to avoid a pedestrian. We weren't so sure.

Afterward, camera crews grabbed footage and television reporters interviewed us to hear what happened. We happily obliged even though we didn't have all the answers. When the drywall dust finally settled and the broken glass had been cleared, one question remained:

What would have happened to Valdez if he had been sitting in his normal spot answering calls?

CHRONOLOGY OF THE SPORTS JUNKIES

- **August 17, 1995** — First episode of "The Sports Junkies" airs for Bowie Community Television.

- **March 25, 1996** — Dick Heller's article, "Sports Junkies: Four longtime buddies talking up a storm on uninhibited cable-access show in Bowie," appears in the *Washington Times*, leading to their discovery by radio station 106.7 FM WJFK.

- **May 4, 1996** — "The Sports Junkies" show debuts at 5 p.m. as part of WJFK's new sports weekend.

- **May 26, 1997** — "The Sports Junkies" take over the 7-10 nighttime slot on WJFK occupied by the legendary "Greaseman."

- **December 5, 1997** — Adult film superstar Jenna Jameson, a frequent guest with Howard Stern and a pioneer in digital erotica, appears on the show and charms the socks off her hosts, leading to porn starlets becoming occasional guests.

- **January 20, 1998** — "The Sports Junkies" hit No. 1 in the Fall ratings book for the first time in men ages 25-54.

- **April 18, 1998** — "The Sports Junkies" broadcast from the NFL Draft at Madison Square Garden, where they interview Peyton Manning. His selection would fuel one of their most intense on-air arguments.

- **May 17, 1999** — Signs three-year contract with Westwood One to nationally syndicate "The Sports Junkies" to 50 affiliates, including stations in Miami, Detroit, and San Francisco.

- **July 12, 1999** — *Sports Illustrated* dubs "The Sports Junkies" as "America's hot new radio show."

- **May 30, 2000** — During a segment of their "Celebrity Shootout" question-and-answer feature, interns Bret Oliverio and "Clank" David Bernad draw the ire of the Orioles' Will Clark, who puts Oliverio in a headlock. Bret nearly blacks out.

- **September 11, 2001** — On a day of infamy in American history, WJFK brass cancels all commercials during "The Sports Junkies" as the guys turn sports talk into public service radio. It's one of their finest moments in show history.

- **October 2, 2002** — Final nighttime show on WJFK.

- **October 14, 2002** — Morning drive debut of "The Sports Junkies" on 99.1 WHFS.

- **September 12, 2003** — Cakes accepts a challenge to spend 48 hours in a makeshift pine coffin, living off beef jerky and water. He wins a $2,500 bet.

- **March 2004** — *The Discovery Channel* may or may not have created a show based on our inane 1998 debate of Croc vs. Shark that aired during their annual Shark Week series program.

- **September 24, 2004** — ESPN shoots the pilot for "Same As It Ever Was," a daily sports show featuring "The Junkies." The pilot for ESPN Classic was bypassed for "Classic Now," hosted by Josh Elliott. The program lasted just 10 months.

- **November 22, 2004** — The Junkies defeat the D.C. Divas women's semi-pro football team 28-6 in a Turkey Bowl football game before 8,000 fans.

- **January 12, 2005** — Final morning show on WHFS before the station shockingly flips programming format at noon and becomes El Zol, "Siempre de Fiesta."

- **January 17, 2005** — "The Sports Junkies" return to WJFK in the midday time slot.

- **January 2, 2006** — Replaces Howard Stern in morning drive on 106.7 WJFK in Washington, D.C., and 105.7 FM in Baltimore.

- **November 30, 2006** — Hosts first Junkies Poker Open at the Borgata in Atlantic City, becoming an annual staple, including tournaments in Las Vegas.

- **December 6, 2006** — Junkie John-Paul Flaim fights Jay Watts in a pro boxing match at the Patriot Center.

- **March 13, 2008** — In a grudge match for the dark ages, Cakes defeats Chad Dukes in a one-on-one basketball game. Both should have been declared losers.

- **July 20, 2009** — Hot talk WJFK flips formats and is rebranded 106.7 The Fan.

- **April 30, 2011** — Married with kids and over 40 years old, "The Junkies" host their final Spring Break Party at the State Theater in Falls Church, Virginia.

- **October 27, 2011** — A car crashes into the WJFK building during the show, smashing into the room where call-ins are handled. Fortunately, the person normally taking calls is on vacation.

- **February 6, 2013** — Weekly television show "Table Manners" debuts on Comcast SportsNet.

- **December 5, 2013** — Toronto Mayor Rob Ford inexplicably appears on the show to talk football amid a scandal surrounding drug abuse, making international headlines.

- **November 21, 2014** — "The Junkies" bury the career of Redskins quarterback Robert Griffin III with a coffin in the studio. Listeners toss their RGIII memorabilia and jerseys into the coffin.

- **June 4, 2016** — The guys celebrate their 20 years on radio at the Junkies Poker Open in Las Vegas.

- **September 24, 2017** — Robert Eatman, long-time agent for "The Sports Junkies," succumbs to cancer at age 65. Eatman elevated the show to new heights locally, nationally, and financially.

- **September 29, 2017** — "The Sports Junkies" hit No. 1 in men 25-54 in the Summer ratings book, a first for the guys in morning drive.

- **June 12, 2018** — "The Junkies" are invited to be part of the Washington Capitals Stanley Cup parade through downtown Washington, D.C.

- **November 2, 2019** — Two parades in 16 months! The guys are part of the Washington Nationals World Series parade.

- **March 25, 2020** — Due to the coronavirus pandemic, the show is moved out of the studio and The Junkies begin broadcasting separately from their homes. It would be more than one year before they are reunited in the same room.

- **May 4, 2021** — Marks 25 years "The Sports Junkies" on the radio. Still barking.

WHERE ARE THEY NOW?

- **Jim McClure** — Assistant program director at 106.7 The Fan who discovered "The Junkies" after reading an article in the *Washington Times*. Currently vice president of Talk and Entertainment programming at SiriusXM.

- **Jeremy Coleman** — Program director at WJFK who gave "The Sports Junkies" their first break. Currently senior vice president at SiriusXM, head of content for the Howard Stern Show and the Howard Stern channels.

- **Jason Veazey** —Show producer at WJFK in 1996. Currently works as creative director at KTAR and KMVP in Phoenix, Arizona.

- **Joe "Slow Joe" Ardinger** — Producer for "The Sports Junkies" 1997-2001. Worked for "The Don and Mike Show" and other radio programs until 2018, when he decided to attend college after two decades in radio.

- **Chris "C.K." Kinard** — Beginning as an intern in 1998, C.K. rose through the ranks and became executive producer while serving as WJFK's program director until July 2009. Currently the operations manager of Audacy D.C.

- **Chad Dukes** —Regular caller to "The Sports Junkies" at nights. Served as an intern before hosting "The Big O and Dukes Show" on 99.1 WHFS. Later hosted shows on 106.7 the Fan with former NFL linebacker LaVar Arrington and his own show called "Chad Dukes vs. the World." Currently hosts "The Chad Dukes Show" podcast.

- **Bret Oliverio** — Served as an intern in 2000 and rose through the ranks to become executive producer until 2012, when he took over Sup Dogs, his late brother's restaurant in Greenville, North Carolina. Bret now runs a second Sup Dog's location in Chapel Hill and has won Barstool Sports Best College Bar in America twice.

- **"Clank" David Bernad** — Intern in 2000 who became a movie producer. He was responsible for getting audio of "The Junkies" in the Jack Black movie "The D Train."

- **Oscar "The Big O" Zeballos** — Worked with "The Sports Junkies" at 99.1 WHFS until teaming with Chad Dukes for "The Big O and Dukes Show." Currently co-hosts "The Mike O'Meara Show" podcast and is co-founder of Podcast Village.

- **Kevin "BDK" McCarthy** — Movie reviewer for "The Sports Junkies" since November 2005. Currently the entertainment reporter for Fox 5 in Washington, D.C., and co-host of the "Reel Blend" podcast.

- **Matt "Valdez" Myers** — Began interning for "The Sports Junkies" in 2008 before ascending to producer. As of 2021, serves as executive producer of "The Sports Junkies."

- **Matt "Drab" Cahill** — Executive producer of "The Sports Junkies" since 2012. Currently serves as assistant program director at 106.7 The Fan.

- **Eric "E-Wadd" Waddon** — Video producer for WatchTheJunkies.com from 2012-'15. Currently a revenue operations analyst at Open Text.

- **Adam "A-Wadd" Epstein** — Video producer from 2015-'20. Currently the live stream video operator for the BetQL Network.

JUNKIES GLOSSARY

- **A-Wadd** — Adam Epstein, former video producer of "The Sports Junkies." Dubbed A-Wadd because he was E-Wadd's successor.
- **Bazilly** — Excellent. *"The Homies gave Boiler Room a Silly Bazilly rating."*
- **Butt** — Adjective: Very, extremely, usually a prefix to emphasize. *"Washington was butt-lucky to win that game."*
- **Cised** — Filled with excitement or joy for something. *"I get cised for Reese's Pieces."*
- **C.K.** — Chris Kinard, former intern and future boss.
- **Drab** — Producer Matt Cahill's nickname, a derivation of "Drab T-Shirt."
- **Donkey** — An idiot. (Also: Donkey Kong or Donk) *"Did you see the donkey who died trying to take a picture while hanging from a 20th-story balcony?"*
- **E-Wadd** — Eric Waddon, former video producer for WatchTheJunkies.com.
- **Grasping** — Trying or shooting for the unlikely. *"Can somebody bring us free breakfast this morning. I'm grasping."*
- **Horns** — Getting something for free. *"Did you get the horns for the concert tickets?"*
- **Hurting** — Something terrible. Opposite of silly or money. *"The Rams' new uniforms are so hurting."*
- **It's a show** — When something is extremely ridiculous or absurd. *"My daughter spent $300 on new shoes. It's a show!"*
- **Joan** — To make fun or ridicule someone. *"Joaning is bullying."*
- **JPO** — Junkies Poker Open.
- **Monkey tilt** — When anger leads to recklessness. In April 2013, Nationals manager Davey Johnson declared, *"I'm real close to monkey tilt right now."*
- **Money** — Excellent. *"That Ben & Jerry's ice cream was so money."*
- **Nubby** — Cheap or in poor condition. *"J.P.'s shoes are so nubby."*
- **Rick** — Perturbed or upset. *"Drab is so rick the Seahawks lost to the 49ers."*
- **Salty** — Similar to Rick. *"Valdez is salty they didn't have any Old Bay in the grocery store."*

- **Silly** — Adjective: Great. *"That Steph Curry crossover dribble was silly."* Noun: Somebody who is extremely attractive. *"Did you see that silly in the bikini?"*
- **Squeaker's Court** — When we expose the cheapest things we've done lately.
- **Tingle** — Deciding with your gut. *"I'm taking the over in this game. No reason, it's just my tingle."*
- **Valdez** — Producer Matt Myers's nickname because he made copies so excessively that he was worse for the environment than the Exxon Valdez oil spill.

ACKNOWLEDGMENTS

I don't remember much from my law school days, but I remember learning you *should* write your closing argument first. Well, on April 1, 2020, I had an acorn of an idea to write this book. Aware that our 25th anniversary was approaching, I started by writing a scant outline, two paragraphs, and the original closing of the book, which was moved to the prologue.

Sending those two paragraphs to my friend Tom Doyle, I waited for his response. Was my idea worthy of a book? Responding quickly, Tom wrote, "In all hot. It is a beautiful story and resonates with every guy who grew up anywhere with his boys. It's a must-tell." That email gave me the confidence to move forward with the project. Thank you, Tom.

More than a year later, I talked with several people about getting the book published. My friend David Falk, formerly Michael Jordan's agent, referred me to New York literary agent David Black, a heavy hitter in the industry. Though David didn't have to call me back, he did and offered sage advice. Then, I connected with authors I knew—John Feinstein, Jake Russell, and Rick Snider—seeking even more guidance. Thanks to each of you for taking the time.

In early July 2021, I met the editor of this book, Dennis Tuttle, a longtime sportswriter, editor, and former colleague of Rick Snider at the *Washington Times*. Rick had read one of the chapters, "Never Ask For Double," and thought Dennis could help me get the book across the finish line.

Dennis, who runs 5editorial, did so much more than carry a baton. When we met, I had an overly long and raw draft. I felt good about the manuscript, but that version has been transformed into what hopefully is a much more readable, enjoyable, and entertaining book. Clap-clap-clap to you, Dennis, for pushing me to elevate the manuscript. I may have groaned along the way when you challenged me to dig deeper into a storyline (e.g., the chapter Gibbs 2.0), and I certainly lost sleep, but I am proud of the work we have done together. I've also learned the answer is always "no" unless you ask.

Kudos to designers Doug Stevens and Jenine Zimmers, who Dennis selected to bring "Still Barking" to life. Doug spent a large portion of his career as an illustrator at the *Washington Post* and *Los Angeles Times* and was asked to make my book cover. Although I didn't know what to expect, I trusted them to find the right concept. When Doug's first draft arrived, I instantly realized why he's so highly recommended. The cover has often served as motivation to make this project better.

And thank you, Jenine, a graphic designer and Etsy marvel in San Diego. She took Doug's cover and made a complementary book composition and a companion website for book sales and promotions. I appreciate her arduous work and putting up with our late-night requests and never-ending page proofs.

I also want to send a special thanks to everybody I interviewed along the way, including: Jim McClure, Mike O'Meara, Chris Kinard, Bret Oliverio, Joe Ardinger, Jason Veazey, Kevin McCarthy, Thomas Block, Tommy Horstkamp, Glen Hardesty, Aaron Schwartz, Cole Policy, Ram the Card Counter, Raymond Lee, Chris Farley, Steve Buckhantz, David Schwab, Doug Hicks, Shirley Bickel, Chad Dukes, Oscar Zeballos, Chris Lingebach, "Cowboy" Todd Myers, Eric Waddon, Adam Epstein, Matt Myers, and Matt Cahill.

Going out of his way, Aaron Schwartz, aka Schwartzy, joined the four of us in the studio to take pictures as well as on the streets of D.C. just outside Nationals Park. Thanks, Schwartzy, for your friendship and contributions to this book.

Beyond that, I want to thank everybody who gave me confidence as I sent random sample chapters. Much appreciation to the P1's, including Chris Farley, John Newton (aka Richmond John), Big Keith, Jon DePompa, Peter from Burke, DeMaris Woods (aka Dee Woods), and John Herr (aka Big John).

Many thanks to my friends who humored me over the last year as I talked about the book. Thank you for reading various chapters along the way and offering feedback, including Eric Shpritz, Fahad Hassan, John Beckley, Michael Taylor, Chris Montanez, Grant Paulsen, Giovanni Barbera, Kareem Washington, Logan Paulsen, Jason Waldman, and many others.

I am genuinely touched by the responses I received from everyone I contacted about writing a testimonial. I was blown away by what you wrote about "The Sports Junkies." Thank you for the kind words and for being supportive of the show to Cal Ripken Jr., Donnie Simpson, Frank Caliendo, John Feinstein, Jason Wright, Mike Rizzo, Ryan Zimmerman, Lindsay Czarniak, Mike O'Meara, Tony Perkins, Eric "Barstool Nate" Nathan, Dan Hellie, DeMaurice Smith, and Rich Vos.

Special thanks to our friend Marc Roberge, lead singer of O.A.R., for writing the foreword. Initially, I asked him a few questions through email about his memories of his first appearance on the show. When I read his response, I immediately thought, "foreword." I'm honored he agreed to write his words.

And, there are my radio partners—John Auville, Eric Bickel, and Jason Bishop. Twenty-five years. Who woulda thunked we'd make it this far? Can you believe how much fun we've had? Thank you for your friendship and support, especially during this last year, when I lost my mom.

As for the book, this project would not be possible without your insights, recollections, and pictures. You answered so many questions about people and events that happened a long time ago—that is, the things you can remember. We'll blame years of alcohol instead of fading memories.

Finally, I want to thank my family. My wife Jessica endured an absentee husband who worked long hours on this project for months and months. I love you, and I love you even more for understanding and carrying the load at home, especially with our little Isabella, who is always energetic. I know this time wasn't easy on our family.

To my kids Kelsie, Dylan, and Isabella. I wasn't as available for stretches, being stuck in the office "working on the book." But, I am thankful for you. You bring me so much joy in life, and, hopefully, you are proud of me.

I also need to recognize my late parents, Paul and Lourdes Flaim. I thought of them constantly during this writing process. Both worked extremely hard to give their children a better life. My father immigrated from Italy when he was just 17 years old. He came to the United States with nothing and learned to speak six languages before becoming an economist. When I received bad grades in school, I would hear the same lecture every... single... time. "John-Paul," he would start, "I used to work 40 hours a week of hard labor as a stonemason, laying brick and cutting stone. And then I went to school at night [at Johns Hopkins], and I never got a C!" Well, I did. Plenty of them.

My mom pushed me hard, too. She came to Washington, D.C., for graduate school at Catholic University. While I flailed in school, she often reminded me that she graduated from college in just three years. My parents set lofty standards. At a minimum, since they both had master's degrees, I had better get an advanced degree too.

So, when I went to law school, it wasn't a significant accomplishment. It was expected. They were proud of me, but achieving higher education is what they expected of me.

When we started "The Sports Junkies," they were proud, too. But mom warned me not to drop out of law school, and dad told me to remain focused on my future. But I also remember them attending "The Junkies" first-anniversary show at Bridges. Later, dad wrote his family in Italy about this crazy idea his son had to step into a professional boxing ring.

When my mom passed away, I had to clean out her house, my childhood home in Bowie. I found many of the articles written about "The Sports Junkies." In addition, I discovered pictures taken of the four of us. I wish more than anything she could read this book.

When I was in high school, dad constantly corrected my papers. It annoyed the hell out of me. What's crazy is English wasn't his first language, but damn, he could write. So if he were still around, he would be helping me.

I know my dad is smiling now; I wish I could tell him Cal Ripken Jr. wrote a testimonial for the book. I wish I could show my mom the finished product. But they are not here, and I miss them every day. But if it weren't for them—lecturing, directing, pushing, expecting—all my life, there is no way I could have achieved writing this story.

Thank you, mom and dad. You gave me an amazing life with such beautiful gifts. I don't wear that suit and tie you envisioned, but I know you are proud of what Eric, John, Jason, and I have accomplished. Thank you for always believing. I love you.

John Paul Flair

ABOUT THE AUTHOR

John-Paul "J.P." Flaim is co-host of "The Sports Junkies" on 106.7 The Fan in Washington, D.C. During his 25 years on the radio, J.P. has done everything from stepping into a professional boxing ring to opening his bar exam results live on the air. Of the four Junkies, he is known for playing devil's advocate, although he'll argue that he often proffers the first opinion. A graduate of the University of Maryland, Flaim received his J.D. from the Temple University Beasley School of Law. The married father of three lives in Gaithersburg, Maryland.

Photo illustration courtesy Aaron Schwartz

Made in the USA
Monee, IL
22 November 2021